ZOLAR'S
BOOK OF DREAMS, NUMBERS & LUCKY DAYS

A FIRESIDE BOOK
Published by Simon & Schuster
New York London Toronto Sydney

FIRESIDE

Rockefeller Center
1230 Avenue of the Americas
New York, New York 10020

Copyright © 1985 by Zolar

FIRESIDE and colophon are registered trademarks
of Simon & Schuster Inc.

15 17 19 20 18 16

Manufactured in the United States of America

First Fireside Edition 1992

Library of Congress Cataloging-in-Publication Data

Zolar.
[Book of dreams, numbers, and lucky days]
Zolar's Book of dreams, numbers & lucky days.
p. cm.
Reprint. Originally published: New York: Arco, 1985.
1. Dreams. 2. Dreams—Dictionaries.
3. Symbolism of numbers. 4. Occultism.
I. Title. II. Title: Book of dreams, numbers, and
lucky days. III. Title: Book of dreams, numbers &
lucky days.
[BF1091.Z64 1989]
135'.3—dc20   89-8790
CIP
ISBN 13: 978-0-671-76599-6
ISBN 10:   0-671-76599-X

CONTENTS

DREAMS
AND THEIR MEANING

The study of dreams is a great realm that may be divided into two territories: that of the observation of dreams, and that of their interpretation. Plutarch and Cicero did not scorn to study it, and following them there are numerous authors from olden times to the present day, not to speak of many writers of keys to dreams, always drawn up at second hand.

Many dreams have become famous, either on account of the position of those who had them or on account of the events that are claimed to have been foretold by them.

No child who has studied his Bible will have forgotten the dream of Jacob seeing the ladder placed on his breast and rising to the sky, prediction of the high destiny of his race; the dream of Pharaoh (the seven fat kine and the seven lean kine), which Joseph interpreted as the approach of seven years of plenty followed by seven years of famine; and so many others in which Jehovah appeared to Moses and the Prophets. He will remember in the Gospels the angel who foretold to the carpenter Joseph the supernatural motherhood of Mary, the other angel who warned Joseph to fly into Egypt to escape the Massacre of the Innocents, and the wife of Pilate who was excited by dreams that drove her to beg her husband to save Christ.

It was in a dream that the mother of Virgil knew, by seeing laurels, that she would give birth to a poet. In a dream Brutus saw a threatening specter foretelling his defeat on the eve of the battle of Philippi. In a dream Calpurnia, the wife of Caesar, foresaw the murder of her husband. In a dream Catherine de' Medici foresaw the tournament in which her husband lost his life. In a dream Henri II of France heard a voice predicting the wound to his eye that would come soon. In a dream the princesse de Condé was present at the battle of Jarnac, in which her son was to perish. In dreams Madame Roland knew the death of her mother and Madame de la Bedollier saw the man she was to marry, whom she did not at that time know.

Are dreams in reality prophetic?

We have all known coincidences between dreams and future events that were at least disturbing and striking. Let us add that some scientists have believed and still believe in dreams as a warning, at least to some extent. On the other hand, there are certain cases in which the dream foreboding can easily be understood. How many wives of fishermen, for instance, see in their sleep their husbands being shipwrecked, when, alas, that same night the men are engulfed by a fate which is only too common to seafarers? But do the wives not forget these same dreams when nothing happens?

Nevertheless, let us remember that, if in some psychophysical condition (especially in hypnosis) the human being shows himself apt to foresee future events, it is not extraordinary that sleep should sometimes be accompanied by a premonitory sensitiveness in which images seen transform themselves into more or less vaguely symbolic forms.

On the other hand, Thylbus remarks in his *Realm of Dreams* that dreams are predictive barely once in a hundred times. These visions of the night are often due, as we shall see presently, to the state of the body, to a physical sensation perceived during sleep, or to a contradesire (Freud's theory). Therefore, before opening a key to dreams to the dream that disturbs you, remember that it is only in cases in which a dream seems inexplicable that it may possibly have any premonitory value.

The Egyptians called such dreams "mysterious messengers," for they took them to be sent by the goddess Isis, who, with the aid of Serapis, thus sent warnings and counsel.

But let us come to more serious explanations.

In the opinion of occultists, the separation of the being into the material self and the psychic or astral self takes place rarely in a state of wakefulness but more often during sleep. And if they see in dreams a kind of presentiment or telepathy, this is, they say, because the soul is

4

freed from the heavy weight of the material body during sleep more often than during wakefulness and thus is more easily able to communicate with the spiritual world.

Scientists, on the other hand—at least the materialists who despise every hypothesis that does not use the scalpel—explain dreams by the rush of blood to the head, allow dreams only physiological causes, and say that they are the result of the nervous system's acting on itself without communication with the outside world. Sleep, by suspending at least in part the exercise of certain faculties (attention, willpower, judgment) releases the control of all the images and thoughts that imagination brings to mind without coordination (hence incoherence).

It cannot be denied that physiological conditions affect dreams, and the ancients were well aware of this, for before accepting signs they took into account the functioning of the organs, the position of the sleeper during his sleep (which must avoid any compression of the liver, the mirror of true dreams), the hour, the day, and the season (autumn and winter, in their opinion, being not very good times). This is why, following the Arab physician Ibn Sirin (who lived in the eighth century B.C.), Moreau de la Sarthe and Maine de Biran distinguished two classes of dreams: the intuitive, and the affective or organic (connected with special conditions, pathological or other, and caused by them, as for instance a physically cold sleeper dreaming of snow).

Let us go into some detail for each of these categories.

As we said, the intuitive dreams are the only ones that have any connection with divinatory science. Even then it is perhaps going too far to believe that the gods busy themselves with our petty affairs to the extent of giving us their advice in this manner, and it may be disturbing to see the contradictions existing between the various keys to dreams that are offered to our eagerness to know the future. And besides, we know that many thousands of dreams have never seen their predictions fulfilled!

We have said that occultists saw in dreams a kind of presentiment or telepathy, which is the faculty of seeing at a distance and without the aid of the senses. By the laws of determinism, events concerning each one of us are

5

undoubtedly always in preparation in the vast field of the invisible world; they are in some way in a condition of germination as the seed is at the bottom of a furrow. But it happens in the spiritual world as it happens in the physical world, and all forebodings do not come true, just as all seeds cast into the furrow do not blossom. Sometimes our willpower, warned by the dream, arrests or precipitates the events in their course.

We should not consider interpretations of dreams as predictions. We must be realistic and consider dreams, rather, reminiscences or the reflection of preoccupations. We must not take keys to dreams literally. Everything we can say about man's search into the future must be based solely on hypotheses and coincidences.

The ancients claimed that it was possible—by recipes, by amulets, by prayers, and by drawings of dreams—to procure sweet and pleasant ones and to avoid unpleasant ones. For this purpose they often advised the placing of a branch of laurel near the sleeper's head. Would you like some more advice on this matter? Good dreams, according to the ancients, result from peace of mind; the righteous man who goes to sleep with pleasant thoughts will have pleasant dreams. To avoid terrifying dreams, they wrote, one should not read at night.

The slightest indispositions as well as the most serious illnesses may give rise to dreams. Unfortunately, their semiological value is very uncertain: we do not know their connections with the seat and the nature of the various affections which they accompany. All that we do know is that during sleep the pathological labor which goes on in the depths of the organism induces dreams which are more or less in direct relation with the affected organ. This is so true that dreams may sometimes arouse suspicions about an illness which are not revealed during wakefulness. To give some instances: An organic affection of the heart or of the large veins is sometimes announced before its obvious occurrence by painful dreams or nightmares followed by sorrowful presentiments. If the dreams are frequently repeated, they may be looked upon as symptoms foretelling a serious lesion already very difficult, if not impossible, to prevent. When the lesion has become actual, the dreams are very short; they usually occur during the first sleep and are quickly followed by sudden awakening. Combined with them, there is an early death in tragic circumstances. According to the observations of various doctors, spontaneous hemorrhages are foretold by red dreams or by dreams of murder. The more these dreams are accentuated and detailed, the more they must be taken into consideration. It is especially during the prodromic period of neurosis and of mental alienation that dreams are found to be of such a bizarre and extraordinary character as to arouse the suspicions of a doctor. Madness, before showing itself definitely, very often reveals itself in terrible nightmares of the worst omens.

The same phenomena accompany illness more often than they precede it. Fever-stricken persons sometimes feel the most dreadful thirst, and dream that they cannot shake it. People have been known to dream that they had a leg cut off or turned to stone and to wake up paralyzed, or become so a few days later. Cold in an organ or its prolonged compression are sometimes accompanied by the same sensations.

Hindu and Chinese medicine, for centuries, has been looking to dreams for information as to the diagnosis of illness. In their system dreams are divided into five classes which correspond to the five great viscera: the heart, the lungs, the kidneys, the spleen, and the liver. Each class is subdivided into two normal conditions of the organ. The normal conditions induce no dreams of any kind. These principles having been stated, the following gives, as an example of this Asian science, a summing up of the various dreams which denote the malfunctioning of each viscus:

1. Dreams of ghosts, monsters, terrifying figures—sign of malfunctioning of the heart (vessels choked), repletion. Dreams of fire, flames, smoke, light—sign of malfunctioning of the heart: giddiness due to weakness in the blood current, and slowing down of the heart's rhythm.

2. Dreams of fights, war, weapons, soldiers—sign of malfunctioning of lungs, repletion. Dreams of plains, sea, country, difficult roads, and journeys—sign of malfunctioning of the heart.

7

3. Dreams of excessive fatigue, pain in the kidneys—sign of malfunctioning of the kidneys; canals overly full. Dream that one is swimming with difficulty and is in danger of drowning—sign of malfunctioning of the kidneys.

4. Dreams of songs, festivities, music, pleasure—sign of malfunctioning of the spleen, starting repletion of the canals. Dreams of dangers, battles, disputes, meals—sign of malfunctioning of the spleen.

5. Dreams of inextricable forests, steep mountains, trees—sign of malfunctioning of the liver, repletion. Dreams of grass, lawns, bushes, fields—sign of malfunctioning of the liver.

Finally, dreaming of brooks, murmuring springs, or waterfalls is a sign of anemia, and dreaming of murderers, hanging, or strangulation is explained by asthmatic suffocation.

It will be seen that this diagnosis by dreams is very similar, in some of its inductions, to that made in similar cases by Western physicians, but it is a little more extended.

In any case, it is generally recognized today that painful nightmares—of suffocation with the sensation of imminent death—reveal a choking in the great vessels of the brain and the heart. It would be wise to remove the threats of congestion indicated, by a modification of the way of living. So, also, in the case of frequent dreams of total and partial paralysis, which indicate a defective circulation of the blood.

Here, at least, dreams offer a sure interest, and it is probable that it was this practical application of oneiromancy which formed in olden times the rightly fundamental basis of this science. We should be wrong to neglect its instructive study under the pretext that the mystics and subsequently the charlatans turned it aside from its most interesting purpose.

Here are some examples of dreams without value:

a. Dreams during the first hours of sleep during the time of digestion.

b. Dreams of a person or a thing of which we have recently heard spoken.

c. The feverish nightmares due to pain, to fright, to a book read, to something seen.

d. Dreams resulting from the manner of sleeping, from the position of the sleeper.

e. Dreams due to illness or some obvious outside cause (noise, cold, etc.).

The true oracle dream: This comes in the middle of sleep, usually between three and seven o'clock in the morning, when the digestive functions are complete, when the body is in a good state of health, when the mind has not been exposed to any excitement, and when the normal position of repose causes no trouble to any organ. According to the Arab Ibn Sirin, author of the first treatise on dreams, "the sleeper lying on the right side will have abstained from all food or of drink. He will have gone to sleep with a light heart, an easy conscience, after having obeyed the precepts of the Koran as to prayers and ablutions."

INTERPRETATION OF DREAMS

These are the general rules as to the interpretation of dreams:

a. The gravity and importance of the events predicted are in direct relation with the depth of impression produced in the dream by its omen.

b. The due date of the event predicted is in proportion: (1) in the case of an animal, to the time of its gestation, incubation, or the breaking of its egg; (2) in the case of a thing seen, to the distance at which it was, in the dream, from the dreamer; (3) in the case of a recurring event, to its recurrence, etc.

c. Apart from fairly numerous exceptions, the meaning is, in general, the opposite of the dream; thus dreaming of death means marriage or happiness; of murder, safety; of a mirror, betrayal.

d. Monstrosities, deformities, and ugliness are, however, evil.

e. The right is good (also odd numbers); the left is fatal.

f. All wild felines and all huge animals are evil.

9

g. All domestic animals, especially if of light color (except the cat), are of good omen.

h. Reptiles are the worst possible omens (slander, crookedness, betrayal).

i. Fishes mean abundance and wealth if they are fine and appear on the surface of the water; but, if they remain at the bottom, serious danger.

j. Interpretation relating to all birds seen in dreams: On the right or east—beneficence; on the left or west—maleficence; flying high—good luck; flying low—bad luck; singing—success; hiding the head—bad luck; turning the head away—an upset; head under wing—illness of much-loved person; coming above the dreamer—reason to beware; wounded—betrayal.

k. Fruit means abundance unless its season is past at the time of the dream.

l. Vegetables are a deplorable omen with two exceptions: mushrooms and peas.

m. The various parts of the body indicate the persons to whom ones dreams refer: A dream of a head is related, in modern interpretations, to the dreamer; a dream of teeth is related to a near relative; a dream of a right hand relates to the dreamer's brothers and sisters; a dream of a left hand relates to his children; a dream of the right foot relates to his parents or grandparents; a dream of a left foot relates to his servants.

n. In the case of a dream of illness or pain, always consult a doctor.

o. Weapons are always omens of a betrayal or break.

p. It is never lucky to dream of an animal of the same sex as the sleeper. The opposite, of course, is a good sign.

q. All dreams of efforts foretell difficulties to surmount. If, however, these efforts are weak or crowned with success, you may expect a happy ending. If, on the other hand, the task dreamed of is difficult, this is a sign of serious obstacles.

r. A light, brilliant, new, or full article is a happy omen.

s. A dark, dull, old, used, or empty article is evil.

t. Going up is always good.

u. Going down is always bad, denotes at least a decrease.

v. It is preferable not to dream of insects (worries, cares).

w. Dreaming of enemies is unlucky.

x. Dreaming of living relatives or friends with whom you are on good terms is a lucky sign.

y. For a girl to dream that she sees herself married means "break": accident, possibly death.

z. All dark or black shades are bad omens; light shades, on the other hand, have cheerful meaning. Any violent color indicates excessive passion; any color mixed with black has meaning contrary to that which it has when alone.

These are the chief color meanings:
Bright red—strong love
Red and black—furious hatred
Dark red—violent passion
Light red—affection
Dark yellow—low desires
Light yellow—material ease
Dark green—evilness, a threat
Light green—serenity, cheerfulness
Dark blue—domination
Light blue—purity, happiness
Warm purple—power
Purple and black—intrigue, treason
Deep purple—sorrow
Light purple—gentleness, wisdom
Orange—happiness in love
Indigo—beneficence
White—family joys
Black—mourning, death
Chestnut—melancholia, danger
White stones—happy omens.

DREAM ANALYSIS

The complete process of dream analysis involves the following steps:
1. the recording of the dream;
2. the dividing of the dream into its parts or elements;

11

3. the discovery, by ordinary memory, of the recent dream material;

4. the discovery, by free association, of the more remote subconscious dream material;

5. the identification of the instinctive wish or fear that is the emotional power of the buried complex and the fundamental cause of the dream.

After a little practice, you will be able to analyze simple dreams merely by a brief free association from the most significant scene or event of the dream.

But if you wish to learn any new art or process thoroughly, it is desirable in the beginning to perform each step of the operation with detailed care. Then you will become more experienced and proficient, and you will be able to omit many of the details, go at once to the heart of the matter, and get results more quickly.

A mind experienced in dream analysis can almost immediately pick the significant element of the dream and, with a few links of the chain of free association, pull up from the subconscious mind the fundamental causes and meaning of the dream.

For illustration: An acquaintance of mine who is quite expert in dream analysis recently related to me his analysis of a dream that he made in a few minutes that morning while dressing.

The dream was a complex one, but the significant element was the taking of his niece to a disreputable resort under circumstances that to others would have looked very suspicious. To a person less familiar with dream analysis, such a dream would have been rather horrifying, as it appeared to involve the dreamer's attempted seduction of his own niece. But the dreamer knew from previous analysis that he had no such subconscious attitude toward the girl, who is rather plain and not in the least the type that would arouse his sexual instinct, even if she were not a relative of his.

The process of free association quickly solved this dream riddle. He had recently been urging his nephew, brother of the niece in the dream, to come to New York City. This invitation of his had the boy's parents, who lived in a small town and considered New York a very wicked place, worried. The dreamer had written to his sister saying, "If he [the nephew] were a girl you might have cause to worry." The nephew is as handsome as his niece is plain, and the subconscious thought of the dreamer had been "My kinfolks are worried for fear that this wicked old New York will ruin their boy. If he were a girl I wouldn't dare ask her to come here, for they think I am a wicked sinner because I live in New York and might even suspect me of having designs on the girl."

This thought becomes the idea which is dramatized in the dream. Without analysis the dream seems to be quite shocking, but analysis reveals the cause to be nothing more offensive than the dreamer's wish that his relatives would quit worrying over the wicked city corrupting his nephew.

Such short cut analyses are safe enough after you have considerable practice; but in the beginning you will do well to give attention to the five steps as outlined. I will therefore discuss these steps in more detail.

There is a very humorous line in an old English cookbook. The recipe is entitled, "How To Bake a Hare," and the instructions begin with this important item: "First you must catch the hare." Presumably one might buy a hare in the market, but I take it the cookbook writer considered it better to go out and catch it so as to be sure to have it fresh.

The same advice is good in our recipe for dream analysis, for a fresh dream is better than a stale one. By stale dreams I mean dreams that you remember having had some time ago, and which you thought peculiar or clever and so remembered. Likely you have told such dreams several times; and dreams, like gossip, frequently get changed in the telling. Dreams that have been written down at the time you dreamed them will be free from fault.

But there is another reason why the dreams should be fairly fresh when analyzed, and that is that in the analysis you are going to delve into the subconscious by free association, in order to find what is back of the dreams. Therefore, the more recently the dream has occurred the more readily you can discover the things that prompted the dream.

13

It might seem, because of the above consideration, that one ought to analyze the dream immediately. In practice I find this does not always work well, especially when one wakes up in the night and tries to analyze a dream he has just had. The mind is still too sleepy, or in case of a dream of strong emotions, too emotionally wrought up. The same thing applies to a dream one remembers on awakening in the morning if one tries to analyze it while lying in bed. It is better to go over the dream in your conscious memory and get it more safely recorded. Better still is to have a pad handy and write it out, then to go to sleep again if it is in the middle of the night or get up and dress if it is in the morning.

Then, any time during the day (that is before you go to sleep the next night) when you have the leisure for it in undisturbed circumstances, recall or reread the dream and analyze it. The one exception I would make wherein you might analyze the dream more promptly is that of a dream you have while napping in the daytime. Such dreams may be properly analyzed as soon as you have stirred about a bit to be sure you are thoroughly awake.

Ordinarily you will probably analyze in the evening the dreams you had the night before. If you wait the passing of a second night, there is some danger of the analysis being more difficult because of interdream memories from one night to the next. During the single day some minor details may be lost; but not essentials, for they are important to the subconscious mind and will be retained. In fact, they may be retained for years or a whole lifetime, as dream analysis itself will show. I have made these suggestions regarding the best time only because I want you to have everything favorable. Stale dreams can be analyzed, but the fresh dreams of the night before will be easier.

The suggestion for dividing the dream up into its elements is needed chiefly to avoid the danger of overlooking some part which may not seem particularly important in the dream but which may prove to be of importance in the analysis.

No hard and fast rules can be laid down as to this division. The elements of the dream are essentially the same as those of a story. They involve the setting, the characters, and the action or incidents.

The setting simply means the place where the dream story seemed to be happening. It may be a familiar place which you can indicate with a few words, as "I seemed to be in a living room in my uncle's house." Later on the dream scene may change: "And then we seemed to be on the shore of a lake, and there was a sailboat coming toward us." These places or prominent objects are elements of the dream. They may be either familiar places or objects that need only to be named in order to be pictured, or they may be strange places and objects that you will have to describe.

The second type of dream element is the dream character. This means the people of the dream, and animals and sometimes objects also assume characteristics of humans, as they often do in fairy stories. "My uncle was in a room, and he wore a full beard as he used to do when I was a child." The character in this is the uncle, but he should be considered with the distinctive feature that at once suggests that the events of the dream are related to some childish experience of the dreamer. "We were fishing and I caught a fish, and when I tried to take it off the hook, it seemed to have changed into some kind of furry animal." The fish and the furry animal are true dream characters, and likely to prove significant as elements of the dream. "And then the boat came up to the shore and a beautiful girl with long golden curls stepped out of the boat; I did not know her and am sure it was no one I have ever known." Here we have a dream character, and the description of her should prove important; perhaps in the analysis her identity may be revealed.

The action, or incidents, of the dream is of course closely related to the settings and characters and often can hardly be separately stated. "I caught the fish," as given above, is action; so is "The fish seemed to change into a furry animal." "A beautiful girl stepped out of the boat. . . . Then she came up to me and jerked the rod out of my hand and threw it into the lake." These items will sufficiently illustrate action or incident.

It is not necessary in dividing your dream into its

elements to rearrange the dream material, as I have done, into three groups of setting, characters, and action. But it will help you to divide it up more completely if you remember these three kinds of elements of the dream story. You can simply go through the dream as it is told in the story form and note these elements without disturbing them from their natural order in the dream. If you are working with a written copy of the dream story, you can simply underline the significant word or phrases.

You are merely one of the dream elements, but your own characterization in the dream is so important that I want to call special attention to it. So note carefully whether you are in the dream yourself and whether or not you are an actor in the dream drama or an observer. Nine times out of ten you will be in the dream scenes. But you may be as you are now, or you may seem to be in some past period of your life or experience. More rarely it will be you in a condition or state in which you have never lived but in which you have in past thought of being. Women, I find, frequently dream "I was married to so and so, or such a kind of man." Men are more likely to dream of love or sex relations without dreaming about marriage.

Occasionally you may be the actor in the dream but living, as it were, in the body of someone else. The transference of your personality comes from the thought, "I wish I were so and so," or "If I were so and so . . ."

There is no sharp distinction between the recent and the more remote dream material. We make the distinction because it helps us, in the analysis, to do so. As you have learned, most, perhaps all, dreams are set off or released by the action of some memory of what has been experienced or thought of during the previous day, or at least very recently.

This material may be discovered merely by going over the dream elements one at a time and asking yourself what recent event or thought could have caused that element of a dream.

Not all dream elements will have such recent events as causes; sometimes only the elements representing events that trigger the dream will be so easily explainable. But strange to say, significant elements do not always appear at the beginning of the dream tale as it is related. In the case of the man who dreamed he was guillotined by the board falling from his bedstead, it seemed that a very recent event started the dream but that the element did not appear in the dream until its end.

This was an exceptional case, but you will often find that the recent event that set off the dream will appear fairly late in the completed dream tale. Hence, if you wish to make a thorough analysis, it will be wise for you to go over each element in the dream and see what recent event or idea might explain that element. This analysis is proper, for which the other steps are only preparatory, and is accomplished by free association.

Take up each element of your dream, and from that scene, character, or action let your mind freely associate back into your subconscious store of memories and experiences. You will be surprised how quickly you will get results and how very clear it will be that the dream was motivated, or its driving energy supplied, from these deeper subconscious sources.

You will usually find a similarity in kind between the more important recent events that have set off or released the dream, and these may have a surprising resemblance to events that have happened many years in the past, even going back a whole life span.

It does not always follow that you will unearth very old memories in this step of the dream analysis, for some dreams, which seem wholly caused by fairly recent events, include some long-existing subconscious elements, which will explain why recent events, represented in the dream, were significant to your subconscious mind.

I will not give illustrations of this step of the operation here, because I am presently going to give you the complete analysis.

Frequently, this instinctive emotional wish or fear will be recognized at once from the recalling of experiences and thoughts back of the dream. At other times this will not be so obvious. The point I wish to make is that the mere recognition of the intellectual elements of dream memories does not in itself constitute the scientific analysis of a dream. Until the more fundamental wish-fear emotion

17

that binds the dream material together and forms the complex of the subconscious is unearthed and comprehended, we have not fully analyzed the dream. When this core of the dream structure has been discovered, the whole dream at once becomes clear and meaningful, and your analysis is complete.

Those dreams which go, for their material, back into your past and which reveal purely subconscious wishes or fears are the ones that will prove of the greater importance in the psychoanalysis of yourself. But it does not follow that all dreams are of this order. It is true that all dreams are wish or fear dreams, but some of them may take all the dream material from your recent life and the wishes and fears that prompt them may also have been recently conscious wishes or fears.

None of these dreams are to be disregarded as unimportant, for they all help you to understand yourself. But the wishes or fears that are the oldest are most fundamental in your nature, and because you are less aware of them, they are the most likely sources of conflict with your conscious thoughts and actions.

I have detailed these five steps of dream analysis as if they were all to be performed separately. But in practice you will combine them to a greater extent, and you will be able to do this even more as you become more expert and experienced in the analysis of your dreams.

As you recall or write down the dream, you can note or mark the elements, and as you note these elements you will often, without effort, recall the recent dream material. Sometimes you will also associate and so discover the more remote subconscious material at the same time, and that usually reveals the instinctive wish or fear. In the following related dream analysis, I give the thought processes approximately as they occur in experienced practice. As I get further on with these examples, I will condense more and omit some of the intermediary details.

The dream: I dream that I meet a man on the street whom I do not recognize. He catches my arm as I pass and calls me by name, and then I realize that it is my old friend Orvis, whom I have not seen for several years. He looks strange, seems younger and more energetic than I would have expected him to be. He asks me to come with him into his office. I do and find that it is a lively place with evidence of his busy prosperity. When my friend removes his hat, I see that his head is covered with a heavy growth of black hair. This seems strange, as he was, when I last saw him, almost wholly bald, and the little fringe of hair he had was turning gray.

Recent dream material: Davis called on me a couple of days before the dream, and we spoke of Orvis and wondered how he was getting along. We remarked that he was getting old, and we feared he wasn't doing well.

Analysis by free association: I didn't recognize Orvis, he looked younger, he had a heavy growth of black hair; but he is bald, he is the baldest man I know. I suppose I will get bald too, as I grow older (wish-fear element suggested). Only a week or so ago I happened to look into a mirror while a beam of sunlight fell on my head, and it revealed that my hair is getting decidedly thinner than it was. (Recent dream material by association and wishful fear element becoming rather obvious.) Orvis's bald head not only had a growth of heavy hair, but his hair, which was really gray, had become black—my wife pulled a gray hair out of my head the other day (more recent dream material and a secondary wish-fear element suggested). Orvis was doing nicely in business, was younger and more energetic looking than I had expected to find him.

It is not necessary to follow the detailed analysis further, for the whole dream is now apparent and its analysis obvious. The fundamental fear of the dream is my fear of growing old. And this fear of the general decay of age is the emotional element of the complex which draws to it the specific ideas of baldness, grayness, loss of youthful energy, and failure in business.

More specifically, the cause of this dream is my fear of becoming bald. Yet I did not see myself as bald in the dream, but saw instead my baldest friend with an astonishing growth of black hair. Hence, the wish element (which is merely the reversal of the fear) is that baldness can be prevented or cured when it comes. There are minor wishes in the dream, one of which I had never been conscious because of its futility: it is that I might have

19

black hair. Evidently, this has been a subconscious wish all my life, for I have always remarked on the handsomeness of black-haired men, my own hair being an indifferent brown.

This dream was simple and very easily analyzed because its material was recent and therefore readily available to the conscious mind. Yet it did require some analysis, for the dream itself, instead of picturing me as bald, showed my bald acquaintance as having hair. The direct meaning of the dream was that Orvis had grown a new crop of hair and was young looking and prosperous. I had consciously wished, when talking to Davis, that Orvis was doing well in business; but I had not thought or cared consciously about his looks or his baldness. My subconscious thoughts were about the danger of becoming bald myself, as revealed by the association of the discovery of how visible my scalp was getting when the sun shone into my hair. The speed with which this memory came into my mind is pretty good evidence that it is my baldness, not my friend's, that my subconscious was concerned with. Yet it is Orvis that gets the new hair in the dream. This is the element of dramatization or symbolism of the dream. My subconscious wished to express itself on the subject of baldness and picked out Orvis as the man who could best play the role. To put heavy black hair on his bald head was good dramatic or symbolic expression of the wish that I would not become bald myself.

Though simple, obvious, and not of great importance, the dream illustrates very nicely the typical dreaming mechanism and the method of dream analysis.

Several writers on psychoanalysis, following in the footsteps of Freud, have made it a business to collect numerous cases of dream symbolism. From these cases they have worked out and published fascinating lists of dream symbols. While it is no doubt true that many symbols have been in the same dreams of different people, there is no reason to believe they will always mean the same thing. Your dream and its analysis will reveal the symbols that you use.

Here is a case in point. The mere statement of dream and its analysis seems a farfetched case of symbolism,

20

yet when all the facts are available, including that of a previous dream, the symbolism ceases to be mysterious.

The dreamer, whom we shall call Smith, dreams he is in a canoe with a man we shall call Jones. Smith and Jones are paddling the canoe, and another, empty canoe is tied on behind.

Now, when I tell you that the canoe the men are paddling is a certain young lady, whom we will call Miss Brown, and that the empty canoe behind is Mrs. Smith, the dreamer's wife, you may say "Bosh!" Yet that is correct, and here is the analysis as Smith worked it out.

"I dreamed that Jones and I were paddling a canoe, and that an empty canoe was tied on behind. This is the only dream, or rather all of the dream, that I recalled on awakening. When I come to analyze it I do not connect Jones with any experiences of canoeing or recall that I ever wished to go canoeing with him. I only know that he is with Miss Brown. But I am rather fond of Miss Brown myself, and I recall that on my vacation last summer I wished she were there and that I could be paddling up the lake, with just her in the canoe. At this point I suddenly remembered another dream, which I must have dreamed earlier in the night, and forgotten when I woke up. In this dream I was in a canoe with Miss Brown, and Jones was in the other end of it, we men paddling.

"I would like to share Miss Brown's love with Jones; that is, I want her for myself, but I recognize him as a fine fellow whom I have no right to cut out. It would be nice if we could both have her. But I am married, and my wife would make trouble. If I had Miss Brown, my wife wouldn't have anyone. She wouldn't stand for that and she wouldn't give me up, she would come along too. The empty canoe tied on behind is my wife.

"The wish of this dream is that I would have Miss Brown, but I would have to share her with Jones, and my wife would have to tag along without anyone. The women were evidently in the canoes to start with but got lost out some way, or rather the canoes came to represent the women. Evidently my subconscious desire to possess Miss Brown is rather ridiculous, considering the circumstances under which I would have to accept her . . ."

21

The analysis of this dream was rendered easy by the memory, recalled in analyzing the first one, of the earlier dream in which Miss Brown was in the canoe. The second dream gives us positive evidence of the symbolism of the canoes as the women, and shows how easily this came about by the continuance of the dream after the women which caused it faded from the picture or were fused into and symbolized by the canoes. In neither dream memory does the dreamer's wife herself appear, and yet her part is obvious enough when the rest of the dream is analyzed.

The psychoanalytical value of this dream analysis is apparent. Smith would probably not have consciously admitted that he was in love with Miss Brown and would have insisted that such a love was ridiculous, as he was married and she had another lover whom he admired and would not wish to cut out. The dreamer was still in love with his wife, yet subconsciously he had developed a secondary love complex. He was splitting his love impulse, and some of his instinctive sex energy was going to the other woman and subtracting that much from the love for his wife. Bringing this subconscious fact into consciousness will naturally have the effect of diverting all his love to his wife, because it is so evident to common sense and reason that his love is wasted on the other woman.

THE DREAM OF THE NIGHT BEFORE THE WEDDING

This dream may not prove to be what you expect from the title. It was dreamed by a girl the night before her intended marriage, and its analysis and what it let to read like a movie thriller. The dream itself was simple, but the way its analysis revealed her subconscious life was important.

She dreamed that a cat and a dog, which she used to have at home when she was a little girl, were having a fight. The cat licked the dog and was chasing him, and the dog was howling dreadfully. She thought how ridiculous it was for the dog to be whipped by the cat and felt that he wasn't much of a dog.

22

She was to be married the next afternoon to a man whom we shall call Henry, whom she had met only a few months before. She wasn't sure that she loved Henry a great deal, but she was sure that she was doing a wise thing in marrying him. The reason she gave herself was that he was prosperous and very much a gentleman, refined and quiet. He thought the world of her, and she felt sure he would always be very tender and kind. But Henry was a little man, an inch shorter than she was; she had taken to wearing low-heeled shoes since she had met him. How different from Albert, the man she had gone with before she met Henry. Albert was so big and rough and a little uncouth; she loved him, but they had quarreled and she was afraid of him, afraid to marry him.

Then she thought of the dream of the cat and dog fighting. And the cat had licked the dog. She could see them now as she used to play with them when she was a little girl. She had called the cat Mama and the dog Papa before she understood sex; and she remembered how embarrassed her mother had been when she had announced in the presence of callers that the dog was the papa of the cat's little kittens. . . . She remembered how her mother and father had quarreled and how small and frightened her mother had seemed.

Now she saw the meaning of the dream. She had wanted her mother to win those "fights," and yet how ridiculous the dog in the dream had looked running and howling in fear of the cat. . . . And how ridiculous a man would look who was afraid of a woman. It was evident that she had refused to marry Albert because she was afraid of him, for he was a big rough man, like her own father. But was it possible that she had decided to marry Henry instead because he was little and gentle and meek and she could "manage" him? In that moment she felt that she would be a fool to marry a man she could not respect because he was afraid of her.

It was all very clear now. She had never before admitted it to herself, but she had refused her big manly lover and come so near to marrying the little man just because in her childhood she had resented seeing her mother bulldozed and browbeaten by a big man. The

23

complex so formed in childhood had prejudiced her against the big man, and this complex was in conflict with her natural instinct of love, which was naturally directed toward that type of man.

These subconscious truths being revealed made it evident that she could not go on with the marriage to the little man, even if he was more wealthy and refined than the man she now realized she really loved more. So she rose and sent a message to Henry breaking off the engagement that had come so near to being a wedding; and when she had removed to another part of the city, away from prying eyes, she sent a note to Albert and asked him to call.

A WIFE'S GUILTY CONSCIENCE

The dream: "It seemed as I was married to my husband and Mary X was also. We were all three of us at home [the dreamer's home on the old farm]. He was painting and I was holding the paints for him, but Mary X was making suggestions on the painting. I wanted to help, but she knew more about his art and he didn't pay any attention to me. So I told Mary X to go out and drive the cows from the pasture. And when she was gone, I said to him, 'Now let's run away before she comes back.' "

The analysis: The dream shows a clear case of substitution of one person for another. Mary X was an art student whom the dreamer and her artist husband had met only a few days before the dream. The wife was slightly jealous, as she was likely to be of any woman artist. There was no real ground for this, as the husband was much in love with his wife and did not care for the women artists he knew but said they were "a silly bunch." The wife had no real occasion to be jealous of Mary X.

The key to the deeper significance of the dream lay in its location at the old home and in the seemingly polygamous relationship. Mary X was a substitute character for the dreamer's own sister. The action of the dream was a dramatic condensation of what had really happened. The two sisters had lived on the old farm, both bright, pretty

24

girls deserving more intelligent husbands than the rural community afforded.

A young man, raised in the neighborhood had gone away to a large city and become an illustrator. He came back to visit the old home community, and his interest in the two sisters was at once apparent. The older girl (the dreamer) had realized that he was really hunting for a wife and that she felt that her younger sister ought to have him, for she was the more artistic.

But she, the dreamer, wanted him for herself. He was handsome and clever and to marry him meant an opportunity to get away from the drudgery of the old farm. So she managed the affair to her own ends and married him, but with the feeling deep down in her heart that she had cheated her sister out of an opportunity that was rightfully hers.

The younger sister had later married very well and was perfectly happy. There was no occasion for a feeling of regret. The artist's wife now realized from his scornful treatment of women artists that, had he married her sister, the latter's slight artistic ability, instead of being an element of happiness, would have made trouble. Consciously she had nothing to regret, as affairs turned out nicely all around, but subconsciously she still suffered from the complex of guilt based on the feeling that she had taken the man that her sister had won. The feeling had lived on in the depths of her mind and had become the source of her own unreasoning fears and jealousies.

Such a dream rightly understood and interpreted should (and presumably did) do much to free her of the inner sense of guilt and make her own married life more wholesome and happy.

THE DREAM OF A BASHFUL YOUNG MAN

A young man relates this dream and its analysis.

The dream: He seemed to be in a pen with a lot of white rabbits. He was eating with them, drinking milk out of a saucer and eating lettuce. He didn't seem to be one of the rabbits but was another kind of animal, a "kitten or puppy, or something." Then the pen seemed to be surrounded by a lot of dogs, which were all barking and laughing at him.

The association: (Recall of some childish feeling): When he was small, the young man had some white rabbits which had to be kept shut up in a pen to keep the dogs from hurting them. Dogs were rough and cruel animals; rabbits were pretty and tame. Nobody ought hurt white rabbits. Boys were rough and mean like dogs, and little girls were nice and tame like the white rabbits. The little girls' mothers were afraid to have them play with the mean and rough boys. But no mother objected to his playing with the girls, he was such a nice little boy. The other boys ridiculed his playing with the girls. They called him "fraidy cat" and "sissy."

When he grew older he moved to a new town and here refused to have anything to do with girls. He grew to be mortally afraid to be seen with them. Lately he had taken lessons in dancing. He could dance fine with the instructors, but the moment he went to a social dance and offered to dance with a girl, the old terror came back to him and he danced so badly the girl wouldn't have him for a partner.

The analysis, now apparent, reveals the retention in young manhood of a subconscious complex of childish fear of ridicule. He was still afraid to be seen playing with girls though he was a fine, handsome fellow with nothing that was sissy about him, in looks or manner. He had overcome his childish sissiness but had retained subconsciously the fear of ridicule.

A DREAM OF DANCING ON A GRAVE

The following dream of a girl stenographer has a double substitution of personalities and the blurring of a name that would seem a pretty clear case of the work of the dream censor. The dreamer is too fearful and ashamed of the real thought back of the dream to permit its more direct expression. Although I do not believe in the universal working of the dream censor or of dream symbolism, I admit the evidence of such an explanation of dreams is very good in certain cases. I can only say that the analysis must determine whether the real thoughts back of the dream are the more evident ones or the more obscure ones that are clarified only when interpreted as symbols.

The dream: "I was in a cemetery with my father, and we were putting flowers on a newly made grave. There was a tombstone freshly put up, and I started to read the name on it. The first name was Elizabeth, but the last name was blurred so I could not read it. I turned to my father; he was smiling and holding out his arms to me. He said, 'There, that's done, little girl, now let's dance.' We began dancing on the grave; but the scene soon changed and I was dancing in a hall with George D."

Recent dream material: She had walked through the cemetery the Sunday before with a girlfriend. There were people putting flowers on fresh graves, but she paid no particular attention to anyone. There was no man with them on that trip. She had never walked with her father in a graveyard. No one had died in her family. Her father and mother got on all right. She had never wished or feared particularly about her mother's death—and her mother's name was not Elizabeth. She did not know anyone by that name to whom the dream might refer. George D. was her friend, and she often danced with him as she was doing at the end of the dream. Dancing with her father was quite unthinkable, and dancing on the grave was "awful."

The search for dream material in the recent experiences does not seem to solve this dream; on the other hand, the dream suggests no particular childhood experiences. Under these circumstances, we have reason to believe that the dreamer's mind is holding back, and that tendency would lead us to suspect that the obvious characters of the dream are substitutes for someone else. Further associations reveal nothing that would help toward a solution. But about George D. we get these comments: "I don't care much for him, he is just a silly kid." This gives us our cue, that the dreamer does care for some other man, an older man, for whom her father is substituted in the dream. To the question whether her father called her "little girl," we get a negative answer. To the next question, "What man old enough to be your father does call you 'little girl'?" we get the revealing answer, "My boss does sometimes; but he doesn't mean anything by it."

Obviously, we have hit upon the clue to the real analysis of the dream. Elizabeth was the name of her employer's wife; the girl at first denied knowing this fact, and yet she recalled that when the wife had been away on vacation the summer before she (stenographer) had taken dictation of her employer's letter to his wife. Consciously the girl may not have known the wife's name, but subconsciously she did, and she blurred the surname in the dream.

This whole dream, put badly, means, "I wish my employer's wife would die, so then he and I could dance on her grave."

As you have seen by the way I have told it, the dreamer had help on this analysis. Without help she might not have been able to analyze the dreams; but on the other hand, we suspect her of holding back in the analysis and of lying because she did not want to admit the truth. The dreamer lied to herself in her dream, and she lied to herself and me a little, I think, in the analysis. If she had really wanted this analysis to come out, I think she could have analyzed the dream more quickly by herself than she did with my help.

I am quite willing to admit that some of you may have a little trouble with dreams of this sort—if you have them— but I insist that if you get over the foolish tendency to be afraid of your own thoughts you will be able to analyze such dreams better by yourself than you could with help. The practical point is that there is nothing of which to be afraid. The young lady in this case did not wish to admit to herself that she was in love with her employer; she wouldn't admit it openly in her dream. But with the analysis before her she is better off than with the love hidden in her subconscious mind; she is more likely to get over it. If she can't, she can change her job; or if she wants to do it with her eyes open, she can go on and have an affair with her employer.

If some of you object to my mention of this latter possibility, I can simply say that there is actually less danger of such an ending with the thing out in the open than there was by her going ahead and lying to herself.

The boss was calling her "little girl" and had dictated letters to his wife to her, evidently not minding revealing to her that there was no great love for him in his home. From such a situation it would be very easy for the girl to drift on, pretending that "he didn't mean anything by it" until the subconscious passion grew to a stage where it would take control regardless of further efforts of conscious suppression. I am holding no brief for illicit love but merely stating that I consider it safer to know what our feelings are than to go on lying to ourselves about them until they rebel and overpower our rational conscious minds.

A DREAM OF LOVE WITH A BROADER SIGNIFICANCE

A middle-aged and happily married friend had told me many of his dreams relating to various subjects, most of which we had been able to analyze with benefit and profit to him. There was one dream, however, or rather a series of dreams, relating to the same person, that for a long time seemed to both of us to be merely memories of puppy love affairs of his childhood and without significance to his present life.

These dreams were of a girl he had known in his early teens back in his home village. They seemed to indicate that he had worshiped from afar and never been able to make much headway with his youthful love affairs.

At my suggestion that these dreams might have some significance with his present love life, the dreamer always scoffed, declaring that he was very much in love with his young, beautiful, and cultured wife and that the other girl was probably married to some farmer or grocer and had a dozen kids.

Then one day he brought me another dream of his first love. "We were having the time of our lives," he said, "and what do you think we were doing? We were running around with torches setting fire to all the churches in town."

The pleasure he took in telling this dream I easily understood, for I well knew that the man was a hater of

29

churches and religion and that this animosity greatly distressed his wife. This was in fact the one sore spot in their otherwise happy married life.

A little questioning brought out these facts. In the strict village life of his boyhood everybody went to church; and the old standby phrase "May I see you home?" at the church door was the accepted, and practically the only way, in which a lad ever got himself a girl. Now the boy had been obliged to go to one church and the girl he was smitten with to another, stern parental authority forbidding even temporary absence from the family place of worship. And so he had come to hate churches, not because, as he had later come to believe, of any genuine lack of religion in his nature, but merely because the rigid church system of the little town had kept him from the girl he loved.

"Well," he admitted, when I offered this explanation, "I guess you have pretty near hit it. I don't know that I have any grudge against churches if they would let people be natural and happy." Needless to say, this discovery to his conscious mind of the complex against churches based on the thwarting of a boyish love led to a happier state of affairs in his own home.

A DREAM THAT FURNISHES PROOF OF SUBCONCIOUS REASONING

The following dream furnishes a curious example of subconsciousness reasoning:

A New York woman dreamed that she was in a subway station. In the space where the trains come through, there appeared a series of long platforms somewhat like a train of flatcars. People were stepping across from the main platform and crowding on these flatcarlike platforms. A gong sounded. People stopped stepping across the platforms, and little protective rails rose from the edges of the main platform, which kept the crowd back. Then a full-length subway train came rushing down the tunnel, its front end open. It ran right on without slacking speed, telescoping over the crowded flatcars and carrying them on with it.

Now another train of empty platforms rolled into place, and the dreamer stepped on with the crowd. As before, the train came through at full speed, running right over them, or rather, the shell of the train running around them; and the dreamer found herself in the full, moving train, which had thus picked up the crowd without stopping speed.

She marveled a little over this new system. She couldn't seem to understand how it worked, but it evidently did work, and she thought it fine.

Before giving the analysis of this dream, I want to call your attention to the evidence it furnishes of subconscious reasoning powers. Fortunately, the dreamer first told me of the dream while the causes that led up to it were still fresh in her memory. Thus I was able to sound her thoroughly on the subject and secure one of the finest proofs I have come across of the power of the subconscious to reason.

First, the dreamer assured me that she had (at the time of the dream and as far back as she could then remember) very little interest in mechanical and engineering problems. She was not in the habit of reasoning consciously on such subjects or of attempting to solve such problems. Her reasons for not doing so were, as you shall see later, subconscious ones. But consciously, that is, so far as she was aware, she had no such ability and no such interest. On the contrary, she distinctly lacked such ability and was bored and annoyed by such reasoning and by all consideration or discussion of such problems.

More specifically, she had positively not taken any interest in the problem of subway congestion; that is, with an inclination to think out a remedy. "I knew that the subways were congested," she said, "because it delayed me, because I had to be packed in with a lot of crude people while the subways often stalled and that made me late for my appointments. But that is all I have ever thought about it. As far as trying to figure out a solution, I never did, and I know I never could and would never try to."

Now, from such a conscious attitude toward the problem, we jump to the dream in which a finished scheme of an effort to solve subway delays and congestion is all figured out. The dreamer does not figure it out in the dream but finds it in complete operation. She marvels at it, wonders how it works, and thinks it rather clever. Certainly she is not in the least aware that it is her own invention.

The fact that the invention in subway operation that she saw working in the dream is a ridiculous and impossible one by no means proves that she did not subconsciously reason, though it does prove that she reasoned rather badly. The very impossibility of a train at full speed picking up the waiting platforms of people further proves that it was not a remembered idea she had heard someone describe or had read about or seen pictured in a newspaper. But impossible as it was, her scheme was rather complicated and ingenious. Not only did she reason subconsciously, but she reasoned upon a mechanical problem and worked out mechanical details, all of which she could not and would not have done in her conscious mind.

Here is the interpretation of the subway dream: In the first place, the recent dream material is quite obvious. Her attention had been turned to subway congestion by the new turnstile, and she was annoyed by the crowded and slow subways and wished they could be improved.

That is interesting but of no great importance to her life. Yet the fuller analysis of the dream by free association unfolded a tragic life story and saved the threatened happiness of a home. This analysis revealed that the real deep-lying wish motive of her dream was sexual in a broad sense and that she wished for more peace, love, and happiness in her married life. This was a conscious as well as a subconscious wish.

A more specific wish, closely related to the dream, was strictly subconscious; she wished that she could be interested in, understand, and reason out engineering problems. Her reason for so wishing was that her husband was an engineer, and such interest and capacity on her part would have enabled her to understand his work and, by so doing, make him more happy and more efficient and prevent his attention to a woman scientist who did understand his work and to whom he went for sympathy and admiration. Now, it would seem that this wish would be conscious, but it was not, for it had been repressed; and

32

she consciously maintained that she was disinterested in and bored by his engineering. She believed that she was sorry she had married the engineer and that he was narrow, mechanical, and uncultured; that she should have married an artist or musician.

Now the dream analysis takes us back to her childhood, and we find the little girl in a refined home with a rather silly old-fashioned mother. The girl is a normal bright child and well endowed with all human instincts of construction: the instincts that lead boys to build things and be interested in machines. The nice little girl with the nice mama, who is trying very hard to make a lady out of her, has a playmate, in the shape of a boy in overalls, who has a good mechanical bent. He is building things in the barn. The girl becomes interested and wants to help. She does help and does so very cleverly.

After a happy afternoon so spent, she comes home with a dainty dress torn and smudged in the boy's machine shop while her mother thought she was over at a nice neighbor's playing with a wax doll. Her mother scolds her and tells her she is unladylike. The mother gossips to a neighbor woman and worries over the tomboy tendencies of her child and the degradation of playing with boys in the barn. The gossip gets to the children, the little girl is called a tomboy, and there are vague, naughty, childish suggestions about being with boys in barns. So by social disapproval and childish ridicule the instinct of mechanical construction is suppressed in this girl child, as it is in practically all girl children, because that is an instinct society has seen fit to assign to men.

Now we skip a dozen years and find a typically well-bred and rather narrowly educated young lady, ignorant of science and mechanics and with little ability to think along those lines but with the native instinct to do so still alive and buried under a heap of acquired ladylike culture.

She meets a young man, and he is an engineer. He is too well bred to "talk shop" while in society (one of the silly restrictions of so-called good breeding). Moreover, he is not yet taking his profession very seriously and is interested in dancing and social life.

So they fall in love. Little is said about his engineering

33

and his chance to rise in the world. Yet the fact that he is an engineer revives for a time this suppressed constructive instinct, and she hopes to take an interest in and help him with his work.

So they marry. One evening the young husband comes home full of enthusiasm for a problem in engineering he is working on. The wife is interested and talks about it, but she is ignorant and unskilled in this sort of mind work, and the husband laughs at her lack of knowledge and understanding. He says "Of course, I couldn't expect you to understand this, pardon me for mentioning it."

So again the instinct is snubbed and suppressed and forced back into the subconscious. This time the suppression, with the resentment of wounded pride to aid it, creates a direct conscious antagonism to the subject. The wife actually cultivates a disinterest and inability to think along mechanical lines. But the husband grows more engrossed in his profession and ignores his wife and her social life. They begin to drift apart in sympathies and interests; she seeks compensation by following artistic lines of thought and culture, and he seeks womanly admiration elsewhere.

Such is the state of affairs when the subway dream occurs. Its analysis reveals to the wife her original instinctive interest in this broadly human passion of devising mechanical things, and she sees how that instinct was twice suppressed and how foolish and unfortunate that suppression was. The analysis of this dream, explained to the husband, shows what an unfair brute he was to kill his own joy in life by snubbing his young wife's first efforts to understand his work. He sees, too, the humor and cleverness of this dainty wife as a tomboy building things in an old barn, and also her remarkable feat of attempting to solve the subway congestion by subconscious reasoning. They laugh at that and laugh, too, at many of her other impossible inventions and impractical solutions, but he is now laughing with her, not at her. And they are going to live happily ever after.

HOW ARE YOU TO KNOW WHEN YOUR ANALYSIS IS RIGHT?

This is a natural question for you to ask when first getting acquainted with the subject. After you have had considerable experience in the analysis of your own dreams, you probably will not ask that question, though someone else to whom you might explain your work or tell one of your analyses would be very likely to ask it.

In the first place, you have the same advantage that you would have in thinking out any other kind of problem. That is, if you follow the methods that have been tested and proven by others and reach certain conclusions, the chances are that you will be correct.

But in the analysis of your own dreams you have a very much more important fact to help you. The answer you are looking for is already in your subconscious mind, so when you work back toward it and find it there is a distinct sense of recognition. You think, "Oh, that's it," and there is a feeling of relief, a feeling that the search is ended. After you have become reasonably practiced in the work this recognition will be sufficiently convincing.

To explain by an example, suppose you are trying to think of some forgotten name that has slipped from your mind, that is deeply buried in the subconscious vaults of memory. You may try rather desperately to remember it and to no avail, but if someone suggests the correct name to you, ninety-nine times out of a hundred you will say, "Oh yes, that's it." The name suggestion immediately reaches the buried memory and is identified.

The correct analysis of the dream reaches the subconscious wish or fear, and is likewise identified.

Here we see another advantage of self-analysis. The professional analyzing another's dreams does not have this advantage except as his patient chooses to give it to him. Psychoanalysis is one of the few instances in which the patient or client knows more than the doctor or expert.

CAN ALL DREAMS BE INTERPRETED?

Yes, if they are completely remembered and you have had sufficient experience in interpreting your dreams. But do not worry, especially at first, if you cannot find a satisfactory interpretation of all your dreams.

If after reasonable effort you do not get on the track of a revealing interpretation, lay the dream aside. Later, after you have interpreted other dreams, you can probably come back to the one that gave you trouble and find that it now has revealing associations. If not, it is probably that you have lost some essential part of the dream in transferring it to the subconscious mind. Hence, to force the interpretation of the fragment that is left would mean to get an inaccurate interpretation.

You can rest assured that you will have plenty of dreams to interpret, for the more interested you get in this work the better you will remember your dreams—and you do dream them, plenty of them, for you dream all the time you are asleep.

Neither should you worry lest you lose some essential messages from the subconscious because of the dream you lose or fail to interpret. If we had to depend on any particular dream our chance of success would be small; for even though we remembered so many dreams that it would keep us busy all day long interpreting them, we would still be getting but a small fraction of the total number of the dreams we dream.

But the subconscious will repeat its fundamental wishes in dreams again and again.

MAKING USE OF YOUR DREAM ANALYSIS

We interpret our dreams to find out what is going on in our subconscious mind, but the purpose of psychoanalysis is not merely to find out what is going on in the subconscious mind but to make use of the subconscious forces to gain our conscious aims and ideals in life.

When you have analyzed your dream and have determined the subconscious wish that prompted it, here are some questions you might ask yourself:

1. How does this wish apply to my present life?

2. Is the subconscious wish also a conscious wish?

3. If so, what forces within my own nature, or in the world outside, stand in the way of realization of that wish?

4. If the subconscious wish is one I cannot consciously approve, what conscious wish can I offer to my subconscious which would serve as a substitute for this wish that cannot be realized?

NEW KEY TO DREAMS

After having given these general rules, there remains for me only to draw up my own key to dreams at once synthetic and reasonable (as far as this is possible)—only by way of information, of course, as my very skepticism does not prevent my being conscientious.

For this task I have consulted the best ancient and modern sources. I have adopted the triple rule:

1. not to waste too much time on dreams which are too vague, too rare, or too bizarre;

2. to broaden the meaning of these images, for here, more than in any other divinatory art, would detail run the risk of landing in a very morass of charlatanism;

3. to neglect explanations which are silly for the very reason that they seem plain, or which have an unpleasant aftertaste, such as that threading pearls in a dream means a love affair.

I shall in the main give those meanings which have unanimous opinion in their favor, this being a sign of tradition and moral value.

AN INTRODUCTION
TO NUMEROLOGY

There are many systems and methods of making predictions but none perhaps as interesting as numerology, since anyone may work it out. No long hours of tedious study are required. There are only a few simple rules to follow.

The Egyptians, the Greeks, the Romans, and the Arabians had systems of arriving at number vibrations, which are remarkably accurate. The teachings of the adepts in numerology have come down to us from the most remote antiquity.

All letters have numerical equations; therefore, all combinations of letters in names respond to certain numerical values. When a name is given to a person, city, book, or *anything*, it immediately lets loose a certain occult force expressed in numbers. Nature in its most primitive form responds to numbers. Note the geometric formation of snowflakes, of growing plant cells, the mathematical precision of the sunrise, the movements of the heavenly bodies, the procession of the seasons, etc. These, and other geometric or mathematical formulas, respond to various numerical values. In everyday life we answer to the numbers of our names, our births, and our locations by our reactions to certain things. Some names appeal to us immediately; others, we pass by unnoticed. It is our reaction to the numerical magnetism which causes us either to ignore or notice them. The universe is operated with exact mathematical precision calculated to a fraction of a second.

Every expression of rhythm responds to a numerical measure of time. When you listen to music that thrills you, you are unconsciously harmonizing with a certain number of influences in the notes of the music; or when you dislike certain types of music, it is because the numerical value of such music is not in sympathy with your own name and birth numbers. Everyday life brings some

41

good or adverse reaction to the magnetic influence of the numbers around. They are in everything you see, hear, or feel. It is impossible to escape them. The sooner you learn the value of these numbers, the better you will be able to harmonize with life and the people around you.

On the following pages I give a very simple system of number calculation so that you may become familiar with their influence in your daily life and get the best out of your newly acquired knowledge.

To find out your fortunate dream number, reduce the key to your dream to a single digit. For example, if you dream of a baby:

$$B = 2$$
$$A = 1$$
$$B = 2$$
$$Y = 7$$

$12 = 1 + 2 = 3$, which would be the lucky number for baby. If you want three numbers you can use any three numbers that reduce to 3. For example, $9\text{-}1\text{-}2 = 3$.

You will note that all numbers appearing before and after each dream in this book have been obtained in this manner.

THE ALPHABET

In any system of numerology the letters of the alphabet respond to the nine digits, or single numbers. Numbers of two figures are not retained except in the cases of 11 or 22, which will be explained later. The letters of the alphabet must be reduced to single numbers; consequently, more than one letter responds to the same number, as shown below:

1	2	3	4	5	6	7	8	9
A	B	C	D	E	F	G	H	I
J	K	L	M	N	O	P	Q	R
S	T	U	V	W	X	Y	Z	

You will notice that the letters A, J, and S have the numerical value of the number 1, while B, K, and T have the value of 2, etc. Whatever number a letter is under, that is its numerical power or number vibration.

EXAMPLE OF NUMERIZING A NAME

We are now ready to begin transfering names into numbers. We will choose a simple name as an example. Preferably, the first name and last name of a person should be written vertically, as it is easier to add this way than horizontally. We choose the name of Mary Smith:

M	=	4		S	=	1
A	=	1		M	=	4
R	=	9		I	=	9
Y	=	7		T	=	2
		21		H	=	8
						24

The name Mary adds up to 21, and the name Smith results in 24. To secure the full name vibration it is necessary to add 21 to 24, which equals 45. This is a double number, so we will add 4 and 5, which equal 9. This young lady then responds to the name number 9. You may now refer to the indications of the numbers in the following pages and find out what number 9 denotes.

We will now suppose that Mary Smith's birth date is June 8, 1912. To transfer this into numerical value, we would write it thus: 6, 8; 1912, because June is the sixth month. Now we add these numbers together: 6 plus 8 plus 1 plus 9 plus 1 plus 2 equals 27. This total is a double number, so we add 2 plus 7, which equals 9. We find that Mary Smith's birth date is 9, the same as her name number. Any number derived from the birth date is called the birth path. Now we wish to find her destiny number. We will add the name number and the birth date number thus: 9 plus 9 equals 18. This is a double number, so we have to add 1 plus 8, which is also 9. Thus, Mary Smith's destiny number is 9. Refer to 9 in the destiny column on the following pages and read her indications.

Certain numbers have an affinity for each other, while others clash seriously. Even numbers harmonize with other even numbers, and odd numbers harmonize with other odd numbers; but even numbers seldom harmonize with odd numbers except in the cases of 11 and 22. These two numbers are apt to be the exception and will harmonize with almost any other number. 11 is a higher octave of 2, because 1 and 1 equal 2, while 22 is a higher octave of 4, as 2 plus 2 equals 4. However, these two numbers are seldom reduced a digit because of their very strong individual powers. Therefore, when you have arrived at an 11 or a 22, you need not reduce it further but look in the indications that follow these pages for those two numbers.

We now propose to find out whether Mary Smith, with a destiny number of 9, would be successful as a typist. Secure the number vibration of the word typist. We find it gives us 2 plus 7 plus 7 plus 9 plus 1 plus 2, which equals 28. This is a double number, so we add: 2 plus 8 equals 10; this, likewise, is a double number; therefore, 1 is added to 0, which equals 1. Since the word typist responds to 1, which is an odd number as is 9, Mary Smith would be a successful typist.

In the same way we can discover whether she would be successful in Chicago, New York, Los Angeles, or any other place by working out the numerical values of such places. We can also find out if a certain street and number is favorable or not; if she should marry her lover or not; if travel by land or water or air is best for her, etc., by securing the numbers of those things the same way we worked out her name number. Many other things will suggest themselves to you that you can work out for yourself or for your friends, such as the proper hotel to select, proper room number to engage, etc.

In figuring the numerical values of names, use the one by which the person is known. If the name James has been given a boy at birth but he always has been called Jim, use the name Jim. If you find the name James produces better influences, he should immediately change his name to James and sign it so at all times, insisting too that his friends call him James instead of Jim. The name by which a person has been called all his life is the name vibration he responds to best, since the constant repetition has stamped upon his destiny the influence of the name even though it is a nickname by which he has been called since childhood. Therefore, when you are numerizing a name, the one by which the person is known is the one to be selected. Changing it, adding certain letters, or spelling it differently produces a new vibration that will bring different results and a different personality if continued for a long enough time. Many famous people change the spelling of their names when they understand numerology, so as to create better harmony.

It is sometimes best, when a woman marries, for her to retain her given name in addition to her new surname. Sometimes it is best to drop the given name and use her husband's full name, placing Mrs. before it. By working out the different combinations according to numerology the best combination can be found quickly and easily. Once the person decides to change his name, the old one must be forgotten entirely and never again used in any future dealings, introductions, or letters.

Remember: Names, articles, places, and things must harmonize—odd numbers with odd numbers, even numbers with even numbers—to be fortunate.

MISCELLANEOUS OPERATIONS WITH NUMEROLOGY

There are various ways in which numerology may be employed to amuse or benefit the many who enjoy working out their numbers. The ideas presented here are just a few suggestions. Others will come to mind as you work with the science of numbers.

SECURING FORTUNATE NUMBERS WITH CARDS

Take a deck of ordinary playing cards and remove the 10 spots. Previous to this you will have worked out your destiny number as directed on the preceding pages. We will take the destiny number of Mary Smith, which we found was 9. After removing the 10 spots and placing them aside, Mary Smith should shuffle the cards, give them one cut, then shuffle them again. She should go through the operation of shuffling and cutting nine times.

She should then deal off nine cards from the top of the pack and put them on one side. The very next card should be turned up and placed face up on the table. If the card should be a 5, her fortunate number would be 5. If she is seeking a number with two figures, she should deal off nine more cards, place them aside, and use the very next card, putting it face up alongside the first one. If she desires a number of three figures, she will deal off nine more cards and place the next one alongside the other two. Now suppose she has laid down the 5 of diamonds, the 2 of clubs, and the 8 of spades; her fortunate number is 528. Face cards are to be considered as 0. Therefore, if the last card had been the king of spades instead of an 8, the number will be 520.

Remember always to shuffle and cut the cards as many times as your destiny number. If you have a destiny number of 4, you should shuffle and cut four times and deal off four cards from the top instead of nine. Your destiny number is the index to use. This process should not be repeated for the same person more than once in twenty four hours, because to repeat it destroys the vibration of the first fortunate number and weakens the one found the second time. Note: The reason the 10 spots are removed is that 10 is a double number, and in numerology you are concerned with single numbers only.

TO FIND YOUR FORTUNATE YEARS

We wish to know if 1934 is a fortunate year for Mary Smith. Add 1934: 1 plus 9 plus 3 plus 4 equals 17. Now add the 1 and 7, which is 8. This results in an even number, so it does not harmonize with Mary Smith's destiny number of 9; consequently, 1934 is not as fortunate for her as odd years would be. The digit of the year must be the same or must be in harmony with your destiny number to be a fortunate year for you.

TO FIND YOUR FORTUNATE MONTHS

It is not necessary to work out the names of months. Merely consider the number of the month; January is the first month of the year, therefore number 1; February is the second month, therefore number 2; etc. October is the tenth month, therefore (1 plus 0) is 1. November is the eleventh month, and you always leave 11 as it is. December is the twelfth month, therefore (1 plus 2) is to 3. Mary Smith's best month is the ninth month, which is September.

TO FIND YOUR GOOD DAYS BY NUMEROLOGY

Any day which adds up to your destiny number is best for you. Mary Smith's lucky days in any month are the ninth, eighteenth, and twenty-seventh. Her fairly good days are those which add to other odd numbers. The days that are neutral or slightly adverse are those which add up to even numbers. Work this out with your own destiny number and check off your good and adverse days on your calendar, to guide you.

TO FIND YOUR BEST HOURS OF THE DAY

Find the time of sunrise from your local daily paper or almanac. For example, suppose the sun rises at 6:15 A.M. The first hour after sunrise will be from 6:15 to 7:15. Mary Smith's best hours are the ninth hour after sunrise and any other hour which adds to 9, which would be the eighteenth hour after sunrise. These hours will vary a few minutes each day as the sun varies in rising time. Always use the hours after sunrise which equal your destiny number.

HOW TO CHOOSE PARTNERS OR FRIENDS

For best results in partnerships or friendships, the destiny numbers should be the same as yours. Those who have corresponding destiny numbers will make fairly good friends, companions, and partners. Those who have destiny numbers which clash will not make satisfactory associates, and relations with them will not be permanent nor very congenial.

HOW TO MAKE MONTHLY PREDICTIONS

Secure the monthly number of any month and year (by month number is meant the number figure for any month reduced to a single digit). Add it and your destiny number together, which is your monthly number for that month. Then refer to the gallery of numbers in the pages which follow for the general indications for that month. As an example, we will see what the indications for Mary Smith are for the month of June 1934:

June 6
1934 added together 17
Destiny number of Mary Smith 9
                                Total...... 32

Three plus 2 equals 5, which is her monthly number for June 1934.

To find Mary Smith's indications for June 1934, refer to the gallery of monthly numbers. Secure your own monthly number in the same way, using your destiny number instead of that of Mary Smith. It will frequently happen that several months will respond to the same monthly number, but they will change from year to year.

GALLERY OF NAME NUMBERS

1: The number of creation, of beginning of first impulses, or of the source of energy. Persons whose name vibrates to this number are trailblazers. Most of their lives they have been leaders and thinkers along pioneer lines, and they are usually popular in whatever sphere of society they choose to move in. They are constructive in thought and like to be doing something new and out of the ordinary. They do not follow in the path of others and generally have the courage of their convictions. There is a lower level to this number also. Those who respond to this lower level are eccentric, egotistical, haughty, dominating, and self-conscious. If your name responds to this number, make every effort to overcome any weak tendencies that might show up in your character.

2: The number of beauty, culture, truth, perception, and consciousness. It is a decidedly feminine number and causes the person to respect and appreciate the refined and intellectual things in life. It is the number of cooperation, attraction, affection, emotion, and enthusiasm. Those whose name responds to this number are warm friends, congenial companions, interesting entertainers, and good judges of human nature. The lower plane of this number causes the person to be hasty, sensitive, and inclined to be too particular. If your name responds to this number, strive to overcome any undignified tendencies that might show up in your character.

3: The number of enlightenment, thoroughness, and refinement. This number causes a person to be tender, affectionate, sympathetic, very cautious about details, prone to self-sacrifice for some idealistic principle, and often willing to do without things to assist friends. It is the number of the Holy Trinity and causes the person to be highly religious, impressionable, intuitive, and magnetic.

4: The number of realization, security, protection, stability, and ambition. Those whose names respond to this vibration are true friends and good company. They possess brilliant and inventive minds and are inclined to reach the goal of their ambitions regardless of obstacles. They usually like a life of activity and variety and have many interesting experiences from which they learn much of the usefulness of life.

5: The number of uncertainty, hesitancy, doubt, and discouragement. Those whose names respond to this number will often become confused, restless, irritable, impatient, and moody. They find it hard to form congenial companionships and frequently disagree with the opinions of others. They sometimes feel that life has been unkind to them, as though they were living an existence against which their nature rebels. If this is your name number and you feel that you do not want to fight against the influences any longer, it might be a good idea to change your

49

name slightly so that it will respond to some other number.

6: The number of dual personality, indecision, temptation, and excess. Those whose name responds to this number have a peculiar nature. They are not always understood and very often cause their own failures. If they will learn to gain from their experiences, they will make this a fortunate number, but drifting through life will never get them anywhere. They like to follow the lines of least resistance, and should overcome a tendency to indiscreet actions. Determination will help them conquer the uncertainties of this number.

7: The number of spirituality, mysticism, wisdom, and success. Those whose names responds to this number are receptive, studious, creative, and intellectual. They possess a deep understanding and desire for the finer things of life. If there are no conflicting influences in their numbers, they make warm friends, valuable employees, and ideal companions or partners. They have magnetic personalities, are very unselfish, and possess rare outlooks on life.

8: The number of justice, evolution, strength, inspiration, and genius. Those whose names respond to this number have strong personalities. They are very magnetic, self-willed, independent, progressive, intuitive, and honest, candid, and straightforward in dealings. The number 8 vibration is an extremely strong one, difficult to overcome. It causes a person to be very active, seldom contented for a great length of time, and eager for changes of events and scenery.

9: The number of dominance, efficiency, psychic powers, humanitarianism, and renewed energy. Those whose names respond to this number are clever, active, philosophical, and intuitive. They have fertile imaginations and high ideals, and are endowed with poetic or artistic ability. They are usually very dignified and pleasant but odd and whimsical. They are refined, gentle, sympathetic, and even tempered. They make friends easily and are quick to solve others' problems.

11: The number of power, courage, success, adventure, impulse, and energy. Those whose names respond to this number are an octave higher than those who respond to 2. They are deep thinkers and fond of exciting adventures. At times they are vague in their statements. Their minds grasp the general outcome of things, but they usually skip details. The number has such a powerful influence that they often find themselves confused by many contradictions, likes, and dislikes. Clear thinking, determination, and concentration are qualities of mind necessary to develop in order to control the restlessness this number creates.

22: The number of rashness, errors, haste and changeability. Those whose names respond to this number should overcome a tendency to be critical and restless. They often do not understand their own peculiarities. They say and do things on the spur of the moment and then wonder why they did them. They usually do not look before they leap. They are inclined to go to the extremes, even against their own better judgments. They have hard struggles with themselves.

GALLERY OF BIRTH PATH NUMBERS
(secured from year, month, and day of birth)

1: If this is your birth, you will have many strange experiences. You will go through life making your own conditions and carrying out your own ideas. You will lead a constructive life.

2: If this is your birth path, you will seem to go around in circles and have repetitions of certain experiences at regular intervals. If you cultivate self-control, you will have an interesting, useful life.

3: If this is your birth path, you will have many of the better things in life. You will travel much and gain from

51

the experiences of others. Yours will be a fortunate, contented life.

4: If this is your birth path, you will have many loyal friends. You will gain some prominence in the business and professional worlds. Yours will be a successful, pleasant life.

5: If this is your birth path, you will have strange experiences, at times difficult to overcome; yet with your strong personality you will win out. Yours will be a long, contented life.

6: If this is your birth path, you are apt to be too careless of your actions and general health and welfare. Success will be attained only through firmness of purpose and stability. Yours is a changeable but useful life.

7: If this is your birth path, you will undertake and usually accomplish big things. New and interesting experiences will present themselves. You will be the master of your own destiny. Yours will be an unusually successful life.

8: If this is your birth path, you will lead an active life but not necessarily a peaceful one. New ambitions will always spur you onward. Frequent outbursts of temper will alter your course of life. Yours will be an adventurous career.

9: If this is your birth path, you will travel extensively and engage in unusual affairs and odd professions. Literature, art, music, and the stage will attract you. Yours will be an adventurous career and an interesting life.

11: If this is your birth path, you will engage in many risky adventures. You will overcome obstacles by sheer force of willpower. You are captain of your soul and master of your own destiny. Yours will be a progressive life.

22: If this is your birth path, you will create many of your own difficulties. Losses may occur through bad judgement and unreliable associates. Learn to think constructively and act with discretion. Cultivate self-control, and you will succeed.

GALLERY OF DESTINY NUMBERS
(secured by adding name number and birth path number)

1: If this is your destiny number, you will achieve great success through your constructive efforts. Some help will be given you, but in the main you will be self-made.

2: If this is your destiny number, you will have many ups and downs in life, but through the aid of friends and relatives you eventually will be successful. You will have wealth if you utilize all your productive faculties.

3: If this is your destiny number, you will experience many successful ventures. The better things of life will assist you to the goal of your ambitions.

4: If this is your destiny number, you will have a life of usefulness, financial success, and honor. Choose your profession carefully and forge ahead. Nothing can stop you if you persist. You will likely acquire much property.

5: If this is your destiny number, you will stand in your own way many times. Guard against accidents and do not trust strangers. Your life is one of varied experiences, some pleasant, others discouraging.

6: If this is your destiny number, do not permit yourself to drift. Control your emotions and make the best of your opportunities. You are apt to overlook them. Success will come to you if you are alert and industrious.

7: If this is your destiny number, you may expect to attain prominence in life. Your light will shine far and you will travel extensively. Friends will be attracted to you.

8: If this is your destiny number, you will encounter financial difficulties often but usually will overcome them with experience and shrewdness. Your life will be very active.

9: If this is your destiny number, you will live a very useful, contented life. You possess many talents, are admired by friends, and enjoy an excellent reputation.

11: If this is your destiny number, you will lead a very active life, will succeed in big undertakings, and be prominent in your sphere of life. You will be the master of your destiny and creator of your fortune.

22: If this is your destiny number, the lower qualities of your nature may control your life unless you strive to change them. Avoid schemes and questionable enterprises. Be deliberate in all productiveness.

GALLERY OF MONTHLY NUMBERS
(secured by adding the destiny number to number of month and year)

1: Any month that responds to this number for you is a month of new happenings. It is a good month to make and start things, take trips, ask favors, start new business ventures, write letters, etc. Anything you can manage to carry on without aid from others should succeed this month. It is a good time to buy, advertise, hire new help, look for new work, and make changes.

2: Any month that responds to this number for you is a month of varied experiences and unexpected turns of events: if unmarried, possible wedlock; slight restlessness; and danger through carelessness. This month holds many arguments, broken friendships, etc., unless you make an effort to control things. Think much but say little. Guard your health and avoid conflicts.

3: Any month that responds to this number for you is ideal for carrying out plans, making changes, taking trips,

54

handling financial matters, dealing with business and professional people. Important, beneficial changes are apt to occur in your domestic and personal life. Make the most of your opportunities.

4: Any month that responds to this number for you is a good month to try and complete unfinished tasks, to make an effort to realize your ambitions, secure the good will of others, deal in lands, property, and legal affairs. If you exercise a reasonable amount of determination and good judgment, you should succeed at this time. You should be able to build a foundation for future activities.

5: Any month that responds to this number is a month in which you should use caution in all you undertake. Guard against fires, accidents, losses, slander, scandal, extravagance, and outbursts of temper. Guard your health and take no risks or chances on anything. Distressing bits of news may come to you this month, but refuse to be alarmed. Avoid litagation, general unrest, and loss of friends.

6: Any month that responds to this number for you is a month which depends upon your own initiative; you can make it either a profitable or an unprofitable month. You may experience some trouble in your domestic affairs and minor delays in carrying out your plans, but if you retain poise you will be able to straighten out everything satisfactorily. Guard your health and control your temper.

7: Any month that responds to this number for you is a month of good results. Follow your hunches and impressions. A good time to read, study, and investigate, it is also favorable for visiting, planning, traveling, starting new enterprises, seeking new work, buying and selling, and investing. New friends and pleasant experiences should enrich your life.

8: Any month that responds to this number for you is a month of radical changes, new ambitions, and much progress. During this month's influence you will be enthusiastic and courageous. Deal with prominent people, develop new propositions, advertise, travel, attend to important financial matters, and push all things of material importance. Avoid undue haste and too much force. Guard against accidents, fires, and minor injuries.

9: Any month that responds to this number for you is a very important month. You will have opportunities to complete tasks that have been pending for a long time, things that you start now rather than having started before. You will have renewed hopes and ambitions and new ideals. Ideas should be carried out carefully. Develop your personality and energy.

11: Any month that responds to this number for you is a month of intense activity. You will be busy yet seem to lack time to finish your plans. However, the headway you gain will be permanent. You will discover that you have a stronger willpower than you realized and that you can conquer obstacles more easily at this time. It is a month of a rise in power, new adventures, and a realization of ambitions, partial or complete.

22: Any month that responds to this number is a month in which you should be careful. You are apt to be influenced by others, to your detriment. Avoid extravagance, rashness, temptations, losses, and controversy over legal matters. Control your emotions and temper. Guard your health and take no risks or chances. You are likely to be impulsive and hasty.

DEFINITIONS

NAME NUMBER—The number secured by transfering the letters in a person's name to numbers. This shows the general characteristics the person has developed from the use of his name throughout his life.

BIRTH PATH NUMBER—The number secured by transforming the month, date, and year of the person's birth and the outstanding events to be experienced.

56

DESTINY NUMBER—The number secured by adding the name number and birth path number together. This shows whether the name adds or subtracts to the birth path indications. If it subtracts, the name should be changed for the future.

MONTHLY NUMBERS—The number secured by adding the destiny number to the number of any month and year. This shows the general indications for that month and year. Monthly numbers change from year to year. Name numbers remain the same always, unless the spelling of the name is changed. Birth path numbers never change; they always remain the same. Destiny numbers remain the same unless the spelling of the name is changed.

A NUMEROLOGICAL
KEY TO DREAMS

A

6 Abandon—This is an unfavorable dream and indicates the loss of friends or the failure of some fortunate expectation. Trouble is indicated, whether you abandon some other person, or whether he abandons you. Abandoning your lover: Will be guilty of foolish actions. 132

8 Abbey—Anything connected with a church shows peace of mind and freedom from anxiety. The more important the structure, the better the prospect. 215

9 Abdomen—It is an omen of contrary meaning. When you are in pain in your dream, your health will be good and your affairs will prosper because of your physical vigor. But if you dream of your unclothed abdomen, then it is an unfortunate omen, especially if you have a lover or are married, for you may expect unfaithfulness or even treachery on the part of some loved person. Do not rashly give your confidence after such a dream. 234

5 Abhor—To dream that you dislike anything or any person is an omen that depends upon the circumstances. If your feeling of distaste disturbs you seriously, then it foretells difficulties in your path; but if you merely dislike any article and can get rid of it, then you will overcome your worries. 931

4 Abortion—A warning as regards the health or the happiness of your partner in marriage; be on your guard as to both. 103

9 Above (hanging and about to fall)—Some danger awaits you, but it may be avoided if the object does not fail. 234

5 Abroad—A change of work is probable. This dream shows that you are in an unsettled state of mind. Others going abroad: Triumph over enemies. 932

5 Abscess—A dream of illness is one of contrary meaning and signifies that you will enjoy good health, or a speedy recovery if you are already ill. An abscess being operated on: A mystery will be solved. 293

4 Abscond—To dream that some person, whether stranger or acquaintances, has absconded with his employer's money or otherwise done some serious wrong is a warning to you of treachery among those around you. If you yourself are the person in question, the injury will be slight and you will recover from your losses. 319

4 Absence—This is usually a dream of contrary meaning. If you dream of the death of an absent friend, it foretells a wedding. A loved one being absent: Danger in love matters. 832

6 Absinthe—Drinking spirits or cocktails in your dream is a warning of coming trouble; the more you drink, the more serious the disaster will be. 357

2 Abstinence—To dream that you refuse to drink is a sign of good fortune coming, but it may not be lasting in its effects. 902

2 Abundance—To dream of plenty is always a good sign and indicates success in your plans. Relatives having an abundance of everything: Approaching money. 353

3 Abuse—To dream that someone is abusing you is a bad sign, but it applies to your business affairs only. To dream that you are abusing others foretells success after hard work. 831

2 Abyss—To dream of any hollow space is a sign of difficulties ahead; it is an obstacle dream. If you escape from the abyss, you will overcome your troubles; but if you fall therein, then be careful in your business affairs. Do not lend money, for it will not be returned to you. 192

7 Academy—To dream that you are master or mistress of an academy indicates that you will be reduced in your circumstances; if you are single, that your intended marriage will be characterized by adversity. 243

3 Accept—To dream that you have been accepted by your lover or, if you are a woman, that your lover has proposed to you and that you have accepted him, is generally considered a dream of contrary meaning. It is

a warning that your love affair will not prosper or at least that it will be a long time coming right. In some localities, however, it is looked upon as a fortunate omen. 687

5 Accident—This dream depends entirely upon the surroundings. If the accident occurs at sea, it means disappointment in your love affairs. But if it happens on land, it concerns your personal and business ventures. Being in an accident: Your life is threatened. An accident in an automobile: Approaching money. 329

6 Accounts—To dream that you are engaged in adding up accounts or checking business figures is a warning to you to be careful or you will lose money by giving credit too freely. 312

7 Accuse—Obviously, there is not much difference between this and abuse, except that the nature of the trouble is more clearly defined. It is a sign of approaching trouble in business, but in this case, if you can prove your innocence, it shows that you will overcome your difficulties. Vague abuse will show undefined troubles or worries, a definite accusation, more serious trouble. 457

8 Ache—This depends entirely upon the circumstances, but it is usually found to be a case of contrary meaning. If it is a trivial ache, it is probably due to some physical cause and is a sign of ill health. But if the pain is severe and obviously imaginary, it denotes some important event that will prove to be beneficial to you. To the business man it foretells good trade and a fortunate season's business. To the lover it indicates a favorable time for him to push his suit. To the farmer it promises a good and profitable harvest, with high prices. To the sailor it shows a successful voyage. 359

8 Acid—to dream of handling acids foretells danger concerning a promise. Fulfill your own promises and do not trust blindly in those of others. Others handling acid: death of an enemy. 953

4 Acorn—As a rule, any indication of Nature's good will is a favorable sign. To the lover it is a sign of future happiness; to those in difficulties, a proof of speedy relief. If you gather the acorns in your dream, it is

63

supposed to indicate a legacy or some good fortune from outside your own life. 652

1 Acquaintance—To dream of some person whom you know is a good sign, but it depends upon the degree of friendship and also upon what happens in your dream. If you quarrel it is a bad sign and often applies to the health of the dreamer. Making new acquaintances: A change in life will soon come. 739

7 Acquitted—To dream of being accused before a court and acquitted foretells prosperity to yourself and failure to your enemies. Others being acquitted will have prosperous business. 124

6 Acrobat—To watch other people performing clever gymnastic feats is a dream of contrary meaning; be careful, or an accident will befall you. Do not take long journeys for seven days after such a dream. If the acrobat in your dream has an accident or is unable to perform the attempted feat, then you will escape the full results of the peril that is hanging over you. 258

9 Acting—To dream that you are acting or taking part in some entertainment is a warning that some slight difficulty will delay the consummation of your plans. Persevere, however, for all will come right. Others acting: Will take a short trip. 216

3 Actor or Actress—To dream that you meet an actor or actress is an indication of trouble of a domestic character. Keep your temper and do not allow yourself to be disturbed if anything goes wrong in the home. A comedian actor or actress: Good success in present business. A tragic actor or actress: Unhappiness. 498

6 Adam—It is claimed to be a fortunate omen if you dream of Adam and Eve and if you see either of our first parents. If you speak to them or if they speak to you, it indicates some delay in the realization of your wishes, but you must be patient. To see both Adam and Eve at once is the most fortunate dream you can have. 384

7 Address—If you dream of writing an address, be careful of your financial affairs and do not enter into risky speculations. Others writing an address: Misfortune in business. 628

64

4 Adieu—To dream that you are saying good-bye to anyone is an indication of misfortune due to ill health. Take no risks, such as chills. Others bidding adieu to you: Will take a tedious journey. 382

4 Admiral—To dream of a naval officer of high rank foretells events of importance to yourself. Being an admiral: Danger in love matters. Being the wife of an admiral: Insurmountable obstacles confront you. 193

5 Admire—If you dream that you yourself are admired, it indicates useful friendships with people whom you like. It is, in that sense, a dream of contrary meaning. If, however, you find yourself admiring some other person, it shows the friendly feeling of some other person for you, but he may not be the person about whom you are dreaming. This point should be borne in mind, as it is very apt to mislead. 590

3 Adopted or Adoption—This is a dream of contrary meaning. If you dream that you have been adopted by someone or that you have adopted some child, it shows that some relative or close friend will appeal to you for help in some crisis. 471

7 Adornment—To dream that you have received a present of some article of clothing such as a frock or a hat is a dream of contrary meaning. Expect some misfortune shortly. The more elaborate or costly the gift, the greater the coming trouble. But if, in your dream, you refuse the present, then you will overcome your trouble. If you accept but do not actually wear the gift, then expect difficulties that will require great care and patience on your part. 853

4 Adrift—To dream that you are adrift in a boat is a warning of difficulty ahead; it is an obstacle dream. If you reach land safely, you will overcome your troubles, but if you fall out of the boat or if the boat should be upset by rough waves, then expect very serious difficulties. Even then you may swim to land or be rescued, which would indicate ultimate success. 292

7 Adultery—To dream of temptation to crime means a virtuous life and success to your plans; to dream of guilt forebodes failure. Committing adultery: Your morals are excellent. 862

3 Advancement—This is a most favorable sign and indicates success in some important undertaking. You may be in some employment and advanced; your success is certain. This dream often occurs in connection with legal matters. But if you dream of a lawsuit, you will lose. 174

3 Adventures—To meet with exciting adventures in a dream predicts a surprising alteration in your fortune. Going on an adventure with a man: New interest and surroundings. Going on an adventure with a woman: Someone is watching you. 507

5 Adversity—This omen has much the same meaning as adversary; it is a favorable dream and indicates prosperity. Fight with an adversary: Doomed for disappointment. Having adversity in business: Will realize high ambition. Having an adversity in love: Be on guard against spiteful gossip. 158

2 Advertisement—To dream that you are advertising in the papers is a sign of difficulties ahead of you. It is a good sign, on the other hand, to read an advertisement inserted by someone else. 893

8 Advice—An indication of useful friendships whether you are being advised or are giving advice to some other person. In this case the dream person concerned is seldom the same as the actual friend; you must seek elsewhere for the real name. 719

6 Airplane—A sign that money is coming to you but that your methods may not be above suspicion. Study your plans carefully. 312

7 Affection—To dream that there is great affection shown between you and some other person is a dream of contrary meaning. It shows that you are not quite straight in some of your plans. Affection between two loved ones: Inheritance. Having the affection of children: Will receive unexpected money. 583

5 Affliction—A dream of contrary meaning. The greater your trouble and difficulty in your dream, the more certain is your success in life. 581

1 Affluence—The greater your appearance of show and wealth in a dream, the heavier will be your loss in business, for this is an omen of contrary meaning.

Others having an affluence of property and everything: avoid rivals. 163

8 Affront—To dream that you feel offended by the conduct of some person is a dream of contrary meaning, unless you quarrel violently and part in anger. To dream that you annoy someone else is a sign of trouble in the near future. 062

1 Afloat—On smooth water a happy destiny is in view; on rough sea, trouble nets of your own making. Seeing someone afloat: Will have troubles caused by others. 613

3 Afraid—Another dream of contrary meaning, since it shows that you realize your difficulties and are likely to overcome them. To the timid lover it foretells success. 786

2 Africa—An unexpected advancement in your fortune will soon take place. Taking a trip to Africa alone: Will make new friends. 183

9 Afternoon—A fine afternoon warns the dreamer to act cautiously in personal affairs. Fortune favors you if you beware of knavery from those around you. 432

4 Age—To worry about your own age when dreaming is a bad sign, and indicates an approaching illness. In a sense it can be looked upon as resulting from physical causes rather than as a dream warning. The more you worry, the more serious that coming illness will be. 238

8 Agony—Authorities differ over this dream, and it might be wise to treat it as an obstacle dream. Some people claim that to feel pain in your dream is a very fortunate sign for business affairs. Others say that it shows domestic troubles. Sometimes both versions might prove true, for example if a married man or an affianced lover gave much too much time to business and neglected his wife and family. 719

9 Agree—This dream is always held to be a warning of some flaw in your plans, some oversight that will upset your calculations and hopes. If you do not actually sign the agreement but only read it, you will get through all right. Canceling an agreement: Will have uncertain profits. 216

1 Air—A dream about the open air depends entirely upon

67

the circumstances. If the air is clear and the sky blue, then it indicates success. But if the air is misty or foggy or if there are clouds about, then trouble is foretold. You should postpone or reconsider any proposed change. 901

8 Airship—A sign of money making, but watch your speculations or you may be caught and lose instead of gaining. Being in an airship with loved ones: Will be guilty of foolish actions. Being in an airship disaster but not killed: Financial gains. 539

2 Aisle—The inside of a church, when forming part of a dream, is considered unfortunate. 398

5 Alligator or Crocodile—To dream of any unusual animal denotes an enemy, and you should be cautious in speculations or in making new business ventures. 761

5 Almonds—This is one of the unreliable omens, since it is looked upon as favorable in the East, whereas in the West the authorities differ. If you are eating an almond and enjoying it, you can look upon it as a good sign, but if the nuts are bitter to the taste, then you should be careful, for your ventures are liable to fail. Should you dream of an almond tree and not of the fruit, it is a good sign, both in your home and in your business. 437

9 Alms—This dream depends upon the circumstances. If, in your dream, someone begs and you refuse him, it is a sign of misfortune for you; but if you give and give freely, then it is a sign of great happiness, either to yourself or to some intimate friend. 378

9 Almanac—To dream you are reading one: A light quarrel with someone dear to you. 036

3 Amber—To see amber is a warning against pride, which may be a barrier between you and someone you love. 706

9 Ambulance—This means speedy realization of your desire. 297

6 Alter—To dream you are inside a church is not considered fortunate; it does not carry the same fortunate meaning as a view of the outside of the sacred build-·ing. 159

5 America—A good fortune is coming to you through your own efforts. 293

8 Ammonia—Danger through illness or accidents; take no risks for a time. Using ammonia: Quarrels with a friend. 602

3 Amorous—If you dream you are of an amorous disposition, it is a sign that you are likely to be a victim of scandal. Others being amorous toward you: Be careful in love affairs. Young girls being amorous: Will make a wrong marriage. 723

9 Amulet—To dream you are wearing one means that you have an important decision to make shortly. Think well before choosing. Receiving the gift of an amulet: Will experience the loss of a lover. 198

6 Ancestors—To dream of your ancestors preceding your father or mother is considered a warning of illness. Grandparents: Speedy recovery from an illness. 483

5 Anchor—If seen clearly, this is a fortunate sight, but the whole of the anchor should be visible to the dreamer. If it is actually in the water, it indicates disappointment. Raising an anchor from the water: Will have good earnings. 356

4 Angels—Another fortunate dream, but it refers to love affairs, partnerships, and friendships. Several angels: Will receive an inheritance. An angel being close to you: will enjoy peace and well-being. An angel coming into your home: Prosperity. 832

9 Anger—A dream of contrary meaning. If you are angry in your dream with some person whom you know, it shows that you will benefit in some manner through that person. If it is a stranger, then some unexpected good news will reach you. Becoming angry with strangers: Will receive unexpected good news. Becoming angry with children: Will get invitation from a prominent person. 216

5 Angling—As with an anchor when seen in the water, this dream indicates disappointment in some cherished project. Angling and catching fish: Good news will follow. Angling but not catching fish: Evil will come to you. 464

6 Animals—To see wild animals in a dream is generally a

69

dream of contrary meaning; but there are a few special animals, such as the lion, the leopard, and the tiger, which carry distinct meanings. Any very unusual creature such as a crocodile is a bad sign. Domestic animals have separate meanings, and the cat and dog are not considered good dream omens. Cows and bulls depend upon their attitudes: if they are peaceful, they are a good omen; but if they attack you, then expect difficulties in your business ventures. 258

6 Ankle—An injury to your foot or ankle in a dream is a fortunate omen, but you will have to face difficulties for some time first. A woman showing her ankles: Realization of her desires. Having beautiful ankles: Will have plenty of money in old age. 519

6 Annoy—To dream that you are annoyed about something is a dream of contrary meaning. Good fortune awaits your plans. 348

7 Anthem—Church music is naturally associated with the interior of the building and is not therefore very favorable. But the combination of pleasant musical sounds with an unfavorable omen will indicate illness in your family circle. Singing the national anthem: Temptation will come to you. Hearing an anthem at an official ceremony: Will receive good news. 176

9 Ants—To dream of these industrious little creatures shows business activity, but in some fresh district or surroundings. Having ants in the home: Illness within the family. Ants on food: Happiness is assured. 657

7 Antelope—To dream you see one means that someone dear to you has placed faith and affection upon you. 421

4 Anvil—This is generally considered to be a good omen, but there should not be much noise connected with the dream. Other people using an anvil: Good times ahead. 931

8 Anxiety—A dream of contrary meaning which shows that some worry will be relieved very shortly. Having anxiety over others or your children: Will have good health. Having anxiety about your mate: Troubles are ahead. 314

70

4 Ape—As in the case of all unusual animals seen in dreams, this is a warning of coming trouble. 193

1 Apology—A change of companionship, possibly a return to a former friendship. Receiving an apology: Happiness in love. Apologizing to friends: Return of a former friend. 793

6 Apparel—It is a dream of contrary meaning to be concerned about your clothes. The newer and more up-to-date your attire, the greater the trouble coming across your path. To see yourself in rags is therefore a very fortunate sign. But the true meaning of a dream concerning clothes often depends upon the color, which you should consult. If you see yourself or other people in a dream without clothes, it is a sign of some unexpected good fortune. 861

2 Apparition—No harm is foretold by a dream of ghosts or other apparations, unless their presence or sudden appearance frightens you or makes you ill. In that case, you must expect financial difficulties or perhaps ill health. 254

8 Appetite—It is not a good sign when you appear to be hungry in your dream; it is Nature's warning of some health trouble. Feasting is also a bad sign but refers to money matters. 872

1 Applause—To dream that you receive the open approval of your friends and neighbors is an omen of contrary meaning. Beware of family quarrels or separation from some friend due to ill feeling. Giving applause: Are unselfish and envious of others. 289

6 Apples—Fruit is generally a good omen in a dream, as with all products of Nature; but if you eat the fruit you will yourself be responsible for some misfortune. To dream of an apple tree is also fortunate. Eating sweet apples means a good and favorable event. 123

1 Apricot—to dream of this popular fruit is a sign of coming prosperity, both in business and in love affairs. 163

1 Apron—It is an omen of contrary meaning when you dream of any mishap to your clothes. If you tear your apron, it means some small benefit, as the garment is not an important one. 982

5 April Fool—To dream that you are made one means that you will soon be given power over another. Be careful to use it well. Fooling others on April Fool's Day: Means a loss of a friend. Fooling children on April Fool's Day: Happiness in the family. Being born in April: Will be happy in love affairs. 131

1 Aquamarine—To dream of this jewel assures you of the affection of a very youthful relative or friend. Buying an aquamarine stone: Happiness is assured. Losing an aquamarine stone: Disappointment in love matters. 208

4 Arab—To dream of a foreign person concerns your love affairs or some important transaction with someone quite outside your family and usual business circle. Many Arabs: Will have a love affair. Going with an Arab: Will have an important and good transaction. 283

3 Arch—It is not a good sign to dream of passing under an arch, since it foretells interference in your love affairs. It is, in reality, a mild form of obstacle dream that concerns your personal affairs, rather than financial. 381

8 Archer—To the single, a speedy engagement; if already married, be true. Danger is near you. 503

3 Arena—A warning of danger. Avoid crowds. If you are not alone in your dream, the danger is lessened. Fighting in an arena: Will realize high ambitions. 381

5 Arm—To dream of an accident to your arm is a sign of ill health in the family circle. To lose one arm generally foretells death or a long and serious illness. To dream of a still arm is usually a sign of some money loss due to ill health. Having arms covered with hairs: Will be very rich. Having an arm cut off: Loss of a relative. Having an accident with the arms: Ill health within the family. 410

3 Army—An obstacle dream, but it only foretells difficulty or a journey followed by a successful issue of your venture. If the men are fighting, it becomes a serious matter. Several armies of different countries: Fortune and joy. 696

8 Armchair—Hasty news. 215

9 Arrest—A sudden and unexpected success will come to

72

you, but you must choose your friends carefully. Being arrested: Will have misery followed by joy. Others being arrested: Will receive an unexpected gift. 369

4 Arson—Not a fortunate dream. News of accidents at sea, possibly to yourself. 427

2 Arrow—To dream that you have been struck by an arrow is a sign of misfortune from some unexpected source. Some person who appears to be friendly is really working against your interests. Throwing an arrow: Unhappiness. Having many arrows: Are surrounded by enemies. A broken arrow: Failure in business. 983.

6 Artist—To dream that you are acting as model for your portrait is a warning of treachery on the part of some acquaintance. If, however, you dream that you are painting a portrait of someone, then your plans should be revised carefully, for you will risk failure by striving to take unfair advantage. 789

9 Artichoke—Vexatious troubles, which, however, you will surmount. Eating artichokes: Dissension within the family. 306

1 Ascent—Any form of progress upward is a sign of success, and if you appear to reach the top of a hill, it shows that you will have great success. 091

7 Ashes—Something lost through your own carelessness. Having ashes in own fireplace: Loss of money. Cremated ashes: Will live a long life. 538

4 Asparagus—Another valuable gift from Mother Nature, a favorable sign. Push on with your plans, and you will be successful. Raw asparagus: Success in own enterprises. Cooking asparagus: Own plans will be successful. 391

3 Assault—False information will be given to you. Be on your guard and prove the facts. Assaulting others: Monetary gain. 858

8 Asthma—A warning to you that some favorite scheme will not prove as profitable as you expect. Revise your plans and avoid all speculation or risk. Having asthma: Will recover soon by change of residence to another state. 629

1 Asters—A warning to you that some favorite scheme

will not prove profitable, as you expect. Revise your plans and avoid all speculation or risk. Picking asters: Will receive a letter with good news. Receiving a gift of asters: Abundance. 802

1 Asylum—This suggestive omen depends for its correct interpretation upon the circumstances of the dream. If you remain outside the building, you should take advantage of every chance you have to help someone in trouble, when you may expect good fortune for yourself. But if you find yourself inside, then look out for trouble of a serious nature. Avoiding being put into an asylum: Take care of your health. A young girl dreaming of an asylum: Will marry soon. 613

8 Athlete—Not a good dream to any but the very strong; beware of overstrain. Being in the company of an athlete: Avoid rivals. 341

9 Atlas—To dream that you are consulting a map or an atlas is considered a sign of business ventures at a distance; in the case of the atlas, it probably indicates a visit abroad. 153

8 Attic—A premonition of an engagement to the single. If married, avoid flirtation. The attic of others' homes: Are confronted with insurmountable obstacles. 269

1 Attorney—Business worries are in front of you. Be careful of your plans and avoid all speculation in stocks and shares. Being in court with an attorney: Avoid speculation in stocks. Dealing with an opposing attorney: Big catastrophe ahead. Having conferences with several attorneys: Troubles ahead. 901

2 Auction—An unfavorable sign, somewhat similar in meaning to attorney or lawyer. Be careful, or some acquaintance will take advantage of you. 672

7 Audience—To dream of having an audience with a prominent person: Will have good earnings. Having an audience with a priest: Will soon be in trouble. To dream of an audience in general: Social pleasures and distinctions to come. 431

8 August—To dream of summer in winter time foretells unexpected news. Being born in August: All will go well in life. Children being born in August: Big fortune. 152

2 Aunt—To dream of close relatives is a fortunate sign

and shows success in money matters. Being an aunt: A successful matrimony is being planned. Visiting with an Aunt: Will receive a legacy. 452

2 Author—To dream of a great author brings unexpected pleasures to the single. To the married: Good fortune in the family. Dealing with an author: Good times are coming. 389

8 Autumn—There are unfortunate and hostile influences around you. Walk warily, and you may avoid them. Autumn in the spring: Unfriendly influences are nearby. Autumn in winter: Good fortune is coming. 458

4 Avalanche—Good fortune of an astonishing nature will soon befall you. Being buried under an avalanche of snow: Good profit. Others being buried under an avalanche: Change of surroundings. 364

1 Awaken—It is a good omen if you awaken some person in the course of your dream, and it will go far to soften any unfavorable omen that may be present. This is especially the case if the sleeper is in bed, as the color white helps good fortune and serves to confirm the fortunate issue of events. Being awakened: Be on guard against coming troubles. 316

B

3 Baby—It is a curious fact that it is fortunate to see children in a dream if they are old enough to be independent but that a helpless baby is a bad sign. It usually shows some disappointment in love, or if the baby is unwell, a serious illness, or even a death, in the family. A married pregnant woman dreaming of a baby: Big success in love. A single woman dreaming of having a baby: Sorrow. A baby sucking milk from mother's breast: Success in everything. A baby taking its first steps: Difficulties in business. A baby being sick: Serious illness within the family. 183

1 Bachelor—If the man is young it is a good sign, but if he is old the dream foreshadows loneliness or the loss of a friend. Being a bachelor: A change in life will soon come. Becóming a bachelor after an annulled marriage: Financial gains. A bachelor getting married: Will find a rich woman to marry. 109

8 Back—If in your dreams some person turns his or her back upon you, it shows opposition and difficulty, though this may not be very serious or persistent. If the person turns around and faces you, it is a sign that all will come well before long. To dream of your own back is a favorable sign, though this is not met so often as dreams of your arms, legs, or body. 728

6 Back Door—To dream that you are making use of the back door instead of the front entrance of your house is a warning of some coming change in your fortune. This may be for good or for evil, according to other circumstances. Friends entering the back door: Caution must be used in business ventures. Robbers breaking down the back door: Approaching money. 060

8 Bacon—An unfortunate omen whatever else happens in the dream, whether you are eating it or merely buying it. Generally, it concerns the health. 278

4 Backgammon—To dream of taking part in it: Test of your character is soon to be made. 427

1 Badge—You are under observation and will shortly be promoted. A badge on others: Warning of troubles. Pinning a badge on a policeman: Family reunion. 352

1 Badger—A typical dream showing that hard work is in front of you. Killing a badger: Will fall in love. Catching a badger: Good luck attends you. 415

1 Bag—A sign of better times, especially if a heavy one. Carrying only one bag: Will incur plenty of debts. Carrying several bags: Treachery from a friend. Bags being in a car: Unexpected money will arrive. 820

5 Bagpipes—As with the most unusual things when seen in a dream, this musical instrument is not a favorable sign, and in particular it indicates matrimonial worry and difficulty. 914

9 Bailiff—To dream that you have trouble with this officer of the court is an omen of contrary meaning. Some

76

unexpected legacy will come your way before long. 126

5 Bait—Do not trust blindly in those who seek to please
you. Putting bait on a fishhook: Will have a great joy.
Others attempting to please by baiting you: Don't trust
them blindly. 536

8 Baking and Baker—To dream of some person baking is
a good sign in every way; you will not have to wait long
for some favorable turn of events. But if you yourself
are baking, it indicates the serious illness of some one
dear to you, either a member of your family or your
betrothed, if you happen to be engaged. 296

5 Balcony—A dream of a balcony should be classed
among the obstacle omens, though the difficulty to be
faced will not be a serious one. If you leave the balcony, all will be well. It is slightly more serious if you
are seated than if you are standing, as your quick
recovery is delayed. 824

1 Bald—A dream concerning your health. The less hair
you appear to have, the more serious will be the coming
illness. In the case of a woman, it indicates money
troubles or some difficult love affair. 316

2 Bale—Good fortune, more or less, according to whether
it is cotton or wool. Owning bales of wool: Will have
many troubles. Buying bales of cotton: Will overcome
enemies. 641

5 Ballad—To hear one: Beware of false judgements. To
sing one: Someone you care for thinks you unkind. 968

9 Ball—This dream depends upon the circumstances. If
you see yourself among the dancers, some favorable
news will reach you. But to watch other people dancing
and enjoying themselves shows that some cherished
wish will fail to realize. Attending a masquerade ball:
Beware of a trap. Playing ball games: Will have many
good friends. Playing with a billiard ball: Good news.
Football: Uneasiness. Tennis or rubber balls: Certain
birth of a child. 729

7 Ballet—To dream of a stage Ballet or other professional
dancing is a warning concerning your health. Take no
risks if the weather is wet or stormy. 142

8 Balloon—Another unusual omen, and therefore an unfavorable sign for the dreamer. Ascending in a balloon:

Will have misfortune during a journey. Descending in a balloon: Will make unfavorable money ventures. 458

8 Ballot—A difference in position and surroundings, possibly for the better. Casting a ballot: Will have a change of companionship. 214

6 Banana—A fortunate omen, though the dream may concern some small affair only. Eating bananas: Will be imposed upon to fulfill some duty. 429

7 Bandage—Fresh influences will surround you. Wearing a bandage: Expect good news. Putting bandages on others: Abundant means. Others wearing bandages: Will receive bad news. 295

5 Banishment—If in your dream you are forced to leave your abode, it is a fortunate sign. The more serious the disturbance appears to be, the greater your future prosperity. Other people being banished: Will soon receive plenty of money. 581

1 Bank or Banking—To dream that you have dealings with a bank is a bad sign. It indicates some sudden loss of money. Owning a bank: Friends are making fun of you. Receiving money from a bank: Bankruptcy is near. 316

3 Bankruptcy—To dream that you have lost money and are now bankrupt should be taken as a warning. Some plan is not very creditable to you and should be abandoned at once, as trouble will follow. Be cautious in your transactions and seek the advice of friends older than yourself. 651

9 Banner or Flag—A good omen, but it concerns your personal position rather than your business affairs. A red banner: Will receive help from friends abroad. A banner on a house: Failure of enemies. Receiving a banner: A promised gift will not be given. 306

8 Banquet—This is usually considered a fortunate omen if the dreamer is young, but not if he or she is old. Being in attendance at a banquet: Pleasures will be costly. Attending a political banquet: Disappointments. 926

8 Baptism—This foretells disappointment through unforeseen circumstances. 314

3 Bar—Your friends esteem you more highly than you know. Having a drink alone in a bar: A false friend is

78

nearby. Drinking with company in a bar: Must control passions. Single woman drinking in a bar: Financial gains. 219

1 Barber—To dream that you are in a barber's shop foretells some difficulty in your business affairs. Being a barber: Will have big success. Having a shave at the barber's: Loss of money. 856

7 Bargain—A warning to be steadfast and trust your own opinions. Being cheated out of a bargain: Own home will be robbed. Having made a good bargain: Advancement within position. 781

6 Barge—You are about to travel some distance. A loaded barge: Triumph over enemies. An empty barge: Troubles will arise from prying into the affairs of others. 852

8 Bare Feet—It is considered fortunate to dream that you are naked. If only the feet are bare, then you may expect some trouble or difficulty, but by perseverance and hard work you will prove successful. Children going barefooted: Shame and sorrow. Feet and legs to knees being bare: Dishonor in social life. 512

9 Barley—A good omen, as with most things connected with nature. 036

3 Barmaid—To dream of a barmaid is a sign of difficulty probably due to your own carelessness. Being a barmaid: Difficulties due to own carelessness, will improve slowly. Dating a barmaid: Beware of jealous friends. Being married to a barmaid: Will soon experience troubles. 543

8 Barn—This is a favorable dream if the barn is full or nearly so; but it is unfortunate to see an empty Barn with open doors. Being in a barn: Will win a lawsuit. Handling grain in a barn: Will live a happy life. 953

1 Barracks—Your difficulties will soon be lessened. Many soldiers living in barracks: Warning of troubles ahead. 721

2 Barrel—An upright and full barrel: Prosperity. Rolling and empty barrel: Hard times to come. An upright and full barrel of wine: Better times ahead. Owning a barrel: Will receive an unexpected gift. 245

6 Bashful—A happy time at large party. Having bashful

children: Joy. Having bashful friends: Warning of troubles ahead. 312

9 Basin—To dream of eating or drinking from a basin is an unnatural dream. If you are in love, you must expect difficulties and may not marry the first object of your affections. Using a full basin of water: Will have plenty money. An empty basin: Will have or incur many debts. 135

4 Basket—An obstacle dream, since it is so easy to upset the contents. Be careful of your business ventures, or you will lose money. 247

4 Bat—Treachery is clearly shown when you dream about these curious nocturnal creatures. Beware of discussing your plans. Don't lend money, and avoid all speculation. 634

7 Bathing—The meaning of this dream depends upon what is happening. If it is in the open and the water is clear, then it shows success in business. But if the water is dirty, muddy, or choked with weeds, then you may expect difficulty and trouble in your work or profession. If you yourself are taking a bath indoors, it is not a good sign. If the water is cold, it shows sorrow; if hot, a separation from a friend or loved one, perhaps a quarrel if steam is seen. To see yourself naked is a good sign in itself, but you must not be in water. 925

6 Battle—This is another unusual event and foretells trouble, a serious quarrel with neighbors or a lover. But if you are on the winning side, whether fighting alone or with others, then things will come right in the end. A naval battle: Will be triumphant. A battle on land: Will live a long life. A battle with fire: Double cross in love affairs. 195

4 Bayonet—A quarrel soon to be made up. Carrying a bayonet: Success in own enterprise. Others holding a bayonet: Will be under the power of enemies. A soldier having a bayonet: Worries will be smoothed away. 109

4 Bazaar—To dream that you are assisting at a bazaar, or any other cause devoted to charity, is a fortunate omen for your love affairs. Buying things at a charity: Will

realize high ambitions. People selling things at a charity: will receive a proposal. 175

5 Beans—Difficulties lie ahead of you, so be careful. 374

8 Bear—An indication of the difficulties ahead of you but that they are within your power if you work earnestly. If you succeed in killing the bear or in driving it away, you may expect success eventually. A bear dancing: Will be tempted into speculation. A bear in a cage: Success in the future. Being attacked by a bear: Will be persecuted. Killing a bear: Will have victories over enemies. 143

3 Beard—If you see in your dream some person with a full beard, you may expect some unexpected success; the fuller the beard, the better for the dreamer. A married woman dreaming of a man with a beard: Will soon leave her husband. A pregnant woman dreaming of a man with a beard: Will give birth to a son. A white beard: Very big prosperity. 732

3 Beasts—Most animals represent difficulties and trouble when seen in a dream, unless in some manner you drive them away. Even our domestic pets, cats and dogs, are not fortunate, but birds, as a rule, are a good omen. Beasts fighting: Sickness. Being pursued by a beast: Vexation caused by enemies. 759

4 Beacon—Avoid misunderstandings, but should you unavoidably quarrel, take the first step toward reconciliation, or you will regret it. 382

4 Beads—False friends or dissatisfaction. 526

3 Beam—If of wood, a burden to be borne; if of light, a well-merited reward. 462

4 Beating—If a married man dreams he is beating his wife, it is a very fortunate sign and denotes married happiness and a comfortable home. But for lovers, it is considered a bad dream. It is also fortunate if a man dreams that he is beating some woman who is not his wife. In the same way, if a father or mother dreams that he is punishing one of his own children, it is a fortunate sign; but it is not if the child is a stranger. 193

2 Beauty—A dream of contrary meaning. If you see

81

yourself as beautiful, it indicates an illness; if some other person, then he will be the invalid. 524

2 Bed—To dream that you are in a strange bed shows some unexpected good turn in your business affairs. If you are in your own bed, it concerns your love affairs. To dream of making a bed is a sign of a change of residence. To sit on a bed is considered a sign of an early marriage. Having clean white sheets on a bed: Will have cause to worry. An empty bed: Death of a friend. Being in a strange bed: Good turn of events in own affairs. A stranger being in your bed: Matrimonial unfaithfulness. 821

9 Bedroom—If the bedroom in your dream is more sumptuous than your own, it shows a change in your circumstances that will eventually prove favorable for you. But you must be prepared for some delay in plans if your dream concerns the earlier hours of the night, whereas the change will come soon if your dream is of the dawn or of the early morning hours. 396

9 Beef—To dream that you are eating beef or mutton, shows that you will remain comfortably well off but never be rich. If you appear to have plenty of food but are unable to eat it, then you will have to spend time to appeal to others to help you. Purchasing beef to cook: Winnings at gambling. Eating raw beef: Long-lasting happiness. 729

3 Beer—If you dream that you are drinking beer or ale, it is a sign of some loss of money in connection with speculation. If you only see the ale or beer or if other people are drinking it, but not yourself, the loss will be small. For all that, you should be careful in betting or speculation. 165

4 Bees—This is a good omen unless they sting you in your dream. They concern business matters, however, not love or friendship. Moving bees in swarms: Will have a fire in your own house. Bees coming into your house: Will be damaged by enemies. Bees flying around their beehive: Will have productive business. Killing bees: Will have a big loss and ruin. 328

5 Beetles—To dream of these unpleasant little creatures is a sign of quarreling with your friends or some difficulty

82

in your affairs due to malice. If you kill the insects, you will put matters right quickly. 923

5 Beets—Some interference with your love affairs is indicated when you dream of beets, but all will go well if you eat them. Buying beets: Will receive an expensive gift. 753

4 Beggar—A sign that you will receive unexpected help, a dream of contrary meaning. Aged beggars: Exercise economy. Many beggars: Will have fortune and happiness. A crippled beggar: Disputes within the family. Giving money to a beggar: Love will be reciprocated. A beggar coming into the house: Troubles and worries will come. 319

9 Belle of the Ball—To dream that you are dancing with the prettiest woman in the room is an omen of contrary meaning. You may expect trouble in your family affairs or from some woman acquaintance. If a woman dreams that she is the belle of the ball, it has a similar meaning, provided she is dancing. But if she finds herself neglected, then the trouble will be short lived, and all will end happily. 828

5 Bells—To dream that you hear the ringing of bells is a sign of coming news, but it may not be favorable. Hearing church bells ringing: Be on guard against enemies. 356

3 Belt—To dream of putting one on is a good omen of a happy future. An old belt: Will have to work harder: A new belt: Honor. A blue belt: Happiness. A black belt: Death. A brown belt: Illness. A green belt: Good wishes. A gold belt: Big earnings. A silver belt: Profit. A yellow belt: Treason. 904

5 Bench—An unfortunate dream. Attend carefully to work, or you may lose it. Sitting on a bench: Will have a comfortable life. Children sitting on a park bench: Good times are coming. 941

8 Bequest—To dream that you are bequeathing money or property to other people is an omen of contrary meaning. You will receive money from an unexpected source. Canceling a bequest: Fights within the family. 602

2 Bereavement—News of a friend's marriage soon to take

83

place. Suffering bereavement: Someone else will benefit from your actions. 524

4 Berries—Social activities of a happy nature. If you dream you are picking many blackberries, financial gains. Eating berries: Abundant gains. Buying berries: Important and very beneficial events to come. 814

1 Best Man—To dream you are acting as best man denotes the failure of a plan of yours through a false friend. A woman dreaming of a best man: Confidence and security. 172

9 Bet—To dream that you are betting is a warning not to allow other people's opinions to interfere with you. Winning a bet: Will have a change for the better. Losing a bet: An enemy is seeking your ruin. 315

7 Betrothed—It is not a favorable sign to dream that you have just become engaged to be married. Expect trouble among your family circle or with your lover, if you are really engaged. Relatives becoming betrothed: Will have family arguments. Friends becoming betrothed: Will realize high ambitions. 628

3 Bible—Reading a bible, family troubles will come soon. Taking a Bible to church: Happiness. Believing in the Bible: With perseverance, will overcome enemies. Children reading the Bible: Joy without profit. 642

5 Bicycle—To dream that you are riding one means that you will have to make a decision. Think well, and then act as you think best. Selling a bicycle: Good wishes. Buying a bicycle for children: Advancement in own affairs. 365

7 Bier—If you are lying upon it, it signifies a triumphant ending to your hopes. Relatives lying upon it: Will receive a legacy. A friend lying in a bier: Advancement in own position. 214

3 Bigamy—Unfortunately, it is considered a fortunate omen to commit bigamy in your dreams. You are assured of a happy and prosperous married life. 723

5 Billiards—Another dream of unusual occurrence, unless you play regularly, when the omen loses all significance. It indicates some difficulty; if you are in love or engaged, it means that you will be opposed by your betrothed's family. Married people playing billiards: Love of mate

sincere. Single people playing billiards: Will soon be married. 239

9 Bills—To dream that you are paying them denotes speedy financial gains; that they are unpaid signifies evil speaking. Being solicited to pay bills: Are disliked by your boss. 279

7 Birds—Usually considered to be of an uncertain nature. If you are poor and struggling, birds indicate a coming improvement in your circumstances. But if you are wealthy, you may expect a reverse. It is a good sign if the birds show beautiful plumage and if the birds are singing, it is always fortunate. 187

8 Bird's Egg or Nest—If you see the eggs in the nest, it is a sign of money coming to you; but if the young are visible, it is not a good sign. People destroying bird's eggs: Business loss. Animals eating bird's eggs: Will soon have a change in surroundings. 134

3 Birth—It is a good sign when a woman who is married dreams of giving birth to a child, but for a single woman it foretells trouble in the near future. Divorced woman giving birth to a child: Will inherit a large legacy. Widow giving birth to a child: Will be guilty of foolish actions. Assisting with the birth of a child: Joy and prosperity. Assisting with the birth of a cat or other animals: Death of an enemy. Twins being born: Will have good luck in affairs. 264

6 Birthday—To dream that it is your own birthday is a fortunate sign for money matters or business affairs. To dream that it is the birthday of a friend or relative is a sign that they will benefit shortly, probably in connection with yourself. Sweetheart's birthday: Abundance of money soon coming. Wife's birthday: Good times coming. Husband's birthday: Abundant means. Children's birthday: Approaching money. 231

3 Biscuits—A prosperous journey; sometimes a warning of coming ill health. Giving biscuits away: Are prone to enjoy pleasures too much. 057

6 Bishop or Clergyman—An omen of ill health or some serious disappointments. Talking to a bishop: Business will be satisfactory. 168

9 Bite—To dream that some animal has bitten you is a

85

sign of trouble over your love affairs. Beware of quarrels. Biting someone else: Will be embarrassed. Biting the tongue: Loss of consideration by other people. Being bitten by a woman: A jealous person is nearby. Being bitten by a man: Beware of quarrels. 351

2 Black—This is an unfortunate color when seen in a dream unless it is in connection with a funeral, when it becomes a dream of contrary meaning. A black dress: Sadness. Purchasing black clothes: Are being deceived. 191

6 Blackberries—Unlike most nature omens, this is bad, owing to the color. Gathering blackberries: Will be unlucky. Buying blackberries: Will be wounded in an accident. Blackberries hanging on bushes: much abundance. A married woman picking blackberries: Will soon be pregnant. 942

1 Blackbird—Another omen that depends upon the color. It is unfortunate. A woman dreaming of hearing blackbirds singing: Will have two husbands. A man dreaming of hearing blackbirds singing: Will have two wives. Unmarried person hearing blackbirds singing: Will soon be engaged. 208

3 Blankets—The importance of this dream depends upon your position in life. If you dream that you are buying or receiving new blankets and you are well to do, it shows that you may expect a loss of money. If you are poor or only moderately off, then expect an improvement in your position. 219

2 Blasphemy—Foretells that a plan of yours will be achieved after great difficulties have been surmounted. Being cursed by others using the name of God: Ambitions will be realized. 416

4 Blot—To dream you make a blot on a clean sheet of paper means a strange bed and a little traveling to come. 292

4 Blunder—This is one of the dreams that go by contraries and means that you will do unexpectedly well in your next undertaking. 823

7 Bleating of Lambs—This is a very fortunate dream and indicates both prosperity in business and happiness at home, but the young lambs must be seen with their

dams, or your dream will show a disappointment at the last moment, just when you expect success. 313

1 Bleeding—An unfortunate omen whatever the details of the dream, a severe disappointment. 208

5 Blind—It does not matter whether you dream of other blind people or that you yourself are blind, it signifies treachery from someone near to you. A young person going blind: False friends are nearby. A baby being born blind: Jealousy and sorrow. Leading a blind person: Strange adventures to come. A woman becoming blind: Some person will appeal to you for help. A man becoming blind: Be cautious in business ventures. 725

8 Blindness—To dream of blind people or that you yourself lose your sight is the sign of an unfortunate love affair. They say that love is blind, and this dream supports the popular view that happiness in love affairs depends upon being blind to the faults of the loved one. 413

3 Blood—To dream of blood in any form is an omen of severe disappointment. The exact significance would depend upon the other details of the dream, but if you yourself are bleeding anywhere it generally indicates an unfortunate love affair or a quarrel with some valued friend. Blood flowing from a wound: Sickness and worry are hovering nearby. Garments stained with blood: Successful career is hampered by enemies. Blood on other people: Severe disappointment. 021

8 Blows—A dream of contrary meaning. If you receive blows in your dream, it shows a reconciliation after a quarrel or some good fortune coming to you from a friend. To give blows to other people is, however, a sign of trouble. Wind blowing: Will have a litigation. Blowing out a fire: Gossip is being spread about you. Blowing in someone's face: Will be tricked by a woman who is cheating. 413

4 Blue—If you see much of this color in your dream, it is a sign of prosperity through other people. The firm for whom you work will thrive and go ahead so that your own financial position will improve at the same time. It may show good fortune in your love affairs and a more

comfortable and happy life owing to your marriage. 526

9 Boar—To chase a wild one: Unsuccessful efforts. To be chased: Separation. Being chased by a boar: Separation from a lover. Killing a boar: Advancement in position. 612

2 Boat or Ship—If you dream that you are sailing and that the water is smooth, it indicates some fortunate business or happiness in married life. If the water is rough, then you will have to face many difficulties. If you fall into the water, then your troubles will prove too much for you. Falling from a boat: Troubles will prove to be too much to handle. A boat sinking: Termination of present love affairs. A boat moving very slowly: Must have patience in life. 389

1 Bones or Skeleton—To dream of ordinary meat bones is a sign of poverty; but if you see a human skeleton, it is a sign of property coming to you under a will. Bones of wild animals: Will have bad business transactions. A few bones of dead people: Will have many troubles. Bones of fish: Illness is near at hand. Animals gnawing on bones: Will fall into complete ruin. 927

8 Books—This is a good sign and indicates future happiness through a quiet way. Reading a book: Will lose a good friend. Reading a mystery book: Will receive a consolation from friends. Reading a religious book: Contentment. Reading schoolbooks: Prosperity. Writing books: Will waste time and money. 737

8 Bookcase—This is a dream of contrary meaning, for if your bookcase is seen almost empty in your dream, then you may expect good fortune through your own endeavors or because of your strong personality. To dream that the bookcase is full is a bad sign. It indicates slovenly, careless work, for which you will surely suffer by loss of employment or by money troubles in business. 143

8 Boots—You can rely upon the faithfulness of your servants or business employees if you dream of new and comfortable boots or shoes, but if they are old or hurt your feet, you will meet with difficulties that are your own fault. 215

1 Borrow—This is a bad dream, for it foretells domestic sorrow, not money loss. If you dream that you repay the loan or that someone repays you then you will sail into smooth waters once again. 217

1 Bosom—To dream that your bosom is inflamed or in pain is a sign of coming illness. Having a beautiful and healthy bosom: Big joy ahead. A woman having hair on her bosom: Her husband will pass away. 109

2 Bottle—This dream depends upon circumstances. If the bottle is full, it shows prosperity. If it is empty, then misfortunes are foretold. If you upset the contents, you may expect domestic worries. A bottle of wine: Will be in a bad humor. A bottle full of liquor: Will be divorced. A full bottle of perfume: Will enjoy much happiness. 128

2 Bound—To imagine yourself bound with ropes is a dream of coming obstacles. Be careful, or trouble will overtake you. Others being bound with ropes: Troubles will overtake you. Binding other people with ropes: Embarrassment and loss of money. 182

2 Bouquet—If you retain the bunch of flowers, you will be all right; but if you throw them away or drop them, it indicates a quarrel or separation from some friend. A withered bouquet: Illness and ensuing death. Preparing a bouquet: Lover is constant. Preparing a bouquet of flowers: Will be married soon. 353

8 Bowls—A fortunate dream, especially if you are taking part in the game, as this denotes further prosperity. 161

7 Bow and Arrows—If you hit the target in your dream, you can rely upon good fortune varying according to the accuracy of your aim. If you miss, then you may expect difficulties resulting from some careless or ill-advised action of your own. Being hit by bows and arrows: Beware of enemies. Having many arrows: money losses. 304

5 Box—This dream also depends upon the circumstances. If you open a box and find something inside, it is fortunate; but if the box is empty, then your plans will be upset. Tying a box: Financial losses. Robbing a strong box: Will lose entire fortune. 176

8 Boxing Match—An astonishing announcement will be

89

made leading to important events for you. Taking part in a boxing match: Loss of friends. Winning a bet on a boxing match: Accord among friends. Losing a bet on a boxing match: You have one loyal friend. 521

3 Bracelet—This is either a sign of money or of some love affair. Where your affections are concerned, it is a fortunate sign to possess, to wear, or to find a bracelet, expecially if it is gold. Otherwise, you will be lucky in some unexpected financial matter. If you lose or drop your bracelet, then you may expect a monetary loss or a broken love affair. Receiving a bracelet as a gift from a friend: Early and happy marriage. 489

1 Branch—Trees are fortunate, being one of nature's own blessings. 901

7 Branches—If in your dream you see a tree with many fertile branches, it is a most fortunate omen, but be careful if you see any dead or broken branches. Gathering branches together: Will have an operation. Burning branches: Will receive a legacy. Cutting branches from palm trees: Big honors. A tree with withered branches: Recovery from an illness. 421

1 Brandy—Some good news is on the way. Owning a bottle of brandy: Beware of untrue friends. Buying a bottle of brandy: Will receive unexpected good news. Offering a drink of brandy to others: Must control passions. 928

1 Bravery—This warns the dreamer to keep a cool head and act with all courage, as an emergency is at hand which will test his nerve. 352

5 Brass—Observe your associates closely and do not let a false friend make you unhappy. Having something made of brass: A friend will cause unhappiness. Buying brass: Advancement in position. 167

3 Bread—If the bread is new and pleasant to the taste, it is a sign of physical well-being, bodily comfort. But if it is stale and hard, then domestic worries of a commonplace character are indicated. To bake bread is an unfortunate omen. Stale bread: Domestic trouble. Having several loaves of bread: Honor. Buying bread: Big success. 156

1 Break—To damage anything in a dream is a very bad

sign, generally concerning health. Breaking furniture: Quarrels within the home. Breaking a drinking glass: Will have a broken leg. Breaking eyeglasses: Unexpected fortune. Breaking dishes: Failure in own affairs. Breaking bottles: Will have bad health. Breaking a bone in the body: Will receive a legacy. 874

2 Breakfast—An omen of misfortune in a dream. Be careful, or your own ill-considered actions will plunge you into trouble. Preparing a breakfast: misery and illness. Having breakfast in a coffee shop: Will have a new sweetheart. Having breakfast in the home of others: Will take a trip before long. 659

9 Breath—If you dream that you are out of breath or exhausted, that is a warning of coming trouble. 252

2 Breast—If you dream that you are resting on the breast of some person, it is a sign that you have a true and loyal friend. Having a beautiful breast: Much joy ahead. The breast of a woman: Wishes will be gratified. A breast covered with hair: Success in love. A baby sucking at the breast: Will enjoy lasting happiness. Breast being wounded by a gun: Will make plenty of money. 425

7 Breeze—To dream that you are in a strong wind presages a successful speculation. Enjoying a pleasant breeze at night: Will receive a gift from a stranger. 142

4 Briars and Brambles—If they prick you, secret enemies will do you an injury; if they draw blood, expect heavy losses in trade. If you dream you pass through them without harm, you will triumph over enemies and become happy. 706

9 Bribe—A dream of contrary meaning. If you accept money as a bribe in your dream, it is a sign of upright and honorable conduct on your part. Refusing a bribe of money: Will be repaid money unexpectedly. Bribing an official person: Big sorrow. 909

2 Bride—unfortunately, this is a dream of contrary meaning. If you are one, it foretells some great disappointment. Kissing a bride: Will have many friends and much joy. Being kissed by a bride: Will have good health. A bride being pleased with her gown: Will have many

children. A bride being displeased with her gown: Disappointment in love. 263

7 Bridegroom—A bridegroom having a rich bride: Loss of a father. A bridegroom having a beautiful bride: Loss of a mother. A bridegroom having a young bride: Sickness in the family. Bridegroom having an elderly bride: Abundant means. 952

2 Bridesmaid—Being a bridesmaid: great disappointment. Several bridesmaids: Happiness and long life. Not being a bridesmaid: Danger through a secret. Girlfriends being bridesmaids: Unhappiness in love affairs. 607

9 Bridge—To dream that you are crossing a bridge foretells a change of situation or occupation in business or a change in district. This will be a fortunate omen if you cross the stream without too much trouble or delay. If the bridge is damaged or being repaired, then be careful and do not make any fresh plans without due thought. 387

7 Brooch—To dream that you are wearing jewelry depends upon the surroundings for its importance. If you are at home, it is a fortunate omen; but if you wear it at a strange house, then expect trouble. Buying a brooch: Will be deceived. Selling a brooch: Loss of a great deal of money. 970

7 Brook or Running Water—Faithful friends, if the stream is clear. Otherwise, be careful. A brook being near your own home: Will receive an honorable appointment. Brook being nearly dry: Discovery of loss of valuables. 412

9 Broom—Beware of a false friend. Having a new broom: Will make plenty of money. Throwing away an old broom: Good luck to one for whom you care. Hitting something with a broom: Will have a change for the better. 639

9 Broth—To dream that you are taking broth is a fortunate sign. Your affairs will prosper. Boiling broth: Will be married soon. Giving broth to a sick person: Abundance of money. 216

5 Brother—This omen depends upon the sex of the dreamer. If a woman dreams of her brother, it is a sign of much domestic happiness; but if it is a man, then

expect a quarrel. A brother dying: Destruction of enemies. A brother getting married: Family quarrels. 239

9 Brown—Beware of treachery on the part of someone whom you trust. 135

3 Bruises—A warning to all but the most robust that their health is suffering from overstrain. Other people having bruises on the body: Beware of enemies. Other people having bruises on the face: Loss of money. 398

5 Brush—Should you touch or use a brush in your dream, your greatest wish will shortly be granted. Having an old brush: Disappointments. Buying a new brush: Good times are coming. 419

9 Bubbles—A sign of gaiety. Avoid dissipation, or you may lose your sweetheart. Bubbles in a bathtub: Will find a protector. Bubbles from boiling water: Dignity and distinction. 819

9 Buckle—For a woman to dream that the buckle of her belt has come unfastened foretells trouble and difficulty. All mishaps with one's clothes are bad signs. Having a fancy buckle: Will have a change for the better. Buying a buckle: Avoid rivals. A broken buckle: An enemy is seeking your destruction. 540

3 Bugle Calls—This announces success in your efforts. Hearing children playing a bugle: Joy without profit. Soldiers playing a bugle: Danger in love matters. 983

4 Bugs—A warning to act cautiously, as there are unfortunate influences around you. Killing bugs: Will have money. Having bugs in the bedding: Prosperity beyond fondest hopes. 139

6 Building—To dream of building indicates some change in life, and your success otherwise will depend upon their general appearance. If the buildings are small, you will not prove successful. Very tall buildings: Will have much success. 861

2 Bull—The sign of some enemy or rival in love or business. Being chased by a bull: Will receive a present. A furious bull: Will have much success in love. 362

1 Bull Dog—Good news from an absent friend. Owning a bull dog: Advancement in own position. Buying a bull dog: Happiness is assured. Selling the puppies: An enemy is seeking your ruin. 154

2 Bull's-eye—To hit the center of the target is a lucky dream, whereas it is unfortunate to miss it. If you see someone else shooting, be careful about giving him your confidence. Others hitting the bull's-eye: Be careful in giving them your confidence. 812

3 Bunion—Presages the return of a traveler from a great distance. Inflammation leaving a bunion: Will have a new admirer. 273

1 Burden—To carry some burden in a dream shows that you will be dependent upon other people. 190

7 Burglar—Beware of treachery among those you trust. A burglar coming into the house at night: Approaching troubles. Catching a burglar red handed: Will gain good fortune. Burglars having stolen valuable things: Good investments. 628

9 Burial—A dream of contrary meaning, for it denotes a wedding, though this may not be your own. Attending the burial of a friend: Are expecting an inheritance. Attending the burial of a relative: Will be married soon. 153

1 Burning houses—A sign of improved fortune. A house burning: Fortune will improve. A building burning: Losses and worries. Friend's house burning: Triumph over enemies. A big store burning: Loss of money. 019

2 Burns—If you burn yourself in a dream, it is a sign of valuable friendship in your life. 389

2 Bushes—A change is indicated. If you push through them, the change will be for the better. Hiding behind bushes: Opposition and imminent danger. Cutting down bushes: Danger through a secret. 290

5 Butcher—You will meet with someone you have not seen for a long time. Act cautiously, as this is not a lucky dream. A butcher killing an animal: Death of a close friend. A butcher serving you with cut meat: Will live a long life. Arguing with a butcher: Are surrounded by unfortunate influences. 428

3 Butter—This is a good dream, but of a material character such as feasting. It is usually something of a surprise. If you are making butter, some money will reach you unexpectedly. Purchasing butter: Will have a

94

change for the better. Cooking with butter: Will be fortunate in business. 804

9 Butterfly—A sign of happiness, if you see a gaily colored butterfly in the sunshine; but if it is a moth and seen indoors, then it means some light trouble. Catching a butterfly: Infidelity. Killing a butterfly: Will receive a gift. Chasing a butterfly: Are surrounded by unfortunate influences. 842

3 Buttermilk—To drink it indicates disappointment in love. To the married, trouble, sorrow, and losses. 102

3 Buttons—For a man, this omen shows delay or difficulty in love affairs, but it is fortunate for a woman. 921

3 Buy—To dream that you are buying a lot of articles is a warning of coming troubles; be careful with your money matters. But if in your dream you are carefully considering every shilling you spend, then it is a fortunate sign. 129

C

6 Cab—To dream that you are riding in a cab or taxi shows good fortune, probably in connection with some distant country or through some friend who is living abroad. A man riding in a cab with a woman: Name will be connected with scandal. A woman riding in a cab alone: Will enjoy average success. Riding in a cab in the rain: Correspondence with friends living abroad. Riding in a cab with wife: Will have a long life. Riding in a cab with children: Happiness within the family. 312

2 Cabin—To dream that you are in the cabin of a ship foretells domestic troubles. Being in a cabin at the beach: Love affairs. Being in a cabin with a lover: Death of an enemy. Being in a cabin with friends: Danger with love matters. 113

9 Cabinet—Beware of treachery among those you trust. Buying a cabinet: Great financial gains. Opening a cabinet: Will receive a long awaited letter. 126

95

8 Cackle—A sign whose meaning varies very much in different localities. It is best to treat it as a warning that care is needed. 341

1 Caddy—You will receive a present which should have arrived sooner. Using services of a caddy: Misfortune is near. 190

7 Cage—To dream that you see birds in a cage is a token of a successful love affair; but if the cage is empty, the engagement will probably be broken off. Wild animals in a cage: Danger of going to prison. 359

2 Cake—Good health is generally denoted by food, provided it is of an enjoyable kind. Baking a cake: Will have a lucky turn of events. Eating a piece of cake: Will lose sweetheart. Buying a cake: Will enjoy the affection of a friend. 182

4 Calendar—To dream that you are worrying about some date is a sign of fortunate marriage, unless you fail to find out what you seek. Buying a calendar: Will receive good news. Tearing off calendar sheets: Will receive an unexpected gift. 976

4 Calf—A good omen for lovers and married people. Owning a calf: Will have a very good future. A calf that belongs to others: Fortune received from parents. 346

9 Calls—To hear your own name called aloud in your dream is fortunate for one in love. It has no money meaning. 414

7 Camel—As with all unusual animals, this foretells difficulties and worries. Many camels: Great financial gain. A camel carrying a load: Inheritance. 673

4 Camera—Looking into one: Someone will deceive you. Owning a camera: Will receive disagreeable news. Buying a camera: Joy without profit. Receiving a camera as a gift: Will have many love troubles. 139

5 Camp—To dream of soldiers in camp is also fortunate for love affairs, for it is a dream of contrary meaning and indicates peace in your domestic affairs. Of camping: Will have good days ahead. 158

9 Can—Good news. To drink out of a can: great joy. 702

4 Canal—This dream follows the rules for all water conditions. If the water is clear, it is a fortunate sign; but if

the water is muddy or covered with weeds, then it is an omen of coming troubles. 913

8 Canary—A certain sign of a cheerful and comfortable home. Owning a canary: Will be deceived by a friend. Buying a canary: Will soon make a trip. A dead canary: Death of a very good friend. 935

3 Candle—This is a good omen provided the candle burns brightly. But if it is extinguished, you may expect trouble. Lighting candles: Will meet with friends. Putting out candles: Will quarrel with a friend. Having colored candles: Will become a widow or a widower. Buying candles: Are inclined to believe enemies. Carrying lighted candles: Death of a friend. 813

2 Candy—Peace and happiness in your home affairs. Making candy: Will reap profit in business. Eating candy: Pleasure in society. Giving a box of candy as a gift: Peace and happiness in the home. Receiving a box of candy as a gift: Are very highly admired. 659

5 Cane—To dream that you have been whipped is a very bad sign. Beware of all business transactions for at least a couple of days. Resting on a cane: Illness in the near future. A woman using a cane: Will have love affairs. 293

4 Canister—Should you enclose anything in a canister, you will soon have a secret to keep. Should you open one, you will discover a friend's secret. 913

3 Cannibals—Disturbing information will vex and hamper you, but you have little to fear. 201

7 Cannon—To dream that you hear the firing of guns or muskets is a certain sign of some vexation and disappointment. A military man firing a cannon: Marriage to a beautiful girl. A man dreaming of hearing a cannon fired: Will have danger in business. A woman dreaming of hearing a cannon fired: Will marry a military man. 241

2 Canoe—A canoe is only intended for one person, and such a dream omen indicates a lack of friends. A canoe overturning: An enemy is seeking your ruin. Being in a canoe with your loved one: Avoid rivals. 326

2 Cap—If you put on your cap or hat in your dream, it

97

signifies difficulty in your love affairs. If a cap or hat is given to you, then you will marry happily. 182

1 Captain—Advancement, prosperity, and hopes fullfilled after great difficulties have been overcome. Marrying a captain: Will be confronted by a big scandal. Being a captain's sweetheart: Security is forthcoming. 874

4 Captivity—If in your dream, you see yourself a captive or in prison, it is a sign of an unhappy marriage. Other people in captivity: Beware of overstrain. Enemies in captivity: Beware of business losses. Animals in captivity: Dignity and distinction. 301

9 Cards—Playing cards in a dream or watching other people playing cards is an indication of coming quarrels. 153

2 Caress—For a mother to dream that she is caressing her children is a dream of contrary meaning. She will have anxious days on account of illness. A wife caressing her husband: Happy events. A husband caressing his wife: Will have good earnings. Sweethearts caressing each other: Will receive dreadful news. 506

5 Carols—To sing them presages a happy marriage. 194

5 Carpenter—To see workmen busily engaged is a sign that you will overcome your difficulties. Being a carpenter at work: Success in financial matters. Hiring a carpenter: Unexpected good news. 131

8 Carpet—To dream that you are in a room containing carpeting is a fortunate dream. Buying carpet: A mystery will be solved. A carpet burning: Be on guard against spiteful gossip. Laying a carpet: Big catastrophe ahead. 413

8 Carriage or Cart—To dream that you are driving a cart is a sign of a loss of money or position. Making a long trip in a carriage: Will be slow to achieve fortune. An overturned carriage: Misery. 683

2 Carry—To be carried by anyone in your dream is an uncertain omen. If you are carried by a woman or by a poor person, it is a fortunate sign, otherwise, it is not. 317

4 Carrots—This dream signifies profit by inheritance.

2 Carving—This omen's meaning depends upon the circumstances. If you are serving yourself, it shows your

98

own prosperity, but if you are carving for other people, then someone else will benefit by your actions. 731

9 Cashier—To imagine yourself in charge of other people's money is a bad omen; expect financial worry or even loss. Watching a cashier: Freedom from want. 585

6 Castle—This omen has varying meanings, but it is generally held to indicate a quarrel through your own bad temper. In some places it is said to show a marriage that opens well but drifts into difficulties. Residing in a castle: Good business ventures. A castle on fire: Quarrels because of bad temper. 158

4 Castor oil—Medicines in a dream are omens of contrary meaning. The more unpleasant the dose, the better it will be for the dreamer. Being ordered to take castor oil by a doctor: Short illness. Giving castor oil to children: Will soon take a trip. 202

6 Cat—An unfavorable dream, as is the case if you dream of a dog. It is a dream of contrary meaning and shows unexpected deceit by someone whom you trust. A black cat: Illness is near. Defending yourself from a cat: Will be robbed. Cats playing: Will be visited at home by enemies. A cat with her kittens: Unhappiness in marriage. 429

1 Catechism—Receiving oral instruction from a catechism: Happiness. Reading a catechism manual: Good business activities. Preaching from a catechism: Dignity and disdistiction. 325

8 Caterpillars—An unfortunate omen, trouble from a rival or enemy. 386

9 Cathedral—The important nature of this building has lead to many contrary definitions. It seems best to treat the outside view of a cathedral as showing good fortune, while if you dream of the interior you should take care, or trouble may befall you. 162

7 Cattle—Sign of prosperity in business, if you see yourself driving cattle, it shows that you have to work hard. Fat cattle: Will have a fruitful year. Lean cattle: Will be in want of provisions. Being rich and owning cattle: Disgrace and loss in business. Being poor and owning cattle: Good profits. 934

8 Cauliflower—Like most vegetables, this is an omen of

good health and a comfortable home life. Eating cauliflower: Joy and honor. Buying cauliflower: Will have good health. 215

1 Cavalry—To dream that you see mounted troops is a sign of good fortune in your love affairs. 316

4 Cave—An obstacle dream. If you escape from the cave all will go well, though you must expect trouble at first. But if you fall into a cave or fail to get out, then expect business worries. 247

5 Ceiling—If in your dream anything happens to the room in which you find yourself, it is an omen of trouble through a friend, probably due to severe illness. 312

5 Celery—As with other useful vegetables such a dream means good health and domestic comfort. 419

1 Cellar—An obstacle dream, unless there is plenty of coal in the cellar, when it indicates good business from a distance, perhaps abroad. Going into the cellar: Will be very fortunate. Many things stored in a cellar: Good news. 802

6 Cement—A present is soon to be given you, which will lead to more important events. Working with cement: Will receive unexpected money. 294

9 Certificate—You do not attempt to see things from other people's points of view. Try to be more sympathetic in small ways, and big events will ensue. 297

4 Cemetery—You will conquer all things. Being in a cemetery: Will soon have prosperity. A bride passing a cemetery on way to marriage: She will lose husband. Elderly people putting flowers in a cemetery: Will have no grief. 283

9 Chains—A dream of contrary meaning, showing that you will escape from some difficulty that worries you at the moment. But a gold chain around a woman's neck shows good fortune from some friend or lover. Cutting a chain: Will have worried for a short time. A person wearing chains in jail: Business will be bad. Succeeding in breaking the chains: Will be free of social engagements. Others in chains: Ill fortune for them. 315

3 Chair—To see an empty chair in your dream indicates

news from á long-absent friend. Sitting in a comfortable armchair: Will have prosperity. 201

8 Chalk—To dream of chalk cliffs means disappointment in some cherished hope. Buying chalk: Will have a long life. Handling chalk: Will soon be married. 908

5 Champagne—This is an unfortunate omen for love affairs. 698

8 Champions—To dream that you are successful at sports or games is a sign of poor success in business affairs. Pull yourself together and be more careful. 134

9 Chapel—As with all religious buildings, it is a fortunate dream if you see the outside but not if you find yourself inside. 783

3 Charity—This is a dream of contrary meaning. The more charitable you are in your dream, the less fortune awaits you in your business affairs. Receiving charity: Domestic affliction. Giving clothing to charity: People are laughing at you. Giving foodstuffs to charity: Will have hard work ahead. 102

3 Chastise—This is a dream of contrary meaning. If you find yourself thrashing your children in your dream, it indicates a happy and prosperous home life. But if you yourself are being thrashed, then it shows bad fortune in money matters. 516

4 Cheating—To dream that you have been cheated is a fortunate omen; but take care if you cheat someone else in your dreams. 814

6 Cheering—The bad sound of shouting or cheering in your dreams is an unfortunate omen. Be careful of your actions. 393

9 Cheese—Annoyance and deception from those around you. To eat cheese shows worry through your own hasty action. Foreign cheese: Are prone to liking only the best things. Homemade cheese: Good luck to one for whom you care. 891

5 Chemist—A chemist's shop is not a good subject for a dream: Be warned as to your business dealings. Being a chemist: Business affairs are not good. 923

4 Cherries—To see cherries growing is an omen of coming misfortune: You will be wise to move slowly in your business affairs. A cherry tree without cherries: Will

have good health. Having cherries in the home: Good health. Rotten cherries: Will be disappointed by lover. A man dreaming of picking cherries: Will be deceived by a woman. 814

9 Chest—To dream of a large box concerns your love affairs. If the chest is empty, prepare for a disappointment. Having a small chest: Love affairs will be good. Having a full chest: Family arguments. 190

3 Chestnuts—Domestic affection. Eating chestnuts: Will have some advantages if careful. Buying chestnuts: Will be dissappointed by lover. 804

3 Chew—If you dream you are chewing, you have to overlook another's fault before you will know peace of mind and happiness. 219

9 Chickens—All very young animals show friendships. Of one fine chicken: Will be fortunate in love. Several chickens: Will have many good friends. Chickens laying eggs: Joy and contentment. A chicken sitting on her eggs: Joy and happiness. A chicken with her chicks: Will receive a favor. Killing a chicken: Profit. 351

1 Children—A lucky dream, showing success in business. Several children: Will have abundance in life. Children at play: Good deeds will bear fruit. Adopting children: Own children will dislike those adopted. Children being killed: Misery caused by parents. Children being sick: Obstacles are ahead. 604

5 Chimney—To see a tall chimney predicts fortunate events. Chimney of own house: Will receive good news. A chimney falling down: Joy. 932

8 China—Financial gains from a long distance. Fine china: Good luck in gambling. Buying china: Happiness in your marriage. 359

1 Chips—A business success or wager won. 307

1 Chocolates—To be eating sweets in a dream is a sign of a coming gift. Buying chocolate: A short period of troubles will be followed by prosperity. Drinking chocolate: Will receive a marriage proposal. 325

8 Choir—As the choir is part of the interior of a sacred

building, it is not really a fortunate sign. If the choir-boys are singing, you will hear from an old friend. 494

4 Choking—Strangely enough, it is a fortunate sign to find yourself choking in your dream. Others choking you: Will be abandoned by lover. Children choking: Recovery from an illness. 310

5 Christ—The birth of Christ: Will have peace, joy, and contentment. Christ in the garden: Will have much wealth. Christ in the temple: Efforts will be rewarded. Christ being crucified: Enemies will be defeated. Resurrection of Christ: Will have good hopes in life. Talking to Christ: Will receive much consolation. 275

9 Christening—This dream also has to do with the interior of a sacred building. It is not a fortunate omen. 216

2 Christmas—A good omen, but it refers more particularly to your friends or your family affairs and not to business. Being at a Christmas party: Will have new good friends. Going Christmas caroling: Great financial gains. 092

7 Church—Here again, it is the outside of the building that is fortunate. To dream that you are inside a sacred building is a warning of coming trouble. Talking in a church: Have plenty of envious friends. Praying in church: Consolation and joy. Being in a church during mass: Will receive what you are hoping for. Hearing a dispute in a church: Will have family troubles. Being with a priest in a church: Happy marriage and success. 475

1 Churchyard—Although apparently unpleasant, this is a fortunate dream, as it concerns the outside of a church. 109

4 Churning—To dream that you are churning is a sign of prosperity and plenty. To the single, happy marriage. 391

3 Cider—Gossip about your own private affairs. Act cautiously. 345

2 Cigar—It is a fortunate dream to see yourself smoking. Prosperity awaits you. Having an unlit cigar: Will have misfortune. Having a lighted cigar: May have good hopes. 371

7 Cigarette—To dream you are lighting one signifies new

plans. A half-smoked cigarette held in the hand is a postponement. To smoke it to the end means a successful conclusion to your hopes. 313

7 Circus—A sign of future unhappiness due to your own careless habits. Watching a circus performance: Loss of money. Taking children to a circus: Important and beneficial events to come. 142

3 City—A large city denotes ambition if in the distance. Ambition will be successfully attained should you enter the city in your dream. A city burning: Poverty. Being in a large city: Conclusion of hopes. A city in ruins: Will have illness in the family. Going through a city: Will receive sad news from a friend. 471

6 Climbing—It is a sign of business prosperity to find yourself climbing, unless the effort proves too great for your strength. Still, even then it shows some sort of good fortune, though combined with difficulties. Climbing but failing to reach the summit: Cherished plans will fail. Climbing a ladder to the top: Success in business. A ladder breaking while climbing: Will have unexpected difficulties. Climbing a tree: Will receive a good position. 609

4 Cliffs—A dangerous dream. Do not take any risks, especially of high places from which you might slip, for some time. Going up a cliff: Conclusion of affairs. Descending from a cliff: Don't trust your friends. 103

8 Clock—To dream that you hear a clock strike the hours is a fortunate sign. You will enjoy a comfortable life. Having a wall clock: Will have happiness. Buying a wall clock: Will receive important business news. A clock being stopped: Will be spared from illness. 359

1 Clothes—This is a dream of contrary meaning. If you have plenty of clothes in your dream, it is a warning of coming trouble. If you are partly dressed or naked, then prosperity is coming your way. To put on clothes is a fortunate sign, but if you make any error, you must not correct it or you will spoil your luck. 352

2 Clouds—This depends upon the circumstances. If the sky is stormy and dark, it betokens many sorrows; but if the clouds pass away, then better fortune awaits you.

Downpour of rain from the clouds: Will have hard days ahead. 254

3 Clover—To dream that you are in a clover field is a very fortunate sign, especially to those who are in love. 147

4 Clown—Others think you witless. Being dressed as a clown: Will receive news of a death. Being in the company of a clown: Troubles ahead. A clown making love to a woman: You have many hypocritical friends. 490

2 Club—You will meet with many people whom you have not seen for a long time. Do not let them influence you. Being refused admittance to a club: Will take good care of business. 605

3 Coach—It is not a very good omen when you dream that you are driving in a coach; be careful or you may find yourself in difficulties. 975

4 Coal—This is a warning of danger. If you dream that you are in a coal pit, it is serious and means heavy business losses or a keen disappointment in love. 535

3 Coat—This is a sign of contrary if you are wearing a new coat, beware of business troubles. If your coat is old, or if you tear it in any way, then prosperity is coming to you. Wearing another person's coat: Will be forced to seek a friend's help. Losing a coat: Will soon face financial ruin through speculation. Getting a coat dirty: Will lose a good friend. 912

3 Coat of Arms—To dream of a shield with a Coat of Arms on it is an excellent sign, a powerful friend will protect you. 723

5 Cobweb—To brush one away means a triumph for you over an enemy. 392

5 Cock—Although a cock is a bad omen by itself, it is considered a sign of some unexpected good news if you hear the bird crowing. Cocks fighting: Will have quarrels. A dead cock: Happiness in the family. 194

4 Coffee—This dream also is favorable and signifies great domestic happiness. Buying coffee: Will have the best reputation in business. Pouring coffee: Security is forthcoming. Being in a coffee shop with good people: Highly considered by friends. 913

8 Coffin—Emblematic of the serious illness of some dear friend, perhaps even death if there is much black seen. An elaborate coffin: Death of a partner. A friend in a coffin: Serious illness of a dear friend. Coffin of the head of the family: Must contend with unpleasant matters. 260

6 Coins—To dream of money in the shape of coins is on the whole favorable, but the more important the coin the less fortunate the dream. Copper coins are more favorable than silver, while gold is often considered a bad omen, as is the case with paper money. 159

6 Cold—If you feel cold it is a sign of comfort and friendship. Having a bad cold: Security is forthcoming. Mate having a cold: Abundant means. Children having a cold: Good times are coming. 582

5 College—It is not a fortunate omen to dream that you are at college. 527

4 Colors—If you dream of flags and decorations in many bright colors, it signifies continued prosperity and success in all your undertakings. White is always favorable, especially in matters concerning other people, such as business affairs. Blue and purple represent prosperity through other people, good fortune in your love affairs, and so on. Scarlet or red is a warning of quarrels, the loss of friends; but crimson denotes pleasant news from an unexpected quarter. Yellow and orange are mental tints and show that you need not expect any important change in your affairs for some time. Green indicates a journey or business with people at a distance. 625

9 Collision—A sign of mental strife. You will need all your self-control to overcome the effect of bad tidings. 054

9 Combat—It is not a good sign to be engaged in a fight in a dream; if you are successful, all will come well, but only after difficulty and worry. Helping others in combat: Reconciliation with enemies. 459

1 Companion—To dream that you are with a pleasant companion is a fortunate omen: It shows immediate success. 208

6 Concert—To find yourself at a concert in your dream is

106

a sign of unexpected news. Singing at a concert: Will receive an inheritance. A sick person dreaming of a concert: Will soon recover. 249

2 Confession—Guard the confidences given to you by others, as you will shortly be strongly tempted to reveal a secret. Going to confession: Will soon be told a secret. 269

8 Congratulations—These signify cause for condolence but better times to follow. Sending congratulations: Joy. Congratulating others: Will have financial gains. 251

2 Confetti—Social disappointments of a trifling nature. Throwing confetti: Will receive a letter with good news. Others throwing confetti at you: Love and happiness. 236

8 Confusion—A dream of confusion presages loneliness and trouble. 269

9 Conscience—It is a dream of contrary meaning if you are being worried by your conscience; all will go well. The more self-satisfied you feel, the less your chance of prosperity. 162

5 Convicted—To be found guilty in a court of justice is a good sign: Prosperity is on the way. 329

9 Consent—If you dream that you consent to the request of someone, it denotes a discovery of lost valuables. Others consenting to your request: Will have good health. Refusing consent: Will have a vigorous mind. 180

3 Convent—An engagement speedily followed by a happy, though not wealthy, wedding. 759

1 Convulsions—To dream you see someone in convulsions means an invitation to a concert. Having convulsions: Prosperous married life. 379

2 Cooking—To dream of cooking, whether by yourself or someone else, is a good sign but only concerns material comforts. Being a cook: Poverty. A young girl being a cook: Will soon become engaged. 506

4 Cord—To knot a cord means the strengthening of a friendship; to unravel it means the breaking of an engagement. 364

3 Corks—If you dream that you are extracting a cork, it

is a sign of some good news of a friend. If you are pushing a cork into a bottle, it shows an unexpected visit to you. 363

7 Corkscrew—It is a sign of illness to use a corkscrew in your dreams. 385

5 Corn—A very fortunate dream, and a sign of money in plenty; according to the state of the growing corn. Eating corn: Success in all your affairs. Harvesting corn: Will hear good news. A field with large ears of corn: Big financial gains. 158

9 Cornet—Family quarrels are foretold when you hear a cornet being played. Playing a cornet: Discovery of lost valuables. 531

6 Corns—To dream that you have corns on your feet is a sign of fortunate business ventures. 240

5 Corpse—An omen of estrangement or separation from friends through your own fault; an unhappy love affair. A corpse in the water: Arguments with your lover. A corpse being lowered into a grave: Separation from a loved one. A corpse at a morgue: Marriage or other happy events. 932

8 Cottage—It is a fortunate sign to find yourself living in a cottage unless you are discontented and endeavor to get away. 593

4 Coughing—This is a dream of contrary meaning and indicates good health, vigor, business prosperity. 526

9 Counterfeit—If you handle counterfeit coins in a dream, you will be asked to help someone who will make you a good friend. 243

5 Court—To dream of going to court means a business loss. Being requested to go to court: High consideration of others. Being punished by a court: Travel and prosperity. Being acquitted by a court: Serious disaster is ahead. 328

6 Courtship—This is also a dream of contrary meaning, for the more fortunate the wooing in your dreams, the worse it will be for your real love affairs. 537

9 Cousin—To dream of your relatives is a sign that you may soon receive unexpected news. 279

5 Cow—Good luck unless you are pursued by the animal, in which case it depends upon what happens. If you

escape the cow, you will survive the evil schemes of some enemy. The greater the number of animals seen, the more serious the warning. 635

6 Crab—As in the case of all unusual creatures, this is a sign of coming difficulties. Many crabs in a fish market: Danger is ahead. Eating crabs: Avoid rivals. 123

7 Cradle—It is not a good sign to dream of an empty cradle; misfortune will come, probably from ill health. A cradle with a baby in it: Avoid rivals. Rocking your own baby in a cradle: Illness in the family. A young woman dreaming of a cradle: Reconsider your present conduct. 682

3 Crawl—An omen of difficulty; your love affairs will not prosper. 534

3 Crew—It is not a good omen if you see sailors on a vessel at work. Expect bad news. 354

9 Cries—These are omens of contrary meaning. If the cries are happy and joyous, then expect bad news. But if they are cries of trouble or distress, then all will go well. 927

4 Crimes—Your undertakings will be crowned with success. 373

7 Cripple—A warning to be kind to those around you. A child being crippled: Will have happiness. Members of family being crippled: Expect too many favors from others. Friends being crippled: Will become a beggar. 241

9 Crochet—A change in your enviroment leading to better times. Your sweetheart crocheting: You are very ambitious. 279

3 Crocodile—Another warning of troubles ahead. Of a crocodile: You are in the grip of a deceitful person. Many crocodiles: Bad catastrophe ahead. 912

2 Cross—An omen of sorrow in the affections. A cross on a grave: You need help. Wearing a cross: You will have the protection of friends. A cross in the church: Big joy. Praying on a cross: Will receive wishes. 794

5 Crow—The sinister color black makes this bird an omen of grief and misfortune. If more than one crow is seen, the matter becomes very serious. A woman dreaming

of a crow: Death of her husband. A man dreaming of a crow: Death of his wife. 518

1 Crowds—Your happiness is assured and will increase. Being in a crowd: Advancement within position. 262

1 Crown—To dream that you have a crown on your head is a sign that you will benefit from people in a better position than yourself. If a cross is seen as well, then you will benefit through a death. Placing a crown on another's head: You are worthy of advancement. Having a crown of flowers: Big success. 190

3 Crucifix—This omen is associated with the interior of a church, so it is not a favorable sign. 597

5 Cruelty—To dream of seeing this means that one near to you is in need of help. 869

7 Crutches—This is an obstacle dream. If you recover and are able to walk without the aid of crutches, all will go well. If not, expect trouble. 232

6 Crystal—You will soon be shown the turning in the long lane that has been worrying you. Buying crystal: Will soon be given nice gifts. Having crystal: Change for the better. 258

4 Cup—An empty cup is a bad omen, but a full one is a sign of prosperity. Drinking from a cup: Good times are coming. Breaking a cup: Death of an enemy. Receiving a cup as a gift: You have faithful friends. 382

8 Cupboard—To dream of an empty cupboard is a bad sign for your business prosperity. If you put things inside it shows that you will recover your losses after some distress. Taking things out of a cupboard: You have many loyal friends. 404

1 Curls—A complete change in your affairs; new environment and better times are in view. 343

3 Curse—To dream of hearing curses and rough language presages a visit of ceremony. Being cursed: Ambitions will be realized. 426

5 Curtain—This is an obstacle dream but refers particularly to bad faith in someone you trust. If you pull the curtain aside, you will be warned in time. Others pulling curtains aside: Warning of trouble. Putting up new curtains: Will entertain a prominent guest. 815

8 Cushions—Signs of comfort in your dreams are not

fortunate. The more comfortable you find yourself, the greater will be your difficulty and business worries. 251

1 Cycling—To dream that you are cycling foretells a visit that you will make at some distance. To see people cycling: Friends from afar will visit you. 208

D

4 Daffodils—All early Spring flowers are fortunate omens. Daffodils particularly concern your love affairs, not your business concerns. A happy future is certain for one who dreams of these beautiful Spring flowers, but for the best results they should be seen out of doors. 184

6 Daggers—Be careful of treachery or you will suffer heavy loss. Being wounded by a dagger: Another person is enjoying what you hoped for. 024

3 Dairy—A fortunate dream. 102

3 Daisies—These simple wild flowers are always a fortunate omen in your dreams. Picking daisies: Great happiness in love. Having them in a vase in a home: Important and very beneficial events. 237

9 Dance—If you dream that you are dancing, it is a sign that money is coming to you or that some cherished plan will meet with success. But if you merely watch others dancing, then you will hear of good fortune coming concerning a friend. 873

4 Danger—This is an omen of contrary meaning. If you face danger in your dreams, you may expect success; but if you avoid it, then trouble will come. 328

1 Darkness—To dream that you are in the dark is a sign of difficulties ahead. If you fall or hurt yourself, then you may expect a change for the worse, but if you succeed in groping your way to the light, then you will face your troubles successfully. 514

8 Darning—To dream you are darning denotes the intro-

111

duction of a new and kindly friend. To see it is a warning against gossip. 638

2 Daughter—To dream of your children is generally considered a contrary vision. What affects your girls in your dream will concern your boys in real life. 425

4 Dates—You are likely to be admired by some member of the other sex. 202

6 Dawn—This omen depends upon the circumstances. To see the dawn means days of storm and stress lie ahead. 537

5 Dead—This omen depends upon the circumstances, but on the whole it concerns other people, not the dreamer. If you speak to friends or relatives who are dead, it means news of some living friend or relative; if you touch or kiss them, the news will be of a sorrowful nature. To dream of a death means a new birth. 806

1 Deafness—To find yourself suddenly deaf in your dream is a good sign. By some unexpected turn of events, you will escape a great trouble or difficulty. 523

5 Debts—To pay your debts in a dream is a good omen, but if other people repay what they owe you, then expect a loss. 194

8 Decorate—To dream that you are beautifying your room or your house is a dream of contrary meaning. Expect losses in your business affairs. Decorating a grave: Will have very little joy. 386

1 Deeds—Should you dream of signing them, avoid speculation and quarrels with those dear to you, as you are in danger of loss of either money or affection. 901

4 Deer—To dream of wild animals in unnatural captivity is unfavorable and indicates quarrels or disputes. A herd of deer running: Financial distress. Killing a deer: Will receive an inheritance. Having the horns of a deer: Will be cheated by friends. 391

2 Defend—To dream of shielding or defending someone denotes at least one loyal friend. Being unable to defend yourself: Will live a long life. Defending children: Luck and prosperity. 857

7 Deformity—To dream that you are deformed signifies shame and sorrow. Others who are deformed: Beware of

false appearances of others. A young lady dreaming of being deformed: She will break her engagement. 925

1 Delirium—To dream of being delirious signifies danger through a secret. To see someone else in that condition means that a friend is trying to help you secretly. 253

2 Delight—Excessive happiness in your dreams is a bad omen. Expect trouble at home and business worries. 236

9 Deluge—A heavy downpour of rain is an omen of bad luck in your love affairs. Avoid quarrels. 207

1 Dentist—A dream of illness. Being in a dentist's chair: Will have cause to question friends' sincerity. Children in a dentist's chair: Will hear false reports about friends. Friend in a dentist's chair: Misfortune in love affairs. 712

3 Derby—A lucky dream; financial gain will come your way. Attending a derby with loved ones: Approaching good times. 237

8 Desert—To dream that you are traveling across a desert or a wide open area signifies difficulties concerning some cherished plan. It is particularly bad if you encounter bad weather or other troubles. If the sun is shining, the final outcome will be successful. 782

3 Desk—The meaning of this dream depends upon whether the desk is locked or open. If it is locked, then you may expect bad news; but if you are sitting at an open desk, then all will go well. 165

9 Despair—It is an omen of contrary meaning. It shows domestic happiness. 456

8 Dessert—It is always a fortunate omen to dream you are eating ripe fruit. If the fruit, however, is not ripe or has been kept too long, expect business losses. 634

7 Destroy—It is a most unfortunate omen if you break something of value in your dream. Having destroyed something: Warning of troubles. Somebody having destroyed your things: Triumph over enemies. 691

3 Detective—You will hear a confession that will rectify an important mistake in your opinion of someone. Being questioned by a detective: You have one loyal friend. Being blamed by a detective: Financial gains. 327

7 Devil—It is a very bad omen if you imagine you see Satan, but the outcome will depend upon the circumstances. Whatever happens, however, it means a long struggle. A young girl dreaming of the devil: A happy marriage will occur soon. An elderly sick person dreaming of the devil: Expect trouble. Children dreaming of the devil: Sickness. Having a conversation with the devil: Will be cheated by friends. Fighting with the devil: You are in much danger. 385

4 Devotion—As with most dreams concerning religion, this is a good sign. Wife and husband having devotion for each other: Happiness is assured. Children having devotion for the parents: Important and beneficial events to come. 563

5 Dew—One of nature's blessings. A very fortunate dream if you see dew on grass. 284

7 Diamonds—There is no certainty about this dream, as some authorities call it an omen of misfortune while others declare that it shows some fortunate deal in business or speculation. Probably it depends upon the financial and social position of the dreamer and should be considered a dream of contrary meaning. 124

3 Dice—To dream that you are playing with dice is a sure sign of change in fortune, but which way things will go depends upon the circumstances. 192

1 Dictionary—This denotes quarrels and the loss of a friend. Consulting a dictionary: Triumph over enemies. Buying a dictionary: Change in environment. 523

6 Difficulty—A dream of obstacles. If you succeed in overcoming your difficulty, all will be well. Having personal difficulties: Good times are coming. Having financial difficulties: Will receive money. Sweetheart having difficulties: Will surely be kind and agreeable. Others having difficulty: All will be well. 465

2 Digging—This dream indicates money, not personal affairs. It depends upon the nature of the soil, for it is emblematic. If the soil is good and easily worked, your plans will succeed. 380

1 Dinner—All meals are dreams of contrary meaning. The better the dinner, the greater the difficulties ahead of you. Having relatives over for dinner: Must control

your nerves. Others giving a dinner party: You have one loyal friend. 892

6 Dirt—To dream that your clothes are dirty denotes sorrow. If you yourself are personally unclean or unwashed, it means illness. 735

7 Diploma—To dream that you are being handed a diploma: Own talents are being neglected. You have probably neglected your talents, which, if properly trained, might lead you to success. 502

6 Disasters—These are always dreams of contrary meaning, favorable for business people. 987

4 Disappointment—To dream you are disappointed assures you of success in the very matter dreamed about. Lovers being disapointed: Danger through a secret. 364

1 Discussion—It is a good omen if you have a friendly discussion in your dream, but if you lose your temper it is a warning of trouble. 357

3 Disease—To dream that you are ill is a warning of treachery; it is a very unfavorable dream in the case of lovers. Having a disease: Warning of treachery. Others having a disease: Will make money illegally. Having an unknown disease: Large financial gain. 723

6 Disfigurement—To dream of personal disfigurement presages an unexpected happiness. 312

3 Disgrace—A dream of contrary meaning. It is a fortunate sign if you find yourself in trouble or in disgrace. Others in disgrace: Are surrounded by enemies. Relatives being in disgrace: Hard work awaits. 102

3 Disguise—Fancy costume is not a fortunate sign. It shows trouble, but not of a serious nature. Having disguised yourself: Will take a long trip and change residence. Others being disguised: Triumph over enemies. 219

4 Dish—To break a plate or dish is a bad sign. It shows domestic trouble. 742

3 Dishonesty—An important document will be mislaid. If you are dishonest in your dream, it will be a document affecting your affairs. Other people being dishonest: Are within grip of deceitful people. Family members being dishonest: Temptation will come to you. 309

7 Dislike—This dream depends upon the circumstances.

115

If you dream that someone does not like you and that you are worried, it is a bad omen. If, however, you do not appear to be upset at all, then your difficulties will be overcome. 421

2 Dismiss—To dream of being dismissed from a business position presages a rise in position. Dismissing an employer: Doomed for disappointment. Others being dismissed: A mystery will be solved. 749

4 Disobedience—To dream of your own disobedience denotes a difficult choice before you, possibly regarding marriage. Children being disobedient: Prompt engagement. 724

5 Disputes—A dream of contrary meaning it signifies success; but there will be obstacles in the way at first. Having a business dispute: Discovery of lost valuables. Others having a dispute: Good times are coming. 365

3 Distance—A dream that you are separated from your friends or family is a bad sign, but if you dream of some person who is separated from you, then you will hear good news. 615

5 Distress—Another of contrary meaning. It is a good sign if you are in distress or in trouble of any sort. Children being in distress: Warning of trouble. Wife or husband being in distress: Will have emotional sorrow. 212

4 Distrust—To dream that you doubt some person is a bad omen. It is just as serious if someone else disturbs you. 706

9 Ditch—All obstacles of a material kind are bad signs. However, beware of unexpected difficulties, especially in money matters. Being pushed into a ditch: Beware of unexpected difficulties. Walking through a ditch: Will be cheated by someone. Digging a ditch: You are going to discover a secret. 531

2 Diving—To dream that you are diving or falling into water is a sign of loss of money. Others diving: Warning of troubles. Children diving: Dignity and distinction. Members of family diving: Business undertaking will be risky. 146

4 Divorce—It is a dream of contrary meaning. If you imagine you are being divorced it is a sign of domestic

116

happiness. Relatives being divorced: Bad gossip by friends. Children being divorced: Much joy ahead. Friends being divorced: Danger through a secret. 346

3 Doctor—A good dream financially. Going to a doctor: Will have mastery over many things. Calling a doctor for yourself: Will live a long life. Calling a doctor for children: New interests and surroundings. Being a doctor: Joy and profit. Becoming a doctor: Financial gains. 219

9 Dogs—This dream depends upon circumstances. If the dog is friendly, all will be well. If he barks, then beware of quarrels, and if he bites you, expect treachery from someone you trust. Own dog: Will receive favors from a friend. Police dog: Quarrels with a business partner. Unfriendly dog: Will receive help from a good friend. Being bitten by a dog: Will be double-crossed by someone you trust. Dogs playing together: You are in danger. A dog and cat fighting: Arguments with relatives. 378

8 Dolls—To dream of dolls is a sign of domestic happiness. Girls playing with dolls: Will have very good luck. Buying a doll: Prosperity. 134

6 Door—This is almost an obstacle dream. If you are trying to enter a house and the door is not opened, you may expect serious business troubles. If the house or room appears to have many doors, then beware of speculation, for you will lose your money. 271

2 Doves—A fortunate dream, for business and home affairs. A woman dreaming of doves: Fortunate affairs at home. 164

4 Dowry—To receive money in a dream without earning it is always a bad sign. A man giving property to his bride: Expect much uneasiness. Giving a dowry to daughters: Will earn more money. A widow dowry: Will make a good change in your life. 913

5 Dragon—To see one: Great riches. Many dragons: Big disappointment in love. A young girl dreaming of a dragon: Much joy. 356

7 Drawers—To dream of an open drawer is a fortunate omen, but if you cannot open a closed drawer, then beware of trouble ahead. If a woman dreams of her drawers or her underclothing, it is a bad sign. She will

not be faithful to the man who loves her. A married woman dreaming of her drawers: Unfaithful to the man who loves her. A single girl dreaming of her drawers: Will soon be engaged. 925

8 Dreaming—To dream that you consult anyone about your dreams shows that you may expect news from a distance. Dreaming of nice things: You have impossible desires. Dreaming of being rich: Will be disillusioned. Dreaming of being poor: Change in your position. 134

7 Drenched—An unfortunate dream presaging danger of fever for you or someone near to you. Others being drenched: You expect too many favors. Drenching by force: A mystery will be solved. 385

2 Dress—It is always a good sign if you are concerned about your clothes in a dream; you will succeed in your plans. Receiving a beautiful dress: Will be helped by an unknown man. Buying a new dress: Health and happiness. Changing dresses: Will suffer because of own foolishness. Wearing a daring evening dress: Sickness. 524

2 Drink—If you dream that you are thirsty and cannot find water, it shows misfortune. If the water is dirty or muddy, it is a bad sign, as also if it is warm or hot. But to drink clear fresh water is a very good sign. It is also fortunate to drink milk. 218

2 Driving—It is a fortunate dream if someone else is driving you; but if you yourself are the driver, then expect money losses. Loved one driving: Avoid rivals. 398

2 Drown—A most unfortunate dream for business people. But if someone rescues you, then you may expect help from a friend. A businessman drowning: Will go into bankruptcy. Rescuing others from drowning: A friend will reach high position. 524

6 Drugs—A successful speculation, much gossip around you. Having drugs: Infirmity. Taking drugs: Affliction. 924

3 Drums—It is a fortunate omen to hear drums in your dreams. You will have great success. Marching in a parade and playing the drums: Luck and prosperity. Buying a drum: Will have a loss of small importance.

Children playing a drum: Will not have sufficient money. 237

5 Drunk—To dream that you are intoxicated is a warning of financial trouble. If you see someone else who is drunk, then you will lose money through some other person. A woman being drunk: Will commit some bad action. Becoming drunk with good wine: Will make acquaintances of high person. Being drunk and feeling sad: Treachery by relatives. Being sick from drunkenness: Squandering of household money. Husband being drunk constantly: Bad future. 491

4 Ducks—A good sign. If the ducks attack you it means trouble in business affairs. Ducks flying: Marriage and a happy family life. Hunting ducks: Big success. Eating ducks: Honor and fortune. A wild duck dead: Don't forget your friends. Ducks swimming: Beware of great danger. 823

5 Duet—To sing in a duet in your dreams is a good sign for the lover or for the married. It shows much domestic happiness. 176

6 Duel—Trouble from friends and relatives. You have treachery from enemies. 284

4 Dumb—To dream that you cannot speak, or to meet a dumb person in your dream, is a bad dream. Avoid speculation and do not discuss your business affairs. 841

8 Dungeon—This is an obstacle dream. If you cannot escape from the dungeon, expect business losses. If you do escape all will come well, though only after some difficulty. 287

1 Dusk—Darkness is not important in a dream as it would be in real life, as it is your natural surroundings when asleep. It represents some slight difficulty ahead of you, possibly in your love affairs. 415

9 Dust—Dust or dirt is a bad omen and shows struggle against adverse circumstances. To dream that you are dusting a room shows that some improvement will come if you persevere. 135

7 Dwarf—If you see a dwarf in your dream, it is a sign of difficulties in your domestic circle. Ugly dwarfs: Illness and misfortune. 421

8 Dye—To dream that you are dyeing your hair or roug-
ing your cheek is a bad sign: You will suffer through
your own folly. 215

5 Dying—If you dream of dying, you will receive empty
promises. Relatives dying: Will receive a big inheritance.
Children dying: Will receive fortune from abroad.
Friends dying: Triumph over enemies. 284

E

3 Eagle—If this noble bird is flying, it signifies good
fortune. If it is dead, or wounded, expect a loss of
money. If, however, the flying bird threatens the
dreamer, then you may expect difficulties. 435

7 Ears—To dream of any trouble with your ears is a bad
sign; it shows trouble from some unexpected source.
Feeling own ears while dreaming: Will discover a secret.
Having ears pierced: Domestic loss. The ears of corn,
wheat, rye, or grain: Will have abundant means. 538

8 Earthquake—This is a rare dream, and consequently
the meaning varies greatly. People in the East think
little of such happenings in real life, so in their dream
they attach little importance to it as some small difficulty to be overcome. But for a Westerner, the omen
should be treated far more seriously and should be
looked upon as a warning. Feeling an earthquake: Death
of a relative. A city destroyed by an earthquake: A
change in life will soon come. 602

6 Easel—It is a happy omen to dream that you are an
artist working at an easel. 916

6 Easter—To dream of this church festival is an omen of
coming happiness. Spending Easter with others: Bad
days are ahead. Being in an Easter parade: Danger
through a secret. 501

2 Eating—An unfortunate omen as a rule and a sign of
family quarrels, but if you see other people eating in

your dream, it shows a valuable friendship. To eat cheese is favorable. Overeating: Discovery of valuables. Eating with the hands: Danger is ahead. Eating broiled meat: Good fortune. Eating salads: Advancement within position. Eating fruits: Happiness is assured. 857

7 Eavesdropping—To dream that you are secretly listening to the conversation of other people is a sign that some unexpected good fortune is coming to you. Others eavesdropping on secret conversation: Money is coming to you. 214

7 Ebony—A voyage to a foreign country. Having ebony wood: Will meet someone from abroad. Buying ebony wood: Success in business. Being given things made with ebony: Will have good earnings. 439

4 Echo—This curious dream is a sign that you will hear some good fortune, but not concerning yourself. In some cases the dreamer may even suffer through the success of some other person. 256

6 Eclipse—This omen is sometimes met in dreams, but it is rare. It indicates the illnes of someone closely connected with you. 492

5 Eels—When seen in a dream, these indicate difficulties which you can overcome if you persevere. Holding an eel: Will be attended by good fortune. Catching a dead eel: Warning of suffering. Many eels in water: You are overworking. 536

2 Eggs—A sign of money unless the eggs are rotten or unpleasant to eat. If the eggshells are broken, it shows loss of money. Eating eggs: Foretells an early marriage. Having very fresh egg: Will receive money. White eggs: Will receive some advantageous news. Having brown eggs: Will receive bad news. The eggs of a fish: Will have hard times ahead. 173

5 Elastic—This dream denotes an improvement in your fortunes. Having something made of elastic: Good times are coming. Putting elastic bands on bundles of things: Beware of jealous friends. 689

2 Election—To dream that you are assisting at one means a speedy success of your own hopes. 352

3 Electricity—Something will happen to surprise you greatly; guard against small losses. 102

9 Elephant—This friendly beast denotes assistances coming from friends, or outside influences. Feeding an elephant: An important person will befriend you. Getting on the back of an elephant: Good fortune. Giving water to an elephant: Will be of service to an influential person. An elephant in a circus: Danger of death for a relative. An elephant escaping from a circus: Family quarrels. An elephant being free: Will enjoy much independence in life. 279

8 Elevator—Coming down in an elevator: Will be overwhelmed by misfortune. Going up in an elevator: Increase in wealth and advancement in position. Being in an elevator with others: Avoid rivals. Being in an elevator with family: Financial gains. An elevator being out of order: Warning of trouble. Being stuck between floors in an elevator: Will have emotional sorrow. 314

6 Elopement—A dream of contrary meaning. If you are eloping with your lover, it shows quarrels and an unhappy marriage. If you see other people eloping, it is a sign of illness. 348

8 Embankment—Your hopes will not be fulfilled, but someone you have known formerly will shortly return to your life. 125

7 Embrace—This is a dream of contrary meaning, for it is not considered fortunate if anyone embraces you in a dream. But if you see your wife, sweetheart, or friend embracing someone else, then it is a good omen for you. 348

4 Emerald—Various meanings are attached to this beautiful gem. In the East, it is considered the greatest possible good fortune, but in the West it is usually treated as a sign of business with someone at a distance or separation from some loved one. Of an emerald: Will experience difficulty over an inheritance. Selling own emeralds: Separation from a loved one. Buying an emerald: Good business with a person far away. 598

3 Employment—A dream of contrary meaning. It is a sign of prosperity in business if you dream that you are out of work. To dream that you employ others shows interest will clash with you. Being in an employment office seeking a job: A change for the better. 293

8 Enemy—To dream that you meet or are in the company of someone whom you do not like is an omen of contrary meaning and foretells good fortune for you. Fighting with enemies: Will be deceived by friends. Hating an enemy: Loss of your fortune. Killing an enemy: Great joy and pleasures in life. Winning out over an enemy: Will succeed in a lawsuit. 152

1 Engagement—To dream of any engagement, business, social, or matrimonial, is considered a bad sign. A broken engagement: May have to endure disappointments. Engagement of others being broken: Will have emotional sorrow. 361

4 Engagement Ring—To see or wear one means a new attraction; to be engaged, a speedy wedding. Returning an engagement ring: A change in life will soon come. 649

9 Engine—To dream of machinery in motion is not a good omen. you may expect difficulties in the near future. Driving an engine: Change in environment. A steam engine: Money will come easily during entire life. A gas engine: Important and very beneficial event to come. An engine being out of order: Watch out for treachery. An engine stopped: Financial gains. 279

2 Enlistment—To dream of enlisting means a postponed success. 317

5 Entertainment—This dream depends upon the circumstances. It is usually a very fortunate omen unless for any reason you feel uncomfortable. If you leave before the entertainment is over, it is a sign that you will miss some good opportunity through your own carelessness. 482

4 Envelopes—Closed envelopes represent difficulties. If you can open the envelope and remove the contents, then some worry will be smoothed away. Putting a letter into an envelope: Discovery of loss of valuables. Receiving an envelope with many letters: Big disappointment in love. Mailing an envelope: Luck and prosperity. Buying an envelope or envelopes: Change for the better. 319

3 Envy—To dream that other people envy you is a good sign. Envying others: Triumph over enemies. Being

123

envied by enemies: Are being watched by one with evil intentions. 543

1 Ermine—This signifies a letter from or some association with those of high rank, but to the sick it means a slow recovery. Owning an ermine coat: Will invest in real estate. Buying an ermine coat: Must attempt to save money. 492

1 Eruption—Good luck is coming to you which will make you much envied. 919

6 Errand—This is really an obstacle dream. If you are out on an errand and successfully conclude it, then all will be well. If you cannot conclude it or procure the article you require, then you may expect business trouble. 492

4 Escape—This is a straight dream that depends upon the apparent happenings. If you escape from any difficulty in your dream, it means success in your personal affairs, a triumph over difficulties. If you escape from fire or water, you may expect anxious moments but a successful issue. If from some wild animal, then look for treachery near you. If in your dream you do not escape, then it is a very bad sign. 715

8 Estates—To dream of your own estate denotes a devoted marriage partner. 251

4 Evening—A prosperous time to come later in life. Your earlier worries will be happily ended. 625

9 Evidence—To dream of giving evidence against a criminal in court denotes a friend whose reputation you will be able to save. 360

3 Evil—A very serious omen unless you succeed in driving it away. Be careful in your business. 750

8 Examination—An obstacle dream. If you find that the examination is too difficult, then expect business worries. If, however, you can answer most of the questions and dream that you are doing well, then some unexpected good fortune awaits you. 404

4 Exchange—If you dream that you are exchanging articles with some other people, expect business losses and difficulties. 634

5 Excuse—It is a bad sign if you find yourself making excuses in your dreams. You will suffer loss through your own folly. Others making excuses to you: Will live

a long life. A partner making excuses: Happiness is assured. Children making excuses: Financial gains. 743

1 Excitement—To dream that you are feeling unpleasantly disturbed denotes a successful ending to your plans. 192

8 Execution—The success of your undertakings will be doubtful. Execution of sweetheart: Avoid rivals. Execution of an innocent person: Will be jilted by lover. 125

7 Exercise—This might be called an obstacle dream. If you enjoy the vigorous exercise, all will be well; but if you feel tired, then beware of money losses. 862

8 Exhaustion—In your dream you may not know why you feel exhausted, but it is always a bad sign unless you recover fully in your dream. 359

8 Exile—To dream that you have been sent away signifies that your lot will be cast largely in foreign parts. A woman dreaming of being exiled: Must sacrifice pleasure to take a trip. Being exiled because of guilt: Will have a skin disease for years. 316

4 Expedition—This omen is only fortunate if you carry out your purpose. If you set out to go somewhere or to do something and fail in your purpose, then expect money losses and worry in business. Planning an expedition but not going: Big castastrophe ahead. Failing to reach goal on an expedition: Expect money losses. 742

9 Explosion—Danger to a relative. Of an explosion: Friends will disapprove of your actions. Being injured in an explosion: Must endure vexation. Face being scarred by an explosion: Will be unjustly accused. Being enveloped in flames after an explosion: Friends trespass on rights. Being guilty of causing an explosion: Friends will lose confidence in you. 247

7 Express—If you are traveling in it, beware of offending those over you in business. Mailing an express letter: Danger through a secret. Receiving an express letter: Will be cheated by friends. 925

4 Extravagance—An omen of happy domestic surroundings. Wife being extravagant: Will realize high ambitions. 283

3 Eyeglass—Good news from some friend or sometimes a fortunate business deal. 831

9 Eyes—It is considered fortunate to see strange eyes staring at you in your dream; some important change will soon take place. But if you are worried about your own eyes, then be careful in your actions, for someone is working secretly against you. Having crossed eyes: Will be short of money. Losing your eyesight: Children are in danger of death. Being worried about the eyes: Be careful of your actions. 594

F

7 Faces—The importance of such an omen in a dream depends upon whether the face is smiling or repulsive, for it is a straight dream and anything coarse or ugly means ill fortune. To dream that you are washing your face shows trouble of your own causing. If you see faces are of absolute strangers, it shows a change of residence or occupation. 286

7 Factory—A factory is a sign of some unexpected happening. If the place shows signs of great activity, then the coming change will be all the more important. An idle factory shows that the change will bring worry and loss. Being in a factory: Great riches in the future. Building a factory: Death of a friend. Selling a factory: Sickness is ahead. 835

9 Failure—This is a dream of contrary meaning, since if you fail in any attempt in your dream you will succeed in real life. 351

5 Faint—It is always a bad omen to see signs of collapse or illness in your dream whether you are the sufferer yourself or whether you tend someone who is ill. 392

9 Faithfulness—A dream of contrary meaning. If you dream that you are false to someone, or they are to you, it is a good omen. Having faithful children: Beware of rivals. Having faithful friends: Sickness. 279

7 Falcon—You are surrounded by enemies who envy you. Falcons flying: Will be cheated by friends. 241

4 Fall—To dream that you fall from a height is a sign of misfortune, and the longer the distance you fall the greater will be the coming trouble. Being injured in a fall: Will endure hardship and lose friends. Falling without injury: Will be victorious in your struggles. Falling on the floor: You are menaced by danger. Falling and rising again: Honor. 823

4 Falsehood—Another dream of contrary meaning whether you are the liar or whether you dream that someone is telling lies to you. 634

7 Fame—This is one of the dreams that go by contraries and warn the dreamer against failure. 673

3 Family—To dream of a numerous family is a good sign of prosperous times in store; it is also fortunate to dream of relatives as long as they are friendly. 264

9 Famine—To dream that you have not enough to eat is a contrary dream; you will live in greater comfort. 315

3 Famous—To dream that you have become famous is a bad sign. It shows loss and change for the worse. Children becoming famous: Rapid success of own hopes. 138

3 Fan—Be cautious. This is not actually a bad sign but a warning that you should not be venturesome. A single lady fanning herself: Will soon form profitable acquaintances. A woman losing her fan: A close friend will drift away. A woman buying a fan: She is interested in another man. 732

1 Farewell—It is generally considered a good sign to dream of bidding good-bye to anyone. 361

2 Farm—To dream that you are engaged in farm work is a fortunate omen: It indicates material success, though after some struggle on your part. If you only visit a farm, it indicates good health. A farm burning: Considerable fortune ahead. A vacant farm: Misery. 938

1 Fashions—To dream that you are studying the fashions either in a magazine or in the shop windows is a sign of some small change, either for good or ill. Watching a fashion show: Will have a long life. Fashion models in a store window: Family quarrels. 712

1 Fasting—Times of good cheer are at hand. Members of family fasting with you: Great wealth. 415

9 Fat—To dream that you are growing fat is an unfortunate sign, especially to a woman. 243

4 Father—To dream that you see your father and he speaks to you is a sign of coming happiness. If he is silent or if he appears to be ill or dead, then you may expect trouble. Father being dead: A big catastrophe is ahead. Father being poor: All desires will be accomplished. 418

9 Father-In-Law—To dream you see your father-in-law either dead or alive signifies ill luck, especially if he uses violence or is threatening. 243

6 Fatigue—To dream that you are tired is a contrary omen, for it indicates a coming success in some venture. 105

6 Fault—It is a dream of contrary meaning if you do wrong and are reproved by your friends. Husband being at fault: A false friend. Wife being at fault: A mystery will be solved. Partner being at fault: Will live a long life. Others being at fault: Doomed for disappointment. 357

8 Favor—This is a dream of contrary, for if you dream that someone has done you a favor it shows a loss of money in some business transaction. Receiving a favor from a loyal friend: Change of surroundings. Receiving a favor from a relative: Warning of arguments. 152

3 Fear—This dream has many interpretations, as naturally it varies so greatly in the circumstances. Fear can be felt and shown in so many forms. Roughly speaking, it should be treated as an obstacle dream. If you dream that you overcome your fears or get over your trouble, all will be well; but if the fear persists and you cannot trace the cause, then expect treachery or deceit on the part of someone you trust. 291

9 Feasting—A dream of contrary meaning. Expect difficulties in the near future. Prepare a feast: Another person is enjoying what you desire. 126

1 Feathers—It is wise to put no meaning into feathers in themselves; they should be treated as emblems of color, such as white, black, red, or blue. Collecting feathers:

Will have joy during life. Wearing a tuft of feathers: Great honors will come to you. 271

8 Feeble—To dream that you are tired or worn out is a fortunate omen. Others being feeble: You are looking for money. Children being feeble: Financial gains. 143

5 Feeding—To dream that you are feeding animals is an excellent omen. Your affairs will prosper. It is not, however, a good sign to dream that you yourself are feasting. Others feeding children: You are being deceived. 824

9 Feet—Feet hurting: Likely to have troubles of humiliation. Burning own feet: Failure in own affairs. Having a broken foot: Loss of a relative. Bathing own feet: Will have trouble and be molested. Feet itching: Joy without profit. 198

6 Fence—A dream of a fence, like all dreams concerning obstacles, is a sign of difficulties ahead. The result depends upon the upshot of your dream. 123

9 Fencing—To dream of a fencing match denotes an adventure in which your wits will be your only weapon. 954

8 Ferns—If you are dreaming of ferns in a luxurious growth, it is a very favorable omen. Mother Nature is helping you to succeed. But if it is Autumn or if the foliage is decaying for any reason, then accept it as a warning of coming trouble. If the ferns are in pots instead of growing naturally in the open, then the success will come only after effort and difficulty. 953

9 Ferry—Danger is around you. Try to do nothing you do not wish known, and do not walk by a river unless necessary. Being on a ferry boat alone: Danger is nearby. Being on a ferry boat with family: Good times are coming. 621

4 Festival—This has much the same meaning as feasting. It is not a fortunate omen. Preparing a festival: Another person is enjoying what you desire. 643

2 Fever—This is generally looked upon as an omen of contrary meaning. If you dream that you are ill, you can rest assured that your health is good. Children having a fever: Will get what you desire. Relatives having a fever: Financial gains. 839

9 Fields—Fortunate happenings of a personal character, agreeable and pleasant friends, hospitality, and merry making. A field of grain: Pleasant friends. A field of oats: Prosperity. A field of corn: Good earnings. 324

8 Fighting—Another example of an obstacle dream. The result will depend upon what happens. If you are beaten in a fight, you must expect misfortune or a love reverse. If you are successful in your dream, then you will overcome your difficulties. Others being in a fight: Recovery from an illness. 260

6 Figs—An unexpected and fortunate event. 726

4 Figures—This omen is a difficult one to judge, as the importance of the dream depends upon the magnitude the figures involved, and these again depend upon the circumstances of the dream. As a rough guide, low figures are figures which are fortunate. High figures are bad, while medium figures or in-between figures show difficulties that can be surmounted if you exert yourself. Obviously, high figures for a girl or for a working man would only be low figures for a wealthy individual or prosperous business man and mean little or nothing. 391

5 File—To dream you are using a file presages new work. A nail file: A mystery will be solved. Putting papers in a file: Are confronted with insurmountable obstacles. Taking papers out of a file: An enemy is seeking your ruin. 635

5 Films—A possible journey abroad in the near future, much discussion. Guard against your tongue. 104

9 Finding—This is an omen of contrary meaning. The more valuable the article you find, the greater will be your loss in business. Finding someone naked: Will find new employment. Finding a child: Will have a very complicated lawsuit. Finding gold and silver: Will have many worries. 519

6 Fingers—To cut your finger or otherwise damage it is a sign of quarreling with your friends or family circle. A finger bleeding: Be careful and do not lose money. Having fingernails cut: Loss of friends. Having burned your fingers: Are envied by many people. Breaking the fingers: Will have a good marriage. 519

2 Fire—An omen of warning. If the fire is small and does no mischief, then expect news of some sort, though not of great importance. If the fire burns you, then expect a serious mischance in your affairs. Lots of smoke but no flames: Will be disappointed. Fireman putting out the fire: Will receive good news. Watching a fire being put out: Poverty. Being in a fire: Triumph. Throwing water on a fire: Will lose your temper. 371

6 Fire Engine—It is a dangerous omen to see a fire engine but its importance depends upon whether it is going to the scene of a fire or is returning. This can be judged by the pace and by the clanging of the bell. Being a fireman on a fire engine: Will realize high ambitions. 204

6 Fish—To dream of fish swimming freely is a sign of coming good fortune; but if you catch them or see them dead, as in a shop, then expect trouble. Cooking a fish: Marriage. Eating boiled fish: Joy. Catching a large fish: Joy and profit. Children fishing: Joy and health. 843

9 Flags—There are different interpretations of this omen in various parts of the world, so it is better to ignore it and study instead the other indications in your dream. Some people consider that the generous display of colored bunting is a fortunate omen; but all colors are not propitious, so this point is doubtful. For instance (see Colors) red is generally considered a warning of quarrels with friends, where black is ominous. There should be plenty orange, green, blue, or white if the bunting is to bring good luck. 927

6 Flames—As a rule, this is a bad sign; but if the flames are under control, all will be well. Dark flames: Danger in love matters. Uncontrolled flames: difficulties ahead. 105

1 Flash—To dream of a flash or light, whether from a searchlight or torch, is a sign of important news that will cause your plans to succeed. 397

8 Flattery—This is much the same as falsehood, for all flattery is insincere and unreliable. It is a dream of contrary meaning. If someone is flattering you, then expect trouble or disappointment. Flattering a fiancée:

Must control passions. Flattering friends: Will experience many ups and downs. 143

3 Fleet—Ships at sea always form a bad omen, and it does not really matter what type of vessels they are. Of course, this does not apply to shipwrecks or other maritime disasters. A merchant marine fleet: Will receive a letter from a friend. A naval fleet in a parade: You are being deceived. A foreign naval fleet: Will entertain an unwelcome guest. 012

5 Flirting—On the whole, a prosperous omen, but not if you carry it to a heartless extent or cause tears. Flirting with married woman: Beware of treachery. Flirting with a married man: Suitable time to pursue courtship. Flirting with an unmarried girl: Avoid rivals. Flirting with an unmarried man: You will be deceived. Flirting with a divorced person: Will realize own ambitions. 419

3 Floating—This is a good dream if all goes well. It is really a variation of the obstacle dream. If you sink or find it difficult to keep afloat, then expect trouble ahead. A dead person floating: Will live a long life. A dead fish floating near the beach: Danger through a secret. An empty boat floating: Will have a change of surroundings. 687

6 Floods—This is a good sign for those whose lives bring them in contact with water or the sea, but for others it should be treated as an obstacle dream, and is especially unfortunate for love affairs. Saving yourself from a flood: You have one loyal friend. Floods causing devastation: Worry will be smoothed away. 394

3 Floor—To dream that you are sweeping or washing the floor is a bad omen for business success. You will not be fortunate, though your losses may not amount to a large sum. To sit or lounge on the floor, on the contrary, is a very good dream. 192

5 Flour—It is a bad omen to buy or to use flour in the course of your dream. Making pastries with flour: A happy life is ahead. Dealing with the flour market: Will make risky speculations. 365

8 Flowers—One of the best of nature dreams, this foretells great happiness unless you throw away the blossoms which means you will suffer from your own care-

132

less actions. A young woman dreaming of receiving flowers: Will have many suitors. Gathering flowers: Will remarry soon. Picking flowers from a plant: Great benefit. Artificial flowers: Misfortune in business. Receiving flowers as a gift: Great joy. 836

1 Flute—It is a very fortunate dream if you see yourself playing the flute, but you may expect difficulties if you see someone else playing. 028

2 Flying—Another obstacle dream, the meaning of which depends on the results. Aviation is of such modern growth, however, that such a dream must indicate ambitious plans, possibly beyond your real power of accomplishing. Being an aviator: Ambitious plans are possibly beyond power to accomplish. Owning a plane: Success in all enterprises. 371

8 Foam—Cheerful scenes will soon surround you. 251

1 Fog—An obstacle dream of great power, especially to those in love. Your prospects of happiness are doubtful. If the fog clears away and the sun shines again, you will get over your disappointment in time. Fog clearing away: Happiness in love. 586

4 Food—It is generally a fortunate sign to eat food in your dream, provided you are soon satisfied. But it is not a good omen to eat like a glutton. Not having enough food: Death of an enemy. People selling food: You will receive some money. Tasting food: Loss of friends. 238

3 Foolish—To dream that you have done some foolish action is a dream of good fortune. Mate being foolish: Financial gains. Lover being foolish: You should mend your ways in life. 732

2 Foot—Beware of treachery if someone trips you up with his foot. Having a broken foot: Loss of a relative. Foot hurting: Likely will have humiliation. Cutting the foot; will have an operation. 326

2 Football—To witness a game of football is a bad sign. You may expect worries, possibly in connection with some friend. It is a good sign to see yourself playing, provided your side wins or you yourself score a goal. 497

8 Footprints—Difficulties which you will soon surmount by your own efforts. Footprints of someone else: A friend is trying to help you secretly. 278

9 Footsteps—You will hear something which will spur you on to greater exertions and success. 819

8 Foreign Country—Your happiness lies at home. Being in a foreign country alone: A change in life will soon come. Being in a foreign country with others: Will have new business ventures. 206

8 Foreigners—To dream of foreigners is usually considered very fortunate for your love affairs. 125

2 Forest—Another variation of the obstacle dream. The meaning will depend on what happens and whether you emerge from the forest. Being alone in a forest: Social activities of a happy nature. Being with others in a forest: Will be cheated by friends. A forest fire: Glad news. A forest with unusually high trees: Good business affairs. 479

4 Forgery—It is a bad omen to dream that you are guilty of forgery; but it is a good sign if someone else forges your signature. 508

5 Fork—To dream of forks is a sign of a quarrel. Receiving a gift of forks: Doomed for disappointment. 167

9 Forsaken—A good omen of the affections of those you dreamed lost. 999

5 Fort—Troubles and losses in store for you. 626

9 Fortune—A dream of contrary meaning. The more fortunate and successful you are in imagination, the greater will your struggles in real life be. Having own fortune told: Great struggle in real life. Being fortunate in business: Gay occasion to come. Being fortunate in love: Will lose plenty of money in gambling. 423

7 Fortune Teller—It is a most unfortunate omen to have your fortune told in a dream, but you will ensure success if you tell the fortune of any other person. Being a fortune teller: Good times are coming. Having own fortune told: Serious disaster is ahead. Hearing a fortune told to others: You have a loyal friend. 214

1 Fountain—A good dream if the water is clear. 352

3 Fowls—To dream of these common domestic birds

shows a commonplace and uneventful life without ups and downs. 534

9 Fox—To see a fox in your dream indicates an enemy or a rival among your acquaintances. If you see the animal killed, you will overcome a threatened trouble. 306

1 Fragrance—It is a good sign to dream of a fragrant perfume, but the results will not be very serious. Some small success is indicated. 253

5 Frantic—To dream of being frantic means a peaceful holiday after strenuous times. 815

5 Fraud—To dream that someone has cheated you is a sign of treachery, but if you dream that you yourself have committed a fraud, it shows coming prosperity. 248

6 French—To dream of speaking and hearing foreign languages is a fortunate sign, especially in love affairs. 312

3 Friends—A good omen, for you will receive unexpected good news unless you dream that your friends are in trouble. Saying good-bye to a friend: Painful experiences ahead. Being separated from a friend: Friends are endeavoring to destroy you. Friends being in trouble: Will receive unexpected good news. A friend being naked: Will have a big fight. Talking with a friend in a room: Joy and consolation. 129

6 Fright—A dream of contrary meaning. The more dreadful your ordeal, the greater your success. Your business affairs will prosper if you preserve your present difficulties. Frightening other people: A change in life will soon come. Being frightened in your sleep: Will discover a secret. 384

2 Frog—Success in business, a good dream. 209

6 Frost—Many troubles ahead of you, be careful what you do in the near future. Frost damaging your plants: Many troubles ahead. 312

2 Fruit—As with colors, the meaning of the fruit in your dreams varies according to its kind. 416

5 Fun—Excessive merriment is a bad sign in a dream and foretells difficulties in business affairs. The more boisterous your amusements, the more serious matters will

be. Quiet homely happiness is a different matter. Having fun with children: Doomed for disappointment. Having fun with friends: Change for the better. Having fun with important people: Honor and happiness. 635

5 Funeral—This dream is associated with the color black, but if you see yourself present at a funeral in black it is appropriate, so no harm need be expected. It is a dream of contrary meaning and indicates a successful love affair. Going to a funeral with family: Loss of friends. Being a pallbearer: Will do something foolish. Attending a funeral of best friend: Long life. A woman attending a funeral in mourning: Unhappy married life. 824

1 Furs—A favorable dream on the whole though it foretells change of some sort. A mink fur: People are being false to you. Being covered with fur: Your lover is faithful to you. 703

6 Furniture—This is generally a good dream, but it depends on the circumstances. Handsome furniture is very fortunate, but naturally this depends upon the person who dreams. What is ordinary furniture for a wealthy woman would be sheer folly for a working class woman, or for a business girl earning her own living. It should be just a little better in quality than what you actually possess. A common person dreaming of nice furniture: Much love. A business girl dreaming of nice furniture: Will earn own living. 789

6 Fury—To dream of a furious person denotes a reconciliation. Of a furious animal: A friend defends your name. 312

1 Future—You may have the chance to make up an old quarrel or mend a wrong. 797

G

9 Gable—Good advice will be given which, if followed, will lead to good fortune. 324

6 Gag—To dream that there is a gag in your mouth is an obstacle dream. If you do not succeed in getting free, then you may expect serious trouble ahead. A young girl dreaming of a gag: Will meet a man who takes her fancy. 654

4 Gain—A sign of contrary meaning. To dream that you have a big income or have pulled off a successful business deal is a bad sign unless you appear to have scored by cheating or by some unfair advantage. 607

7 Gale—Better times to come. Do not take present vexations too seriously, especially quarrels. Being on a ship in a gale: Will realize high ambitions. 214

7 Gallery—Worries will soon pass unless you should dream of falling from a gallery. A gallery of paintings: Big honors and fortune. 628

8 Gallows—This unplesant dream is one that carries a contrary meaning and is generally considered very fortunate in every way. Hanging on the gallows: Dignity and money. Someone you know being on the gallows: Avoid rivals. 287

2 Gambling—Do not act on the ideas of others or you will incur loss. Winning at gambling: Social activities will be of a happy nature. Losing at gambling: Will be relieved of pains. Gambling with dice: Inheritance. Gambling with cards: Loss of prestige. Gambling at roulette: Vain hopes. Gambling at a slot machine: Doomed for disappointment. 920

8 Game—To dream that you are taking part in a game is a mixed omen; for it depends upon the result, for one thing, and it is contrary in its meaning. If you win for yourself or your side, it is an unfortunate sign and means misfortune in business; but to lose indicates that you will be prosperous. 746

6 Gangway—Should you cross it, you have aroused the hostility of a rival. Take care not to lose what is now your own through overconfidence. Coming down the gangway on a ship: Avoid rivals. Other people going up the gangway: Loss of money. 429

4 Garden—A very fortunate dream, nature at its best; but of course it must be a garden that is well kept and not neglected. It concerns money matters. A beautiful gar-

137

den: Increase in fortune. Walking in a garden: Joy. 391

5 Garlic—This is generally considered a fortunate omen; but there are many people who detest the smell of onions, and in such cases they should be treated as signs of ill success. Cooking with garlic: You are disliked by those working under you. 914

6 Garret—An advancement in position should come speedily. Being in the garret of own house: Happiness is assured. 312

6 Garter—To dream that you have lost your garter indicates coming misfortune. If both garters should be loose and come down, the omen becomes more emphatic. If someone picks it up and returns it to you, it is a sign of a loyal friend that will help you in your difficulties; but if the person retains the garter, then your troubles will be increased by treachery on the part of someone near you. 402

9 Gas—This concerns your love affairs or domestic happiness. If you dream that the light is bad, then your interests will suffer accordingly. If the light goes out suddenly, expect a catastrophe. 279

8 Gems—Jewels are not favorable omens in a dream, nor are any excessive displays of luxury. Selling gems: Misfortune in love. Receiving a gift of a gem: Danger through a secret. Relatives having gems: Sickness within the family. 296

8 Geraniums—Those popular garden plants are often seen in dreams. They can be taken as omens of variety. Buying a geranium plant: Will have plenty of money. Red geraniums: Sickness. 521

6 Ghost—This is unfortunate only if the sight of the apparition appears to cause fright. Then you may expect a troublesome time ahead of you. If you do not fear the ghost, however, you will pull through your difficulties, especially if the spirit disappears. A ghost speaking to you: Beware of enemies. 438

6 Giant—One of the many obstacle omens. It signifies difficulties that can be overcome if met boldly, but the result depends on the circumstances of the dream. Killing a giant: Abundant means. A monstrous giant: Much success. 483

138

6 Gift—A dream of contrary meaning. Beware of the person from whom you receive a gift under such circumstances. Giving a gift: Bad luck. Receiving a Christmas gift: Treason from friends. Receiving a gift from a woman: Close friendship. Receiving a gift from a man: Change of fortune. 564

3 Gin—To dream of drinking gin denotes short life and many changes. Buying gin: Will have many changes in life. Serving gin: You have false friends. Receiving gin as a gift: Family quarrels. Giving gin as a gift: False favors. Breaking a bottle of gin: Will be visited by a friend. 102

4 Gypsy—An omen of varying meaning. If the gypsies offer any of their wares and you buy, it shows good fortune coming to you, but probably after some change or from a distance. 607

1 Girl—Surprising news; a reply long delayed will reach you at last. A beautiful girl: Increase in business affairs. Kissing several girls: Great success. A girl crying: Will be embarrassed by a friend. 145

4 Glass—This dream depends upon the detail of whether the glass is clear or cloudy. If all is well, it is a fortunate dream, especially in matters of business. Breaking a window glass: Trouble is ahead. Cleaning window glass: Your happiness is in danger. Breaking a drinking glass without water in it: Death of a woman. Spilling a glass of wine: Good news. 427

8 Gloom—A possible change for the better will come your way. Do not hesitate to grasp a chance. 296

8 Gloves—This omen is very similar to that concerning garters, but any good or bad fortune will be short lived. Carrying gloves: Prosperity and pleasure. Buying gloves: A false friend is nearby. Losing own gloves: Will be thrown onto own resources. 935

9 Glue—This portends faithful friendship from one whom you trust. Buying glue: Will realize own ambitions. 891

8 Goats—Many trials, but you will face them bravely. If the animals are black, white, or piebald, then you must take color into consideration as well. 179

8 God—To hear His voice or to dream that He speaks to you: Happiness and joy. Praying to God: Much prosper-

ity. Seeing God face to face: Will have much joy. 917

2 Gold—A dream of contrary meaning as far as the metal itself is concerned, for it signifies loss of money; but if your clothes are of gold cloth or if they are embroidered with gold ornamentation, it is a good sign. Losing gold: Financial distress. Working with gold: Misfortune. Counting gold: You are attempting to deceive friends. 902

8 Goldfish—Trouble in business. Dead goldfish: Disappointments to come. Having goldfish in a bowl in own house: Financial gains. Buying goldfish: Matrimony within the family. 314

4 Golf—To dream that you are spending your time playing games is a warning that your business affairs need attention. Playing on a golf course with others: Unfit to fill your position. 472

5 Gondola—This presages a happy but unromantic life. Being in a gondola with lover: Love will not last very long. 815

7 Gong—An exciting event in the family. Avoid trifling with important matters. 214

5 Good—To dream that you do good signifies jollity and pleasure. To dream that others do good to you means profit and gain. Saying good things about others: Will be embarrassed. People saying good things about you: Will be deceived by friends. 914

9 Gout—Avoid overstrain; you are not too strong at present. Having gout on the feet: Will have misery. Having gout in any other joint: Financial losses because of relatives. 819

7 Government—To dream of a post under government is an omen of a precarious living and much poverty. 583

5 Gown—A dream of contrary meaning. The more handsomely you are dressed, the worse the omen. In fact, the most fortunate dream a woman can have is to imagine herself naked. If, however, your clothes are shabby or torn, it is a fortunate sign, though not so good as nakedness. 329

4 Grain—This is a very fortunate omen, although your success will come to you from hard work and endeavor. Persevere and you will be richly rewarded. Harvesting

grain: Big gains. Grains standing in the field: Will receive plenty of money. Carrying the grain to the barn: Luck and prosperity. Grain catching on fire: A serious disaster is ahead. Sowing grain in a field: Much joy. Selling grain: Financial gains. 841

1 Grandparent—To dream that you are a grandparent or that your grandchildren are present is a very favorable sign. 784

1 Grass—As in the case of a garden, this dream is fortunate if the grass is seen green and flourishing but not otherwise. 127

7 Grasshopper—Loss of harvest. Grasshoppers in your own yard: Bad omen for sick people. Killing grasshoppers: Rivalry by an unexpected person. Others killing grasshoppers: Expect the arrival of a theft. 421

6 Gratitude—Surprising events will happen to you should you dream of being exceedingly grateful to someone; but should you dream of another expressing gratitude to you, the events will happen to someone dear to you. 240.

8 Grave—News from afar. If the grave space is open, news will not be good. A newly prepared grave: Will suffer through the sins of others. Walking on a grave: Unhappy married life. Digging a grave: Big obstacles are ahead. The grave of your father: Inheritance. 125

2 Gravel—To dream that you are walking on a rough gravel path is equivalent to an obstacle dream, but naturally it concerns small affairs. If you complete your journey, all will be well. 794

1 Gray Hair—These signs of advancing age are most fortunate, especially if you are in the company of a gray-haired person in your dream. If you imagine that you yourself are gray, it is still fortunate but indicates difficulties for success. 280

9 Greyhound—You will win more than a race, despite keen rivalry. A greyhound belonging to others: Will win at a lottery. A greyhound racing: Will receive a letter with good news. 324

9 Grief—This indicates joy and merry times. 612

2 Groans—It is not a fortunate dream to hear people groaning unless you assist them. 083

5 Groom—Legal affairs will be made known to you, probably to your advantage. 914

7 Ground—To dream that you are stretched out on the ground signifies a humble status for some time to come. 790

6 Guard—To dream of keeping watch against a peril of some kind is a warning to avoid ill-considered speech which may put you in a difficult position. Being a security guard: Will be saved from a big danger. A guard taking away a prisoner: Will be insulted by friends. 708

1 Guests—Not a fortunate dream. The more visitors to come to you, the greater will be your business difficulties. Others having guests: Beware of illness. Unwelcome guests: Unhappiness in love affairs. 415

1 Guide—To be guiding someone else in a dream signifies a kindly assistance in your own difficulties from good friends. 631

1 Guitar—This is much the same omen as a violin, and it is a fortunate dream if the music pleases you. Any interruptions are a bad sign. Being pleased by guitar music: Love and joy. A young woman dreaming of hearing a guitar: Temptation through flattery. 820.

5 Gum—Someone will stick to you in an emergency. Financial delays are indicated. 516

6 Gun—To hear the report of a gun is an omen of illness concerning some loved one, but it will pass away. If you hear several reports, the illness will last for a longer period. If you yourself fire the gun, you will be the invalid. Shooting a person with a gun: Dishonor. A rifle with a bayonet: Separation of partners. Traveling with a gun: Will soon get married. 915

7 Gunpowder—To a man this dream means a speedy change of residence. To a girl, a wedding with a soldier. 178

1 Gutter—To dream of being in the gutter denotes hard times to come. Should you find anything valuable in a gutter, financial reward will come later for hard work done now. 802

1 Gymnastics—Any violent exercise is a dream of con-

trary meaning. Your plans will fail because you will not be able to put sufficient energy into your work. 937

H

4 Habit—To dream of putting on or wearing a riding habit indicates a great effort which you will have to make to escape from some unhappy position. Be brave, as you have more friends than you think you have. 841

7 Hag—Gossip and scandal about women friends. 439

3 Hail—This is a bad dream and foretells difficulties and disappointment. 309

9 Hair—To dream about your personal appearance is a sign of continued prosperity if you are satisfied with your image. If your hair is getting thin or falling out, it is a bad sign. If you worry because your hair is turning gray, it shows that difficulties are ahead of you and that your affairs need careful attention. 468

6 Hall—To dream of a great hall in a strange place means important decisions to be made shortly. 249

9 Halo—Present pain will lead to good fortune later. Be brave. Seeing a solar halo: Rapid success of own hopes. Seeing a lunar halo: Change in own environment. 819

4 Ham—A fortunate dream, but it concerns trivial matters. Buying a ham: Will incur debts. Boiling a ham: Big profit. Slicing a ham: Financial gains. Eating ham: Joy and profit. 157

4 Hammer—Unlike hearing the noise of a gun being fired, it is a fortunate sign if you hear the sound of a hammer. It is a good sign for business and love affairs. 913

1 Hammock—This is a sign of a loss and also of a gain of more value than the loss, probably to do with a lover. Children being in a hammock: Misfortune in love affairs. 901

9 Hand—Another dream that concerns your personal appearance. If your hands are dirty, you should be care-

143

ful over your affairs, for success is doubtful. If your hands should be tied, you will have great difficulty in overcoming your troubles. But to dream that you are shaking hands with some person is fortunate, for some unexpected event will enable you to put things right. 909

1 Handcuffs—This is a dream of contrary meaning. Good fortune awaits you. A dangerous prisoner being handcuffed: Will receive a letter with money. 316

2 Handkerchief—Someone has a gift for you. Losing a handkerchief: Serious troubles. Giving a handkerchief as a gift: Will cry for a long time. Using a handkerchief to blow your nose: Will be loved by people. Buying a handkerchief: Be careful of new ventures. 254

1 Handwriting—It is not a good sign to see written documents in your dream. Be careful of new or untested ventures. 613

6 Hanging—To dream that you are being hanged denotes good to you. To dream that you see a person hanged is an omen of good to him. He will attain wealth and great honor. A criminal hanging: Will make money in a shameful manner. Someone hanging without a cause: You are prone to be stingy. Being freed just before hanging: Will realize own ambitions. 213

3 Happy—Any excessive pleasure or merrymaking in a dream is an omen of contrary meaning. The more boisterous your pleasures, the greater your business difficulties will prove. 246

8 Harbor—Means a happy time to come with one you care for. Falsehood will be exposed. Being alone in a harbor aboard ship: Financial gains. Being with loved one in a harbor aboard a ship: Falsehoods to be exposed. 242

5 Hare—This is not a good sign. Things will be difficult, but a change of residence or occupation will help to put matters right. Shooting hares: Happiness. 248

9 Harem—Truth will out. Things you believe unknown are the subject of much gossip, but you will triumph in the end. 162

3 Harness—A pleasant evening and an introduction which

144

will lead to a friendship. Buying a horse's harness: Will be tempted by a new love. 903

7 Harp—All pleasant music is a favorable omen in a dream. Playing a harp: Do not trust friends too far. A harp being played at a theater: You have one loyal friend. 313

3 Harvest—To dream that you see the workers busy on the harvest is a most favorable sign; nature favors you. It is very fortunate for those in love. 435

2 Hat—New clothes are generally excellent omens, but shabby things are a warning of trouble. If you lose your hat, beware of false friends. A women's hat: Recovery from an illness. A man's hat: Will have emotional sorrow. Wearing a new hat: Wealth. Wearing a straw hat: You are prone to conceit. 218

8 Hatbox—To dream of opening one denotes a gay occasion unless you find it empty, in which case it means disappointment about a festivity to which you will not be invited. 413

2 Hatchet—You will be in danger soon. Anxiety and trouble. 317

7 Hawk—Birds of prey are omens of coming losses. Be careful about your business ventures and speculations. 097

7 Hay—A very fortunate dream. Nature helps you, and you should be successful both in business and love. 925

9 Head—Pains in your head or dreams about accidents are warnings of difficulties ahead of you. Persevere, but be prudent and do not take any risks. Washing your head: Overwhelming misfortune. A bald head: Will be loved. A head with long flowing hair: Big honor. Having a clean-shaven head: Will be ashamed. Having your head cut off: Pleasure and honor. 549

2 Hearse—Beware of fire and deceit. Save your pennies and trust few people; you are shortly making an important change. 128

7 Heart—Warm affection is felt for you where you least expect it. Having pains in your heart: Long sickness. Being out of breath because of heart trouble: Will surpass friends. 196

7 Heart—You have no reason to worry over your circumstances; but avoid angry thoughts or words. 475

1 Heaven—A dream of heaven is a sign of prosperity and happiness in this life. The heavens being dark: Recovery of money. The heavens without the stars: Will receive bad news. Being in heaven: An immediate marriage. Going to heaven: Prosperity. 208

5 Heirloom—An answer postponed. Do not be dominated by a friend. Putting an heirloom away: You will be humiliated. 329

2 Hell—There are many interpretations concerning this omen in a dream, but it is a sign of disturbed health and not a true dream at all. 091

9 Helmet—Pleasant visitors; avoid extravagance; you will need all your savings. 216

9 Hen—A dream of commonplace affairs. If you see the hen laying eggs you may expect good luck. Chickens, however, are not considered fortunate. 423

7 Herbs—Signs of good fortune in almost any case, as they are favored by nature, but they must be growing vigorously. If flowers are seen, it is a very good sign. 853

2 Hero—A change of heart in someone who has hitherto been cool to you, especially should you dream of some great hero of historic times. 218

7 Herring—Fish are always good omens; you may expect success in business, but you will have to work steadily in order to secure it. 853

2 Hiccup—To dream you have a fit of hiccuping predicts travel. To dream a friend has hiccups means a parting. 308

8 Hide—To dream that you are hiding shows that bad news will soon reach you. 728

6 Hills—These must be looked upon as obstacles. If you succeed in climbing a hill, you will put things right with perseverance. The easier the ascent, the better for your future. 519

8 Hive—Dangerous undertakings which you will bring to a successful conclusion. 107

4 Hoarding—Be on guard against misfortune through de-

ceitful companions. Your affairs will improve before too long. 975

4 Hogs—To dream of hogs if they appear well fed: You have prosperity to come. If they are thin, prepare for bad times. Buying hogs: Joy. Selling hogs: Will be hated by friends. Wild hogs: A friend will try to cause harm. 193

4 Hole—To creep into one or to fall into one: You will come into contact with undesirable people. 328

3 Homicide—Misfortune and heavy loss. 309

9 Holly—A prickly plant. Beware of vexations. 126

5 Home—To dream of your home or school indicates continued prosperity, especially to the lover. Building a home: Honor without joy. Changing homes: Small fortunes. Your home burning: Honor and dignity. Own new home: Prosperity, especially for lovers. 329

4 Honey—If you eat honey, it is a good sign. As the bees are industrious so must you be, and then you will thrive. 319

7 Honeymoon—Changes, journeys, and disappointment. Being on your own honeymoon: You are being deceived. Friends going on their honeymoon: Much disappointment. 304

9 Hoop—To dream of a hoop or anything of a circular nature is a fortunate sign. 207

2 Horns—To dream one has horns on his head signifies dignity, dominion, and grandeur. Blowing a horn: Social activities of a happy nature. Animals with large horns: Expect sorrow. Animals with small horns: Joy and happiness. 218

9 Hornets—A spiteful rival will seek to injure you; be on your guard. 819

2 Horse—These animals are generally good signs but the color must be noted, such as black, white, brown, and so on. This affects the omen. If you are riding a horse and are thrown, it is a bad sign. If someone on horseback comes to visit you, expect news from a distance. It is a very lucky dream to dream of a horse being shod. 470

4 Horseshoe—To find one indicates a legacy; to see one, travel over land and water. 841

5 House—It is a most fortunate omen to see a house being built; but take warning if you see one being pulled down. 734

6 Horoscope—To dream of a chart of your starry influences is a sign that a stronger mind than yours will dominate you unless you resist with all your might. Buying a horoscope book: Approaching money. Being told your horoscope: Will be badly tormented. 105

1 Hospital—A warning to alter ways of living which lead to ill health, or a serious misfortune may befall you. 136

6 Hotel—It is not a favorable sign to dream that you are staying in a hotel; any omens of luxury are bad signs. For a wealthy person the dream will carry no particular meaning. It is the sense of luxury that means disaster to your plans. 519

8 Hunchback—A period of many trials and changes to come, to be followed by a happy love affair. 107

1 Hunger—A dream of contrary meaning, for to be hungry in your dream is a sign of prosperity but only through hard work and much effort on your part. 523

3 Hunting—If you are hunting small animals, such as hares, it is a sign of disappointment; but if you hunt a stag, it is an omen of coming prosperity. The dream of hunting a fox shows, however, a risk from clever competition. If you are present at the kill, you will conquer all difficulties. 912

9 Hurry—Danger of fire or accident. Care will avert it. 783

7 Hurricane—A most unfortunate dream both for business and your home life. Be careful of your actions. 673

4 Hurt—A dream of warning. The result depends upon the nature of the accident and whether you recover from it. 526

6 Husband—An omen of contrary meaning in the case of lovers, for if you dream that you are married when you are not, then expect a quarrel with one dear to you. Losing husband by death: Important and very beneficial events to come. Marrying a second husband: Luck and prosperity. A husband divorcing his wife: Quarrels with

148

one dear to you. Others flirting with your husband: Will live together all your life. 168

7 Hymns—To dream that you are singing hymns is a fortunate omen; your plans will be successful. Hearing others singing hymns: Recovery from illness. 241

9 Hysterics—Be firm and do not allow yourself to be dominated by others if you would achieve success. 297

I

8 Ice—This is always an unfortunate omen; expect many difficulties. Breaking through the ice: Anxiety without cause. 341

4 Iceberg—Every test will be made of your strength; make a big effort, and you will triumph. 742

6 Icicles—Good luck, happiness, and success in love. 159

3 Idiot—It is a good omen to dream of idiots; some unexpected good fortune awaits you. 219

6 Idols—Your eyes are about to be opened. Do not show your feelings too plainly. 483

5 Ignorance—To dream that you are ignorant or cannot understand some matter is an omen of contrary meaning. Success will crown your efforts. 536

9 Illness—A warning of some great temptation that will not work out favorably for you, however promising it appears at first. Having illness: Misfortune in love affairs. Children having illness: Consolation and happiness. 603

5 Illumination—Great good fortune. To a lover, it is quite exceptionally fortunate. 671

8 Image—Not a fortunate dream. Postpone important decisions. The image of a dead person: Expect the death of a relative. The image of a saint: Failure in business and in love. The image of your own children: Misfortune in love affairs. The image of dead relatives: Postpone an important decision. 413

6 Incense—It is considered a favorable omen if the

149

incense is pleasant to your senses, as in the case of all perfumes. But incense is so closely associated with the interior of a church that I am inclined to treat it doubtfully myself and suggest that success will only come after effort and anxiety. 384

5 Income—To dream that you possess a comfortable income is an unfavorable omen. 518

5 Income tax—Financial loss, probably through assisting a friend. Receiving a refund on income tax: Success in own enterprises. Cheating on payment of income tax: Beware of big losses. Having income tax raised: Will be assisted by a friend. 203

1 India—Strange happenings, a message of an unfriendly woman. Going to India: Will have emotional sorrow. Being in India: A big catastrophe is ahead. A native of India: Will have an adventure soon. 361

1 Infant—Children are good omens in a dream, but a helpless baby is generally looked upon as a warning of coming trouble. A beautiful infant: Peace and joy. A newborn infant in diapers: Good events to come. The infant of someone else: Unhappiness in love affairs. 235

7 Injury—To dream that you have been injured by someone shows that you have a rival in business or love who will prove a danger to you. Injury of someone else: Danger is ahead. Children having an injury: Joy without profit. 529

7 Ink—If you spill ink in your dream, expect separation from friends; but to be writing and using ink is a good sign. Buying ink: Financial gains. Writing love letters with ink: Treason. Writing business letters with ink: Loss on business affairs. A young woman dreaming of ink: She will be slandered. 493

6 Inquest—To dream of being at an inquest denotes prosperity. 267

4 Insanity—A dream of contrary meaning. Your plans will prove successful. Relatives being insane: Long life. Friends being insane: Unhappiness. A woman dreaming of being insane: Will be a widow. A man dreaming of being insane: Will divorce his wife. A young girl dreaming of being insane: Will have a happy marriage. A

young single woman dreaming of being insane: Her child will be prominent. 139

8 Insect—The interpretation of a dream concerning insects depends on the circumstances of the dream. If the insects fly or crawl away from you, it is considered that a disappointment awaits the dreamer in his business affairs. Having insects in own home: Be concerned with others. Killing insects outside own home: Financial gains. Killing insects with poison: A mystery will be solved. 926

5 Insult—A dream of difficulty, the result depending upon what happens. If someone insults you and you do not resent it, beware of trouble ahead. There may be a change of residence or of occupation. Insulting friends: Will suffer through own foolishness. Being insulted by enemies: Change of occupation. Being insulted by relatives: Change of residence. 814

6 Intemperance—To indulge to excess either in eating or in drinking foretells trouble. It is equally as bad to see someone else doing this. 735

8 Invalid—This is best treated as an obstacle dream. If you recover from your illness, then all will go well; if not, you must expect to find difficulties in the path of your success. Children being invalid: Expect difficulties on the way to success. Being invalid for the rest of your life: Will soon receive money. 296

6 Invitations—Written or printed documents are not good omens in dreams. Receiving an invitation from a loved one: Financial gains. Sending an invitation to business people: Financial gains. 420

1 Iron—Most metals indicate difficulties when they are prominent in a dream, but the color may be held to affect this. Silver or gold would carry the significance of white or yellow, whereas iron would be similar to black. 712

4 Ironing—A change for the better. Keep yourself free from ties and responsibilities for a time. Help will come to you in an unexpected way. 562

5 Island—Another omen of difficulties ahead, but if you get away from the island you will conquer in the end. 104

4 Itch—Your fears and anxieties are groundless. Having an irritation or rash: Unexpected arrival of friends. Having a sore caused from itching: Trouble from several women. 931

8 Ivory—A very fortunate dream when ivory is concerned. Giving ivory as a present: Money will come easily during life. 539

2 Ivy—Good health awaits you unless the ivy is pulled away from its support. Ivy growing on a house: Wealth. Having ivy in a pot in the house: Happiness is assured. 596

J

4 Jacket—Hard work with little reward. Be patient, but take the first opportunity of a change. Wearing a dark colored jacket: Infirmity. Wearing a sport jacket: Financial gain. Wearing an evening jacket: You will be deceived. 265

2 Jade—To dream of jade ornaments is a fortunate omen, though the color green indicates hard work in front of you if you want to succeed. Wearing jade: Prosperity. Buying Jade: Financial gain. 236

5 Jail—This is generally considered an unfortunate dream unless you are released in due time. Being in jail for a long time: Bad destiny. Being in jail for life: Will receive a big favor. Friends being in jail: Family happiness. A woman dreaming of being in jail: Must endure much suffering. 347

2 Jealous—To dream that you yourself are jealous of some other person is a bad sign; difficulties of your own making are shown. To dream that someone else is jealous of you shows that their attempts to defeat you will turn to your advantage. 452

7 Jeers—To dream that you are being jeered at by companions foretells triumph over enemies. 259

7 Jellyfish—A scheme is on foot to injure you; be on guard. 304

3 Jeopardy—If you dream you are in jeopardy, it will be very fortunate for you. Children being in jeopardy: Financial gains. Sweetheart being in jeopardy: Immediate success in love affairs. 984

2 Jewels—Always a very fortunate dream, especially for lovers. The omen is just as good whether you give the jewels to someone else or receive them yourself. Stealing jewels: Are in danger of committing some disgraceful act. Admiring jewels: Will experience extravagance. Selling jewels: Loss of money. 326

8 Jig—To dream you are dancing a jig portends at least one lover; be careful not to cause jealousy. 917

3 Jingle—To hear the jingle of small bells—either cattle bells, dog bells, or sleigh bells—foretells innocent flirtations and amusements. 354

6 Jockey—If a woman dreams she sees a jockey riding at full speed, she will have an unexpected offer of marriage. A jockey winning a race: Money will come easily during life. A jockey losing a race: Will be cheated by friends. A young girl being fascinated by a jockey: Proposal of marriage. 402

6 Jilted—A dream of contrary meaning. Expect good luck in your wooing and happiness in your married life. A woman jilting a man: Frivolity. A married woman jilting a secret lover: Will have worries over love. An unmarried woman jilting a lover: Unhappiness. 159

9 Journey—A change in your circumstances is shown, but the details of the journey will show the result. If your voyage is a pleasant one, all will be for the best; but if the road is rough or the weather is stormy, then be careful. Taking a journey by steamer: Accord among friends. Taking a journey by plane: Family quarrels. Having stormy weather during journey: Be careful of own affairs. Taking a journey with children: Happiness is assured. 612

5 Joy—A sign of good health when you are happy in your dreams. 428

2 Judge—An obstacle dream. It denotes trouble and difficulty ahead unless the judge takes your side of the case,

in which event you will pull through in time. Being found guilty by a judge: Will have high social standing. Being acquitted by a judge: A big fortune is coming to you. 839

8 Juggler—An advancement in position will come within your grasp. Do not hesitate. 368

9 Jumping—Another of the many obstacle dreams. You will meet difficulties but will overcome them if you persevere. 513

6 Jungle—Financial affairs will cause you anxiety. Economize while there is time. 654

2 Jury—It is considered unfortunate to dream that you are one of a jury, but if you merely dream that you see a jury from the court, then you will overcome your difficulties. 308

K

1 Kangaroo—The hostility of something or someone influential will cause you great anxiety. 532

5 Keg—Filled with liquid: A bad sign in business. With fish: Prosperity. Empty: A change of surroundings. 923

7 Kennel—You will be invited to the house of a man you know well. Do not go alone, and avoid quarrels. 298

1 Kettle—A very happy omen if the kettle is bright and clean. Troubles and losses if the water boils over. 892

9 Keyhole—It is not a good sign to peep through a keyhole in your dream or to see someone else spying in this way. Losses will follow quarrels. 396

6 Keys—To dream that you have lost a key is a bad sign. To give a key to someone shows good fortune in home life. Having a lover's key: You will come out well from present danger. Finding several keys: Peace and happiness in the home. 258

4 Khaki—Anxieties are around you but will be speedily dispersed. Wearing khaki uniforms: You are prone to

frivolity. Buying a khaki uniform: Approaching good times. 907

7 Kick—It is a bad omen to be kicked in your dream, for you will have many powerful adversaries; but it is a good omen if you kick another person. Kicking friends: A friend is trying to help you. 907

2 Kidnapping—Your circumstances are about to improve, and many of your worries are needless. A boy being kidnapped: A catastrophe ahead. 893

2 Killing—Someone wanting to kill you: Will have a long life. Killing a serpent: Separation. Killing a businessman: security. Killing a friend: Will have good health. Killing your parents: A big catastrophe is ahead. Killing a beast: Victory and high position. Killing birds and bees: Damage in business. 704

5 King—To dream of royalty is a very favorable sign unless the royal person shows signs of displeasure. Sending a letter to a king: Danger. Having an interview with a king: Rebellion in own home. 419

4 Kiss—This is a fortunate omen provided you have a right to kiss the person; otherwise, your own ill-judged actions will cause your downfall. Kissing a sweetheart at night: Danger. Kissing a husband or wife: Marital happiness. Kissing a friend: Failure in your affairs. 139

7 Kitchen—News from a distance is generally a good omen unless the kitchen is very bare and untidy. A very neat kitchen: Arrival of a friend. A fire lighted in the kitchen: Will have a change in your help. A coal stove in the kitchen: Misfortune in business. Preparing a meal in the kitchen: Will soon be divorced. 925

7 Kite—This omen depends on the circumstances. If the kite flies easily, you may expect success; and the higher up it goes, the better the omen. 214

7 Kitten—A favorable dream unless you hurt the young creature. Of a newborn kitten: Recovery from an illness. Kittens with their mother: Will have emotional sorrow. 124

4 Knapsack—An obstacle dream unless you feel no strain from carrying it on your shoulder. But at best it means difficulties ahead for a time. 328

8 Knee—Any injury to your knee should be treated as an

obstacle dream. If it is not serious, then you will come through all right. A broken knee: Poverty. Falling on the knees: Misfortune in business. The knees of a woman: Good luck. 791

2 Kneel—To dream of praying on your knees to God is an omen of happiness to come. Kneeling in church or tabernacle: Desires will be accomplished. 308

9 Knife—Quarrels with friends will lead to much misfortune. A sharp knife: Many worries: A broken knife: Failure in love. Having many knives: Quarrels. Cutting yourself with a knife: Must curb your emotions. 108

5 Knitting—Your undertaking will be crowned with success. If you see someone else knitting, you will be deceived. 419

3 Knocking—Guard your tongue, and you will be well on the way to happiness. 561

7 Knots—You will meet with much to cause you anxiety. Tying knots: Will soon meet a true friend. Untying knots: Will escape from danger. 358.

L

5 Label—Fixing a box with a label or trunk with a label shows that you may expect a surprise. 275

1 Laboratory—Danger and sickness. People working in a laboratory: Be cautious in business ventures. 415

8 Laborer—A laborer working; prosperity in own business. Laborers resting: Loss of wealth and mate. Laborers fighting: Will undergo a public crisis. Punishing laborers: Persecution. Hiring laborers: Profit. Paying laborers: Will be loved by people. Firing laborers: Beware of actions of neighbors. A laborer tilling the ground: Profit. 962

8 Ladder—Climbing a ladder is a good sign, but the reverse is an indication of troubles ahead of you. The number of rungs should be noted, for this increases the

power of the omen. To feel dizzy when on a ladder is always a bad sign. 125

2 Lake—This is a dream that depends entirely upon the conditions. If the water is smooth, and the sailing or rowing is pleasant, then you may expect comfort in your home life and success in business. If the weather is stormy or unpleasant, then you are faced with difficulties which you may overcome with patience and industry. 902

1 Lamb—A dream of similar importance to that of playing with a kitten: it signifies good fortune unless you spoil your luck by your own action. A lamb particularly concerns your home life. Lambs in a field: Much tranquility. Killing lambs: You will be tormented. Finding a lost lamb: You will win a lawsuit. 361

4 Lame—An omen of business troubles if you find yourself lame or see a lame person in your dream. The result will depend upon what happens, and it can be classed as one more of the obstacle dreams. 609

7 Lamps—This is a fortunate omen, but the result can only be foretold by studying the circumstances of your dream. If the light is dim, you will have to work hard and face the difficulties if you wish to succeed; but if there are many lamps, then your path will be an easy one. If the light goes out, then expect ill health or the failure of your plans. 619

4 Land—A good dream if you possess land and retain it; but if in your dream you move away, then expect a change of occupation, not necessarily for your own good. If the owner of the land orders you away, then expect bitter disappointment. 913

1 Landlady or Landlord—This is not a favorable dream and indicates domestic trouble. 019

3 Lantern—This is usually a fortunate omen, but the light must be good. If it is dim or if it goes out altogether, then expect worries and difficulties. 408

8 Larder—Expect happiness and a joyful time. 125.

7 Larks—It is one of the best omens possible to hear a bird singing happily; it is nature in her kindest mood. But if the songster is shut up in a cage, then your own greed will cause the failure of your plans. 142

157

2 Late—To dream of being late means that your opinions will be asked. Friends being late: You are being deceived. Employees being late: Warning of trouble. 524

7 Laughing—A dream of contrary meaning. It is especially serious if you laugh immoderately or without good cause. Be careful with your love affairs, for laughter in a dream means tears and sorrow in your life. 493

5 Laundry—A sign of a quarrel, parting, or loss. 563

5 Lawn—To dream you see a smooth green lawn portends prosperity and well-being, but should you walk on it the meaning is anxiety. 239

9 Law, Lawsuit, Lawyer—An omen of serious business trouble ahead of you. Do not start upon any fresh or hastily considered plans, for the stars do not foretell your success. Do not lend money, for you will not receive it again; nor should you spend too freely. 315

1 Lazy—To dream of idling denotes trouble to those near you, affecting you indirectly. A legal matter will end in marriage. Children being lazy: Will marry wealthy people. Others being lazy: Warning of trouble. 451

4 Lead—The significance of metals depends largely upon the general color. Lead is not a fortunate dream, so be careful and consider your plans once again before you act. To the married it is a sign of domestic squabbling. 103

6 Leaf—To see trees with full leaves in your dream is a happy omen. Your affairs will prosper. Nature is favorable. It is a very good dream for lovers, especially if a blossom is seen in addition to the leaf. With fruit it is a sign of a happy marriage. But if the leaves are withered or falling, as in Autumn, it shows loss in business, disappointments in domestic affairs, or quarrels with friends. 915

7 Leakage—You are wasting time. Find a wider scope for your activities. 124

2 Leap Year—Frivolity in matters that should be taken seriously. Getting married in leap year: Marriage will not last long. Being born in leap year: Will live a long life. 101

9 Leaping—Another obstacle dream, the full meaning of which depends upon the circumstances. If you sur-

mount the obstacle, your plans will succeed. To those in love it foretells trivial disagreements; or possible rivals, if the obstacle is a serious one. Leaping in the air: Loss of your present position. Leaping into water: Will be persecuted. 315

3 Learning—To dream that you learn something readily is a good sign, but if it proves a difficult task, then you are undertaking more than you can carry through. Learning a foreign language: Unhappiness in love affairs. 705

6 Lease—If you dream that you are taking a house, a shop, or some land on lease, it is a very fortunate omen for both business and love matters. 484

6 Leather—It is an unfortunate omen to dream of leather in any form, whether as a strap or bag, harness, or anything else. Buying leather: Happiness within the family. Giving a gift of leather: Family quarrels. 159

6 Ledger—All written documents or books are unfavorable omens in a dream. This includes keeping or using a ledger or cash book. 213

8 Legacy—It is always a fortunate sign to dream of a legacy or a gift; but naturally the extent of the good fortune will depend entirely upon the nature of the legacy. Receiving a legacy and arguing with relatives about it: Loss of money. Making a legacy to relatives: Will be upset because of difficulties. 413

7 Legs—To dream that you have bruised or injured a leg foretells money difficulties which will last for a short or long period according to the seriousness of the mishap. 394

6 Lemons—They are not fortunate omens unless you see them growing on trees, when it is a sign of an important journey which will affect your affairs seriously. 105

2 Lending—A dream of contrary meaning. If you appear to be lending money or other articles, it foretells that you will want before long; it is an omen of loss and poverty. Lending articles and clothes: An enemy is seeking your ruin and trouble is ahead. Lending your car: Change of environment. Lending household items: Doomed for disappointment. Others lending you money: Failure of affairs. 452

9 Leopards—Difficulties and dangers are ahead of you. It is probable that you will go abroad on business. Hearing a leopard roar: Will suffer grief. Leopards fighting: Sickness. 405

2 Leprosy—This signifies that it is in your power to overcome your worries. 290

4 Lessons—A sign of good fortunes of every kind. 220

9 Letters—To dream that you receive a letter is a sign of unexpected news; but if you post or send a letter, then you will meet some unexpected difficulty that will upset your plans but may not cause any real loss. Letters are a sign of something unexpected. Receiving a letter from a lover: Prompt engagement. Receiving a letter from children: Abundant means. Receiving a business letter: Be cautious in all your affairs. Receiving letters with money: Hopes have been accomplished. 405

5 Lettuce—Difficulties ahead that can be overcome by prompt and vigorous action on your part. 797

4 Libel—A dream of contrary meaning. The more severely you are libeled in your dream, the greater your success in life. 535

4 License—A change of occupation will lead you to better things. Applying for a license: Change of surroundings. Having been refused a license: Important and beneficial event. 625

•2 Lice—To dream of lice and that you are killing a great number of them is a good omen. Finding lice in hair: Will be very rich. Finding lice on own clothes: Approaching money. Having lice on own body: Will have money very soon. 803

4 Lie—It is a bad omen to dream that you are telling a lie, as your coming troubles will be due to your own misconduct. 490

1 Lifeboat—This wonderful vessel is an omen of contrary meaning in a dream. If you see it on shore, then expect difficulties. If you watch it at sea saving a life, then all will be peaceful and quiet in your business affairs. 109

2 Light—A good sign unless the light goes out or becomes obscure, when it shows difficulties in store for you. A light in a distance: Safe return from travel. Turning a light on: Success in business. Turning a light out: You

160

are being cheated by your lover. A light on a ship in a distance: Will take a trip with your sweetheart. Lighting a lamp: Happiness. 704

8 Lighthouse—This is a fortunate dream and is not often encountered. Seeing a lighthouse through a calm sea: Will have a peaceful life. Seeing a lighthouse through a storm: Happiness will come soon. 134

1 Lighting—This is also a favorable dream, though you will have to face worries, as indicated by the dark clouds from which Nature's unexpected light is poured. Persevere, and you are certain of success. 172

7 Lily—Happiness and prosperity await you but only as the result of your own industry. Do not expect help from others; you must depend on your own exertions. If your dream shows the flowers withering or if you throw them away, then your own thoughtless actions will cause your downfall. 304

2 Lilac—Conceit. Do not think too much of appearance, either in yourself or others. 731

5 Limp—This is an obstacle dream. If you are forced to rest and cannot complete your journey, then the signs are more favorable for business ventures or speculations. 392

9 Linen—To dream that you are dressed in clean linen is a favorable sign; you may expect good news before long. If your linen is soiled or stained, it denotes serious loss in business unless you see yourself change the garment, which means you may expect to get over your worst difficulties. The meaning of a dream about linen also depends upon the color of the garment. 909

5 Lion—This dream is not the same in significance as if you see a leopard. The lion signifies some purely personal honor or success not necessarily involving a gain of money; but if you hear the lion roaring as if angry, then expect some misfortune near you through the jealousy of someone. A lion cub is a sign of valuable friendship. Being attached to a lion: Success. Killing a lion: Will have many changes but finally achieve victory. A lion being in a cage: Enemies will fail in their attempt to injure you. Hearing a lion roaring: Will suffer grief. 365

2 Lips—To dream that you have handsome lips is a sign that your friends enjoy their health. To have them dry and chapped means the contrary. 317

3 Liquors—Drinking freely in a dream shows a change of circumstances, and the other surroundings will decide whether this is in your favor or otherwise. 453

7 Lizard—Treachery. Killing a lizard: Will regain lost fortune. Having a lizard in a cage: Will have a good reputation. Having a belt made of lizard: Will have money during your life. Having shoes made of lizard: Will be very healthy. 250

1 Lobster or Crab—Both these are favorable omens for your love affairs or your domestic happiness. 325

6 Locks—This is another obstacle dream, and you will encounter difficulties in the near future. If cabinets or drawers are locked and you cannot find the key, it is a bad sign. You should be very careful in money matters and avoid speculation or risk of any kind. If later you find the keys, you will pull through; but even then it should be taken as a warning. 429

3 Locomotive—To dream of a railway express is a certain sign of travel or the arrival of some friend. This depends upon whether the engine is traveling from you or to you. If you find yourself burdened with luggage, it becomes an obstacle dream. If your luggage is light and easy to handle, then your difficulties will be overcome. 102

9 Locust—Your happiness will be short lived. 612

8 Logs—Logs of wood or the fallen trunks of trees are favorable omens in your dream, but you must not interfere with them or cut them up. 471

2 Lonely—Feeling alone in a dream is a favorable omen, but it shows that you must depend on your own exertions, not on the influences or help of friends or strangers. 731

6 Looking Glass—A woman looking at herself in a looking glass: Friends are cheating you. A man looking at himself in a looking glass: Be careful in business. A lover looking at a mirror: Sweetheart is not faithful. A widow looking in a mirror: Should find out the real underlying motive. A looking glass: Treason. 213

7 Lottery—To dream that you are interested in a lottery or hold a ticket for such a chance is a bad omen. There will be an unhappy attachment or an engagement to some person who will not be worthy of your love. 592

9 Love—This is a dream of contrary meaning as far as sweethearts are concerned. To dream that you do not succeed in love is a sign that you will marry and have a happy life; but to dream that your friends are fond of you is a very fortunate omen and indicates prosperity. To dream that you are in the company of your lover is also fortunate. 972

8 Love Letter—Unpleasant explanations have to be made, and a great deal will rest upon your decision. Remember, frankness is an admirable quality. Reading love letter: Will receive good news. Receiving many love letters: Frankness is an admirable quality. Tearing up love letters: Unhappiness. Saving treasured love letters: You will find out the truth. 305

2 Love Token—A love affair in which you will be greatly interested. Several others know more about it than you think; be circumspect. 290

9 Lucky—This is an omen of contrary meaning, for if you dream that you are lucky in business or in love affairs, it is an unfortunate sign. Be cautious and use your brains; do not trust your affections. 306

6 Luggage—A dream that signifies difficulties in your path though it depends upon the quantity of luggage you have with you and whether you are able to deal with it successfully. For the lover it foretells quarrels slight or important according to circumstances. 690

8 Lumber—Trouble and misfortune. Having plenty of lumber: Unhappiness. Burning lumber: Will receive unexpected money. Piles of lumber: Will face a troublesome task.

8 Lunatic—Surprising news which will lead to different surroundings. Being a lunatic: Warning of troubles. Keeping company with lunatics: Will be guilty of foolish actions. Being in an asylum: Danger in love matters. 512

4 Luxury—Another dream of contrary meaning; for the more your surroundings are luxurious in your vision,

the greater the difficulties you will have to face. You are not likely to be successful in business and will probably lose money through bad debts. In love it foretells a rival, who will probably supplant you. To the married it shows domestic and family quarrels and trouble. 202

4 Lie or Falsehood—It is a bad omen to dream that you are telling lies, as your coming trouble will result your misconduct. Others lying to you: Being cheated by friends. 623

6 Machinery—This dream depends upon whether you feel interested in the machinery. If so, it is a favorable sign, though it means hard work; but if you feel afraid of the machinery, then be careful in your ventures, for you will surely fail to carry out your purpose. 915

3 Madness—To dream that you are mad or in the company of insane people is a good sign. You will prosper in your affairs. It is a good omen for everyone—those in bad health, those in love, businessmen and speculators. 507

4 Magazine—Printed papers are not favorable omens in a dream. Be careful if you would avoid loss. 823

6 Magic—To dream of things happening by supernatural or unknown means is a sign that changes are coming in your affairs through some unexpected source. The ultimate result, fortunate or otherwise, will depend upon the details of your dream, but as a rule the result will be beneficial. The unexpected happening may mean the loss of a friend or some event that appears at the time to be unfortunate. 591

5 Magistrate—To dream that you are being charged with some crime or offense depends upon whether you are convicted or set free. If convicted, fortune is against you. 212

6 Magnet—Personal success and security in business. Be careful not to trust too recklessly. 321

8 Mail—Mailing a package: Will receive a gift. Mailing a letter with a check: Will receive good news. Mailing documents: A false friend is cheating you. Mailing items of value: Will become jealous. 314

1 Man—It is a fortunate omen to dream of a strange man but not of a strange woman. A tall man: Good luck. An armed man: Sorrow. A bald-headed man: Abundance. A fat man: Bad ventures. A naked man: Beware of whom you meet. A man with a beard: Loss of temper. A dead man: Loss of a lawsuit. 325

3 Manicure—A marriage with a much older partner. It will prove a happy one. 768

4 Mansion—All luxury dreams are bad omens. The greater the apparent prosperity, the worse your troubles will be. 823

9 Manure—To dream that you are cultivating the soil is a good sign for those in subordinate situations, but it is not so fortunate for the wealthy. 234

3 Map—To dream that you are studying a map indicates a change of residence and probably also of business or employment. If the map is colored, the omen is a fortunate one. 561

6 Marble—This is really a luxury dream and indicates disappointment and loss. Polishing marble: Will receive an inheritance. Buying marble: Will attend a funeral. 519

1 Marching—To dream of marching predicts advancement and success in business. 307

7 Marijuana—Will be melancholy. Smelling marijuana: Will have protection. Smoking marijuana alone: Will dream of unattainable things. Smoking marijuana with a member of the opposite sex: Security in love. Be arrested for smoking marijuana: You love amusements too much. 312

5 Market—To dream that you are in a market doing business or buying goods is a fortunate sign and shows that your circumstances will be comfortable; but if you are idly looking on, then it is a warning of lost opportu-

nities. If the market is empty and unattended, then it means you can expect difficulties and troubles. Going to a fish market: Will have a prominent position. Going to a meat market: Will receive honors. 419

9 Marriage or Marrying—To dream that you are a witness of marriage is a warning of ill health; but if you assist at the ceremony, it shows some pleasing news, not of great importance. To dream that you are being married, either as bride or bridegroom, is a most unfortunate omen. Giving a daughter away in marriage: Good times ahead. Being a bridesmaid in a marriage: Will be married soon. 423

6 Marsh or Bog—This is another obstacle dream, and its meaning depends upon what happens to your troubles and difficulties. If you find it hard to move along but if you get out all right onto firm ground, then you will be able to put most of your misfortunes right. 654

8 Mask—To dream that someone comes to you wearing a mask or a disguise is a sure sign of treachery. 431

6 Matches—Financial gains are at hand. 591

7 Mattress—A warning of poverty ahead: Guard against it. Buying a mattress: Will lead an easy life. 475

3 Meat—It is not considered fortunate to eat meat in your dream, though it is all right if you cook it for other people. Broiled meat: Good times ahead. Raw meat: Will receive news of a friend's death. Eating raw meat: wealth. 102

9 Medals—To dream of wearing them: Merry times are to come soon. Army and navy personnel wearing medals: Financial gains. 594

8 Medicine—To dream that you are taking medicine is a warning that your troubles are not serious, persevere and you will succeed. Taking bitter medicine: Will attempt to injure one who trusts you. Giving medicine to children: Hard work awaits. 782

9 Melancholy—A dream of contrary meaning. All will go well. A young girl being melancholy: Disappointment from a broken engagement. 504

2 Melody—All pleasant music is a fortunate omen. Per-

severe, and success will attend you. Playing and hearing a melody: Affairs will prosper. 812

3 Mending—To dream of darning clothes portends an inferior and miserable position. 390

9 Mermaid—An unlucky dream, particularly for those in whose lives the ocean plays an important part—seaman, fisherman, etc. 297

3 Mice—An indication of trouble through a friend or a business associate. A cat killing mice: Victory over enemies. Mice being caught in a trap: You will be slandered. A dog catching mice: End of troubles. 516

2 Midwife—This portends news of a birth and the discovery of a secret. 182

9 Milk—To dream that you are drinking milk is a fortunate sign; but it is unfortunate if you sell milk in your dream. To give milk to some other person is a good omen for one in love. It also is a good sign to dream that you are milking a cow, provided that the animal is docile and quiet. 405

9 Miracle—Unexpected events will astonish and occupy you for a little while. 459

8 Mirage—Signifies the loss of one friend in whom you have trusted. 782

1 Mirror—Discouragements. Seeing yourself in a mirror: Illness. Seeing your husband in mirror: Will be unfairly treated. Seeing others in mirror: Unhappy marriage. Seeing a loved one in a mirror: Wealth. A broken mirror: Unexpected death of a relative. A woman seeing herself in a mirror: Friends are cheating you. A man looking into the mirror: Be careful of business. A young girl looking into the mirror: Should change boyfriends. A business executive looking at himself in mirror: Employees are not loyal to you. A widow looking in a mirror: Find out her ulterior motives. 451

1 Miser—An unfortunate dream, for the more you hoard, the more unfortunate you will prove in business. It is a bad sign, particularly for those in love. 208

5 Misfortune—This is a dream of contrary meaning. If you dream that some misfortune happens to you or to someone you love, it shows some fortunate stroke of

business that will result in a far greater success than you expect. 392

9 Mistletoe—Take no chances of any kind. You are not in favor with fortune. 621

7 Missionary—A change to more interesting work and to truer friends. Do not be made unhappy by the desertion of a fickle companion. 817

6 Mistake—Avoid conceit and make sure of your information before acting. Take counsel of those who are willing to guide you. 429

8 Moans—Be on your guard against doubtful friends or dubious actions. 314

4 Monastery—Worldly affairs will prosper. 202

9 Money—To dream that you pay or give money to other people is a fortunate omen; prosperity awaits you. To dream that you receive money also foretells personal success due to hard work. To find money in your dream is not so fortunate, however; there will be some sudden advancement or success, but it will prove disappointing. If you change money it is a sign of difficulties that are your own fault, as if you exchange notes for silver or silver for copper. It is a very bad sign if you dream that you borrow money, either from a friend or from a moneylender. 758

7 Monument—Any handsome monument is a good omen. Success is coming your way as a reward of effort. Monuments in a cemetery: Discovery of lost valuables. 205

3 Moon—This dream depends upon the circumstances. If the moon is bright, shines clearly, and is free from clouds, it foretells success in love and personal happiness. If the moon is clouded over, it shows ill health or some other interruption to your comfort and enjoyment. A new moon is a fortunate sign for business; a full moon, for love affairs. 138

6 Mop—You will need forethought and carefulness to avoid coming trouble. 222

3 Moss—Take care of your correspondence. Write guardedly; seal and post carefully. Someone has an attraction toward you which will soon be expressed. 921

2 Moth—A warning of rivals who will harm you if you

are not careful in your speech and actions. Expect quarrels with your lover, husband, or wife. To those who employ others it is a sign that they are not being faithfully served. 101

7 Mother—To dream that you see your mother and converse with her is a very fortunate omen. Mother being dead: Danger to property and to you personally. Embracing own mother: Expect good fortune. 475

9 Motor—If you are riding in a vehicle powered by one, new surroundings are portended. 837

8 Mountain—Another dream indicating obstacles in your path. The ultimate result depends upon the circumstances. If you climb to the top, all will go well, although it means hard work as unexpected difficulties will confront you. 723

3 Mourning—A dream of contrary meaning. Great prosperity is before you if you are a business man, or married happiness, if you are a lover. 237

5 Mouth—To dream of your own mouth means a hint to guard your tongue. To see a small mouth signifies money to come; A large one, a companion worth more than money. 824

3 Movies—Frivolous invitations. Do not trust fair women. Going to a movie alone: Be cautious in love affairs. Going to the movies with a sweetheart: Great joy. Performing in a movie: A change in life will come soon. Someone you know performing: Warning of troubles. 345

2 Mud—A dream of contrary meaning. Good fortune awaits you. Mud in the street: Advancement within own position. Walking in mud: Family disturbances. Having mud on clothes: Your reputation is being attacked. Others having mud on their clothes: Good fortune awaits you. 839

4 Mummy—Be confident. Success is not far off. 364

7 Murder—Naturally, this dream is even more serious in its warning than manslaughter, for it shows that you have lost control of your difficulties. You cannot expect to succeed so should do your utmost to lessen your liabilities and risks. 412

6 Mushrooms—If you see yourself gathering mushrooms,

169

your ventures will be fortunate, but if you are eating them, be cautious in your business affairs. 132

2 Music—To dream that you hear pleasant music is a very favorable omen; all your affairs will prosper. It often indicates pleasant news from an absent friend or the renewal of some old friendship; but harsh and unpleasant music is a warning, especially to lovers or married people, for it shows some cunning and under-handed action that will cause you great discomfort and loss. 416

8 Musician—If you dream that you are a musician when this is not the case, it is supposed to show a sudden change in your life. Probably you will move to another area. If you really are a musician, amateur or professional, then the dream is of no importance. 215

1 Mystery—A dream of some happening that puzzles and disturbs you is really an obstacle dream. Solve the mystery, and all will be well. 363

1 Mustard—Danger from free speech. Try to avoid hearing or repeating confidences. 901

3 Mutiny—Your undertakings will lead you into odd company. Keep your promises, but avoid making rash ones. Taking part in a mutiny: You are unhappy in your present position. Being wounded in a mutiny: Infidelity. 363

N

5 Nagging—To dream of being nagged signifies that you will be the recipient of pleasing information. Be careful in whom you confide. 203

8 Naked—It is most fortunate to dream that you are naked or only partially clad. Any troubles will be of your own making, and you will not find it easy to get anyone to help you in your difficulties. It is particularly fortunate for lovers, as it shows reliability. To married people it foretells great happiness. 629

6 Name—If someone calls you by the wrong name in a dream, it is an unfortunate omen for your love affairs. 123

2 Napkin—Some pleasant news is coming to you soon. Having an embroidered napkin: Marriage will take place. Receiving a gift of napkins: Family quarrels. 146

3 Naval Battle—Promotion in the service for a great friend or relative. 642

8 Navy—Dreams of the navy foretell love troubles. Being in the navy: Success. Being in the navy and released: Honor. A wife dreaming of her husband being in the navy: He commits adultery. High-ranking naval officers: Troubles in love. 359

9 Necklace—To dream that you are wearing jewelry around your neck is very fortunate. Your love affairs are more favored than your business ventures. If the necklace breaks or falls from the neck, then there will be quarrels and disappointments in married life. 531

1 Needles—Disappointments in love. It will be very serious if you prick yourself. Threading a needle: Family burdens. Losing a needle: Disappointment in love. Pricking yourself with a needle: You are overly affectionate. 991

7 Neighbors—To dream of your neighbors is an omen of coming misfortune or business loss. Visiting your neighbors: Family quarrels. Being very friendly with neighbors: Loss of money. 619

8 Nervousness—The solution of a puzzle will occur to you after long thought and bring you great good luck. 305

4 Nest—One of nature's most fortunate omens. Prosperity and honor are certain to come your way unless the eggs are broken or the nest contains dead youngsters. A snake's nest: Dishonor. 328

4 Nets—Omens of prosperous times to come. Using a net: Success in business. Catching something in a net: Will receive a surprise. Catching fish in a net: Change of temperature and much rain. 215

7 News—It is not a good omen to hear news in your dream unless it is painful or worrying. In fact, it is a

dream of contrary meaning. Hearing bad news: Satisfaction. Giving good news: Great curiosity. Giving bad news: Will learn of the loss of relative. Hearing good news from children: Honor in life. 214

9 Newspapers—If in your dream you are reading a newspaper, it is a sign that a fortunate change will come in your circumstances, but from a distant source. A daily newspaper: Common gossip. A Sunday newspaper: Will have a short life. Throwing a newspaper away: Dishonor. 423

1 New Year—An improvement in circumstances is at hand. You will have an unscrupulous rival; be careful of your confidences. Being drunk at a New Year's Eve party: Love affairs will improve. Proposing on New Year's Eve: Marriage will last forever. Getting married on New Year's Eve: Marriage will not last long. A boy being born on New Year's Eve: Will become a prominent person. A girl being born on New Year's Eve: Will marry a wealthy person. Committing adultery on New Years Eve: Imminent separation. 937

4 Night—To dream that you are suddenly overtaken by night or by an unexplained darkness is a bad sign; misfortune will be your lot. But if you persevere in your dream and once more see the light of day, then you will recover your losses. 652

9 Niece—Mutual affection and assistance between you and a relative. 801

5 Nightmare—To imagine that you are dreaming or have a nightmare, in your dream, is a warning to you of treachery on the part of someone you trust. 869

8 Noise—To hear a loud noise in your dream is a sign of quarrels among your friends or relatives. The louder the noise, the more serious the result. 125

8 Nose—To dream that you are bleeding at the nose is an omen of failing business; be careful in your investments and speculations. It often shows trouble in your home circle. Do not travel, for it will not be fortunate for you; and avoid lending money for the next few weeks. 215

5 Novel—All printed matter is unfortunate in your

dreams. Be careful of your business affairs and speculations. Writing a novel: Unhappiness. Buying a novel: Refrain from speculation in the stock market. 158

5 Noose—Obstacles and competition with which you must hold your own. 896

9 Nosebleed—Not a good omen. Take the utmost care of yourself for a time. 360

2 Numbers—To count the number of persons present in your dream foretells power, satisfied ambition, and dignity. 758

5 Nurse—It is a good sign to dream of a nurse, and your business affairs will prosper. 392

2 Nuts—As a rule, it is a fortunate dream that includes nuts, whether they appear in a dessert or are on a tree; but they refer to the family fortunes rather than to your business affairs, generally. Some important wish will be gratified. 524

O

9 Oak Tree—Any dream that includes a flourishing tree may be looked upon as a fortunate omen. The finer the tree, the better the immediate prospects. If, however, you see healthy young trees, you will not be benefited fully for some years, although it is still a good sign. If the tree is withered or the leaves have fallen, it is a warning of business losses. If the tree has been felled and is lying in your path, it is a very serious omen. 324

7 Oar—It is a good omen in your dream of rowing a small boat. If others are also rowing with you, then expect to face difficulties before success. It is a bad sign if you lose or break an oar. 241

9 Oasis—To dream of wandering in a desert and finding an oasis is a sign of one friend on whose help you can always rely. 126

8 Oath—A comfortable salary and good position will be yours. 593

1 Oats—Success in commerce follows a dream of a growing crop. If the crop is still green or unripe, be careful for a few months or you may make a serious binder. 109

5 Obeying—You have an admirer who is seriously attracted. Do not be depressed by sad tidings from a distance; brighter days are ahead are in store. 923

3 Obituary—To read of a death of someone you know well means news of a marriage. 129

7 Occupation—To dream of doing work you detest means good fortune in every way. 403

6 Oculist—You are being watched; do not be ensnared. Buying glasses from an oculist: Dignity and distinction. Taking children to an oculist: Prosperity. 303

2 Ocean or Sea—The meaning of this dream depends entirely upon the circumstances. If the water is quiet and peaceful, it is a good sign, whether it is the sea, a lake, or a river. But if it is stormy or rough, then beware; for you have a difficult time before you and will need all your courage. 452

8 Odors—Fragrant scents signify contentment; unpleasant odors mean vexations. Pleasing odors: You will excel in everything. Offensive odors: Unreliable servants are in your employ. Smelling odor on hands: Will suffer because of own foolishness. Smelling odor of the body: Will be guilty of foolish actions. 278

9 Offense—To dream that some person has offended you is a warning of family quarrels that will affect your position or your domestic comfort. If you have given cause for offense, then the fault will certainly lie at your own door. 495

5 Offer—It is considered fortunate if someone makes a good offer for your service in your dream. Expect an improvement in your position, but you must work hard. 491

8 Office—To dream that you have lost your situation or that your landlord has turned you out of your office is a warning of trouble in your love affairs or married life. 407

8 Officer—Guard your speech and letters alike. Important happenings will claim your attention. 413

9 Oil—To dream that you are using oil in any way is an unfortunate omen, except for women, for those who use it normally, such as artists, painters, or contractors. Digging for an oil well: Profit. Taking castor oil: Happiness. Artists and painters using oil: Large earnings. 729

4 Old—To dream that you are very old signifies fame. A dream of old clothes: You should take courage and think more highly of yourself. 247

1 Olives—An omen of peace and happiness in domestic life. 256

4 Onions—A very mixed dream. You will encounter some unexpected good fortune, but it will prove disappointing to you in the end. Pulling onions out of the ground: Revelation of a secret. Eating onions: Quarrels with employees. Cooking onions: Will be visited by a friend. 256

1 Opera—To dream of an opera signifies that success will not be easily obtained. Going to the opera: Family disorder. Being at the opera: Confusion in your business. Hearing grand opera: A long-absent friend will return soon. 235

5 Operation—It is a hospital dream if you imagine that you are undergoing an operation. Success will come to you if no trouble comes in the dream. It is, however, considered a sign of unexpected news if you watch an operation performed on someone else. Neither of these meanings apply in the case of a nurse or medical man. 725

2 Opium—Worries, bad news from the sea, or serious illness of someone dear to you. It is portended by this dream. 128

4 Orchard—To dream that you are in an orchard is always a favorable sign; but the actual extent of your good fortune will depend on the condition of the fruits. If it is ripe and plentiful, you may expect great success; if it is green or scarce, then your fortunes will mend; but it will require time and patience. 589

8 Orchestra—Music is generally considered a fortunate

omen in a dream, but in the case of an orchestra there will be too many difficulties, and failure usually results. 368

1 Organ—This is a fortunate dream unless the music is too loud to be pleasant to you personally. If a funeral march is being played, it is very fortunate for love affairs. Playing an organ: Loss of a relative. 352

9 Orient—To dream of oriental people or countries is an omen of romantic interest which will not prove lasting. Do not be too absorbed in it. Traveling to the orient: Take a little less stock in people's promises. Being among oriental people: Good marriage chance. Bringing back things from the orient: Waste of time. 459

1 Orphans—Whoever dreams of orphans will receive profits or riches by the hand of a stranger. Adopting an orphan: Happiness is assured. 262

2 Ornaments—A dream of contrary meaning. The more ornaments you wear in your dream the greater will be the coming trouble. Giving ornaments to others: Extravagance. Church ornaments: Will have a good spirit. Flower ornaments: Will have pleasure and fortune. 110

2 Ostrich—A slight ailment will worry you; look to your diet. 495

2 Oven—To dream that you are baking or cooking some food in an oven is a sign that your affairs have reached a standstill. If you burn the food, you will drift to the bad; if the result is a pleasant meal, then in time you will prosper. But in any case you should be very careful for some time and certainly take no risks. 902

5 Overalls—To dream of working in overalls means you will be well paid for some kindness. To tear it means ill luck. 429

9 Overcoat—The more clothes you wear the greater the coming trouble. Taking off an overcoat: Disgrace. Buying one: Will be a person of honor. 315

4 Oxen—To dream that you see a herd of oxen is a very fortunate sign; your affairs will prosper. If they are grazing peacefully, your speculations or investments should be watched, as they should show signs of favorable development. Buy and sell shares carefully. 823

4 Oysters—To dream of eating oysters is a sign that you

have hard work in front of you and that you will need courage, if you are to succeed. But in love affairs it promises happiness if you are patient. Gathering oysters: Will make lots of money. Buying oysters: Someone new will fall in love with you. 283

P

8 Padlock—This is an obstacle dream. Note carefully whether the padlock fastens you inside or whether you use it to fasten some door. 395

2 Pageant—A warning against judging by appearances or paying too much attention to outward things. 181

4 Pain—A dream of contrary meaning. The greater your suffering in your dream, the more successful you will be in real life. To lovers it is extremely fortunate. Having pain in teeth: Unhappiness. Having pain in stomach: Pleasant social activities. Having pains in legs: Will receive good news. 832

9 Painter—Good fortune. 333

7 Painting—Domestic affliction. Painting another's portrait: Friends will be false to you. Painting a landscape: Will make good purchases. 250

2 Palace—It is a good sign for those in lowly circumstances to dream of palaces or showy houses and big estates. It is also favorable for love affairs. Living in a palace: People esteem you highly. 128

1 Palm Trees—Successful speculations and flourishing business ventures. Some unexpected difficulty will be overcome. Young girls dreaming of a palm tree: Will soon be married. A woman dreaming of a palm tree: Will have children. A man dreaming of a palm tree: Will enjoy success and fame. 145

6 Pancake—To dream that you are eating pancakes shows some unexpected success; you will see your way out of

some difficulty perhaps by the assistance of some friend or business associate. If they burn while cooking: Your venture will fail. 249

4 Pantry—To dream that you are in the pantry is not a good omen. You will succeed up to a certain point but will always have obstacles to overcome. 913

2 Paper—To dream of paper is a sign of some trouble. If the paper is clean, you will escape with a light money loss, but if the paper is soiled and dirty, then your own questionable action will prove your undoing. If the paper is folded, it denotes some small disappointments. 875

3 Parachute—Be careful of all extremes and do not overwork or overplay. Yourself coming down in a parachute: Sorrow within the family. Many people coming down in parachutes: Increase in the family. 093

9 Parade—To see a parade of soldiers drilling means that you will quarrel with someone. A union parade: Improvement in family conditions. A parade of protest: Great satisfaction will come to you. 945

1 Paradise—Happy marriage; to the farmer, abundant crops; a good omen to all. Being in paradise: Forgive those who have wronged you. Young girl dreaming of being in paradise: Will have sorrow. Woman being thrown out of paradise: Misery. 415

3 Paralysis—If you dream that you are paralyzed it is a sign of a broken engagement. Having paralysis: Dishonor. Children being paralyzed: A change in life will soon come. 048

5 Parasol—It is considered fortunate if you see yourself with your parasol open. In other words it is a direct indication of favorable weather and sunshine. Borrowing a parasol: Misunderstandings with friends. Lending a parasol: Will be hurt by false friends. A beautifully colored parasol: You will be displeased by your lover. 293

1 Parcel—To dream that you receive a parcel is a very fortunate omen, but if you open it, you may affect your luck. If you are carrying a parcel, expect a change of circumstances. 109

1 Park—This dream of a fine open space is a favorable

one. If you are accompanied by one other person, it shows a happy love affair; but if several people are with you, you can expect difficulties for some time. Children playing in the park: Happiness in love. Sitting in a park alone: Increase in your fortune. Sitting in the park with sweetheart: Enemies will be punished. 397

7 Parrot—Hard work is before you; you will suffer from the idle talk of other people. Children talking to a parrot: You have confidence of friends. A parrot chattering too much: Will be flattered by someone. A young engaged girl dreaming of a parrot: Inquire about fiancé's family. 529

8 Party—It is considered a fortunate omen to dream of being at a party. But it is unfavorable if you yourself give a party, and the smarter the function, the worse the omen. Being at a wild party: Will be a victim of gossip. Someone getting hurt at a party: Will have a long life. 134

3 Passion—It is a warning of trouble, generally domestic, to lose your temper in a dream. A woman being passionate: She will be justified. A man being passionate: A passing love. A wife being passionate: A better future awaiting her. A husband being passionate: Changeable in love. 264

9 Path—This is another obstacle dream, as the meaning depends upon circumstances. If you can walk easily and comfortably, then your affairs will flourish. If you meet obstacles to your progress, then you may be certain that there are difficulties to be faced in the future. 315

6 Pawnbroker—This dream certainly foretells heavy losses and disappointments. Your sweetheart will prove unfaithful; or if you are married, some indiscreet action of your partner will cause great trouble. 762

6 Peach—A dream of personal pleasure, not of business affairs. Of peaches on a tree: Promised attainment of fondest hopes. Many trees loaded with peaches: Earning will be good. Eating peaches with others: Love worries. 249

9 Peacock—A dream of contrary meaning. Your fine plans will fail, and you will be disappointed; but to the

farmer this handsome bird foretells a good harvest after much hard work. A dead peacock: Own good plans will fail. A woman dreaming of a peacock circling: Riches. 531

8 Pearls—A very fortunate dream, but you will have to earn your success by hard work. Be patient, for you will surely succeed. If pearls are given to you in your dream, it is a sign of a very happy and successful marriage. If the string of pearls should break, however, it shows grief and sorrow unless you thread them again in your dream. Buying pearls: Will succeed in your goal. Losing a set of pearls: Will make new friends. Giving a gift of pearls: Are trying to gain favors by a gift. 134

5 Peas—This is a fortunate dream on the whole, but you must exercise patience, particularly if the peas are raw or not cooked sufficiently. It is most favorable when you see peas growing in the garden. Dried peas show money acquired in a doubtful manner. 131

1 Pedlar—To dream of a pedlar signifies deceitful companions. 109

5 Pencil—Take note of the friend who gave it to you in the dream, as a parting from that person is indicated. 212

7 Pendulum—A sudden message will cause you to take a long journey. 304

9 Pens—News about absent friends. 513

6 People—People coming to your house: Will have sorrows and tears. People coming uninvited: Unhappiness. Blind people: Misfortune. People dressed in white: Loss of friendship. People dressed in black: Unhappy events in the near future. People in high office: Honor and dignity. 132

9 Pepper—Talent in your family, particularly if you sniff the pepper until you sneeze. 369

3 Perfume—This is always a favorable dream, both for the man of commerce or the lover. Spilling perfume: Loss of something that brings pleasure. Buying perfume: Will find a new lover. Breaking a bottle of perfume: Disaster to fondest hopes. Receiving a bottle of perfume as a gift: Will be embraced by unknown person. Giving

180

a gift of perfume: Big profit. Smelling perfume: Frivolity. 642

6 Peril—It is an obstacle omen if you find yourself in peril in your dream. If you come off successfully, then all will go well. 762

7 Perspiration—Great efforts will be required of you and duly rewarded. 826

6 Pest—To dream of house or garden pests is a token of prosperity beyond your hopes. 753

3 Petticoat—A dream of warning against conceit and dissipation. Keep to moderate ways and feelings. Having petticoats: Will soon have a love affair. Buying petticoats: Exercise moderate mode of living. Losing a petticoat: Difficulties in married life. A white petticoat: Will receive a beautiful gift. Colored petticoat: A marriage will soon take place. A torn petticoat: Unhappiness for a long time. 102

3 Photo—It is always fortunate to look at a photo of some other person in a dream, but if it is your own it is a bad omen. 750

5 Physician—This is a very fortunate omen. It is always a good sign to see or speak to a doctor in your dream. Being a physician: Joy and profit. Calling a physician for children: New interests and surroundings. A physician visiting patients: Great wealth. 257

1 Piano—To dream of piano: All of your own affairs will prosper. Owning a piano: Beware of jealous friends. Selling a piano: Loneliness and disappointment. Playing the piano: Disputes. 190

9 Picnic—A doubtful sign concerning your love affairs. The meaning depends upon what happens at the picnic. 342

3 Pictures—To dream of pictures is a bad omen, for it warns you of treachery by one you trust. The more pleasing the pictures appear to you, the more dangerous the omen; it means work without profit. Pictures of naked women: Public disgrace. Pictures of naked men: Unhappiness in love affairs. 651

3 Pie—To dream of cooking one means homely joys; to eat one, dissension in the family. Receiving a pie as a gift: A friend is seeking your ruin. 912

6 Pigs—A very mixed dream, for good and bad luck will both be present in your affairs. Many of your cherished plans will fail, yet others, apparently less important, will succeed and restore the balance. Watch over the members of your household, as trouble may reach you from this source. 897

4 Pigeons—News of importance from afar, but it may not be very favorable and will mean changes in your affairs. Pigeons are favorable for love affairs. It is better to see them flying than walking or settling on ledges. 625

6 Pillow—A clean pillow is a good sign; but if it is soiled and untidy, then expect troubles of your own making. 195

7 Pills—A journey abroad with many pleasures at the end of it. 160

9 Pilot—Cheery scenes and good times ahead, but you will be defeated by a rival in the end. 531

2 Pine Tree—This signifies good news to elderly people but danger to the young. 209

4 Pineapple—Comfortable domestic surroundings, invitations, and pleasure seeking. 580

1 Pipe—A sign of unusual events resulting in good fortune to the smoker. Breaking a pipe: Security. Dirty pipes: Misery. Receiving a pipe as a gift: Advancement in own business. 532

6 Pirate—Exciting times, journeys and financial gains; the deceit of an associate will cause you gain. 420

1 Pistol—To hear the sound of firing foretells misfortune. If you yourself fire a pistol, it is a sign of hard work with very little result therefrom. Carrying a pistol: Will be disliked by people. Other people firing pistols: Will learn of schemes to ruin you. Being an officer and carrying a pistol: Treachery. 514

9 Pit—This is really an obstacle dream. If you descend into a pit or deep hollow, it shows that your business affairs will decline. To a lover it means that he will meet with coldness and indifference. If you fall into a pit, it is a most unfortunate omen, for you will suffer a long time from troubles confronting you. 999

6 Pity—To dream of being pitied means humiliation. Pitying someone else: Small vexations. 124

9 Plank—A sign of a restless state of mind which only travel will satisfy. 126

6 Plaster—False accusations will be made against you if you dream that the plaster is upon you; but if you dream that the plaster is coming off the walls of your house, the trouble is for your family. 348

2 Platform—You will marry when you least expect to; beware of hasty judgments. 371

9 Play—It is more fortunate to watch a play than to dream that you are taking part in one. 216

7 Poison—To dream that you have taken poison is a warning of financial loss through the dishonesty of some person whom you trust. Be careful how you give credit or lend money. Do not speculate or buy shares of stocks. If you recover from the effects of the poison, you can get over your difficulties by exercising care and paying attention to the facts. 241

6 Police—This might be called a dream of contrary meaning, for if you dream of trouble with the police, it shows that some present difficulty will be overcome. Being arrested by police with cause: Misfortune will attend you. Being at a police station for questioning: Happiness. Being with friends at a police station for questioning: Happiness. Being with friends at a police station: Loss of money. 825

9 Portrait—A warning of danger regarding the person whose portrait or photo is envisioned, especially if it is faded or injured. 243

8 Postman—Some unexpected happening. Being a postman: Loss of real estate. Giving a letter to a postman: Listen to the advice of friends. Receiving special delivery letter from a postman: Great love. 512

6 Post office—A change of residence or companions. Mailing a letter at the post office: Will have obstacles in your path. Registering a letter at the post office: Change of companions: Buying a stamp at the post office: Unpleasant things awaiting. Finding the post office closed: Dissension in love affairs. 132

3 Potatoes—Do not try to play Providence for other people, or you may do more harm than good. Planting potatoes: Dearest plans will materialize. Digging potatoes: Big success in own efforts. Boiling potatoes: Will entertain an unwelcome guest. Frying potatoes: Will marry a husky girl. Baking potatoes: Will have arguments with sweetheart. Eating potato salad: Investments will bring profits. 120

1 Poultry—A very fortunate dream. Buying poultry: Consolation. Cleaning poultry: Someone will give you money. 325

4 Poverty—A dream of contrary meaning: Good fortune is coming your way. Other people in poverty: Will give beneficial service to others. Family falling into poverty: Future riches. Friends being in poverty: Health and joy. 139

2 Preacher—The result of your plans will be satisfactory at last although worrying at present. 317

3 Precipice—This is another dream very similar in meaning to that of a pit. It is a warning of trouble ahead, and you should avoid traveling or any change of plans. Take warning and act with prudence. If you fall over the precipice it is a bad sign; but if you walk away from the edge, you will overcome your troubles. 831

7 Pregnant—Being pregnant means that your health will soon improve. A married woman being pregnant: Marital unhappiness. Unmarried woman dreaming of being pregnant: Trouble and injury through scandal. A widow dreaming of being pregnant: She will marry very soon. A young girl dreaming of being pregnant: Won't get married for a long time. 295

6 Priest—To dream of a clergyman is a sign that some quarrel will be cleared up, thus increasing your personal happiness. Confessing sins to a priest: You are dealing in dangerous affairs. A priest being aboard a ship: Bad weather or shipwreck. Family going to see a priest: Family quarrels. 213

1 Prison—This is a dream that indicates much happiness in your home affairs and success in business. To dream that someone is put in prison through your efforts is not a fortunate sign. You are being too venturesome in your

money matters, too eager to secure profit; and it may mean a loss instead of a gain. 109

2 Prize—This is a dream of contrary meaning that forebodes loss through sharp dealing. Be on your guard when offered something cheap. 137

8 Promise—An important decision for you to make. The right answer will lead to happy times for you, so think well. 743

4 Proposal—If you dream of receiving one, be careful not to be drawn into another person's schemes. Should you make one, exciting times are ahead. 319

7 Property—This means you will be disappointed in your hopes. Possessing property: Fortune. Having a large estate of property: Unhappiness. Inheriting property: Will be in mourning. A prospective buyer of property: You are a dreamer. Selling property in the country: Disgrace. 934

1 Prostitute—Being a prostitute: An enemy is seeking your ruin. A prostitute who thinks she is a man: Will give birth to a boy. Embracing a prostitute: Will take a long trip. Receiving a prostitute into your house: Good business ventures. A prostitute dancing: Will go back to your sweetheart. Seeing a prostitute: Good times ahead. 725

4 Puppy—An invitation to a jolly party. Laugh with the people you meet there, but do not become intimate. 526

3 Pump—To pump clear water is a good sign. Your business will prosper. If the water is soiled, however, worries and evil speaking will annoy you. 210

8 Punch—To dream of drinking it is a warning of unpleasant news to come concerning loss of money and, possibly reputation. 269

7 Punishment—To dream of being punished signifies unexpected pleasure. 399

7 Purse—To dream that you find a purse is a good omen if money is inside and a very fortunate omen for lovers; but if you have lost your purse, then expect difficulties or illness as the result of your carelessness. 601

1 Push—To dream of pushing against a door or other heavy object signifies that some overmastering obstacle will be removed from your path. 811

7 Puzzle—An obstacle dream. If you cannot solve the puzzle, then expect heavy losses in business, for trouble is ahead. 394

9 Pyramids—A successful future and a high position in the world are assured to you. 828

Q

7 Quack—To dream that you are under the care of quacks is unfortunate and foretells to the person dreaming that he must beware of these nuisances to society. 124

3 Quarrels—This is one other dream of contrary meaning and foretells prosperity in your business affairs, but there will be opposition for you to face at first. Quarreling with wife or husband: Will be guilty of foolish actions. Quarreling with a sweetheart: Will make up very soon. Quarreling with a friend: Loss of money. 390

8 Queen—A sign of valuable friendship. Going to see a queen: Good fortune. Having an interview with a queen: Rebellion within the home. A queen surrounded by her court: Will be deceived by friends. 548

2 Questions—To dream that someone is asking you questions is an obstacle omen. If you can answer properly, all will go well. 308

7 Quilt—This is a fortunate dream provided it is properly placed on the bed. 124

9 Quicksands—This dream denotes that you are surrounded by many temptations. Do not be imprudent. 216

R

9 Race—One of the ever-recurring obstacle dreams, warning you to persevere if you desire success. Running a

race and winning: Distinction and honor. Running a race and losing: Will have many competitors in your affairs. A jockey running a race: A change in life will soon come. A dog race: Will have mastery over enemies. 135

9 Racecourse—Jolly company but danger of losses through sharp practices. Friends being at a racecourse: Death of a loved one. Important personalities at a race course: Hard work awaits you. 918

2 Racehorse—Seeing a racehorse means you should try to economize while there is time. To ride one: Do not speculate; luck is not with you. Your racehorse winning: You have a lot of enemies. Your racehorse losing: Will have many competitors. 110

4 Racket—This dream betokens loss of leisure which will, however, be well repaid later by a new friendship. Creating a very loud racket: Frivolity. Others making a racket: Warning of troubles. A tennis racket: Good luck to one for whom you care. 931

3 Raffle—This dream of risk and chance is a warning to you that you do not deserve success. Mend your ways and be more generous in your treatment of others. Taking part in a raffle: Small risks ahead of you. Lovers holding a raffle ticket: Unhappy association. Losing a raffle: Engagement will be called off. 624

9 Raft—To dream that you're on a raft means enforced travel. To see a raft: Varied life for some time. Saving your life on a raft: Will have mastery of your own affairs. A very big and long raft: Will travel for a long time. 126

9 Rags—This is a fortunate dream; any display of wealth in a dream is generally a bad sign. A woman dreaming of herself in rags: Unhappiness. A girl dreaming of herself in rags: Will meet an arrogant man. Washing rags: Unhappiness. Gathering rags: Big arguments. Buying rags: Will be in the company of happy people. 594

5 Raid—An excellent omen of pleasant times to come. A police raid: Change of environment. An air raid: A change of life will come soon. Own home being raided: Will have emotional sorrow. Other people being raided: Happiness is assured. 149

6 Railroad—To dream of a railroad means good times ahead. Being on a railroad alone: Rapid rise in business. Being at a railroad with relatives: Abundant means. Being at a railroad with friends: Hard times ahead. Walk on railroad ties: Distress and worry. Being forced to walk the rails: Affairs will bring unmeasured happiness. 312

1 Rainbow—A fortunate dream showing that there will certainly be a change in your affairs for the better before too long. A young girl dreaming of a rainbow: Will have an agreeable sweetheart. Lovers seeing a rainbow together: Happy marriage and riches. A rainbow being over your head: Family inheritance.

6 Rain—An omen that foretells difficulties in the near future. If the downpour is a heavy one, it beomes a serious warning. Getting wet in a downpour of rain: Suffering caused by suspicion of friends. Rain dripping into a room: Beware of false friends. A very bad rain and windstorm: Great joy. Women being out in the rain: Disappointment in love. 321

8 Rake—To rake hay: A wedding to come. To rake leaves: A happy home. 854

4 Rape—To dream of being raped means you will receive a marriage proposal. Raping someone under age: Misfortune. Raping someone over the age of twenty-one: Joy and prosperity. Being raped by a woman: Will receive inheritance. Friends being raped: Will be highly embarrassed. 211

3 Rat—An omen of enemies whom you do not suspect. If you see more than one rat, then the coming trouble will be a serious one and may overwhelm you. To the lover it foretells a fortunate rival. White rats sometimes may be seen. They mean you will get through your trouble successfully. 372

6 Raven—This is really a dream of the color black. Trouble is coming, though you may not deserve it. A raven flying: Your life is in danger. A raven flapping its wings: Death of a friend. Hearing the noise of ravens: Unhappiness. 312

6 Razor—Any sharp cutting instrument is a warning of a coming quarrel. Keep control over yourself. Cutting

188

yourself with a razor: Must control your emotions. Buying a razor: Persecution. 186

4 Reading—It is not a good sign to dream that you are reading; it foretells a dangerous venture, in which you will probably lose money. 814

9 Rebellion—An inferior who has caused you much trouble will soon cease to annoy you. Watching a rebellion: Be cautious with business affairs. Taking part in a rebellion: Much satisfaction. Being wounded in a rebellion: Infidelity. People being killed in a rebellion: Will win at gambling. A foreign rebellion: You are too ambitious. 297

3 Reconciliation—This is a favorable sign in a dream. 309

8 Reflection—To see your own reflection in water means a lonely life; but should you dream of a strange face reflected, it is a sign of meeting and marrying the owner. 305

6 Refreshments—To offer them: A happy marriage. To partake of them: Small vexations. 942

1 Refusal—To dream of a refusal signifies a most certain acceptance. Being refused by relatives: Prospects of better times. Being refused by friends: Jealousy and dissension. Refusing a gift: Will receive another one. Others refusing a gift from you: Will be embarrassed by sweetheart. Refusing to accept a letter: Secret plans. 190

8 Religion—It is generally a bad sign to be troubled by religion in a dream. 287

3 Rent—Unexpected gains will be yours following a dream in which you cannot pay rent or any other debt. 318

8 Rescue—To be rescued is not a good sign, especially if it is from drowning. Avoid travel on the sea. Rescuing others: Will have a good reputation. Rescuing others: Will make big financial gains. Rescuing one who wants to die: Beware of insincere friends. 269

9 Resign—To dream of resigning your work means advancement in the near future and also money gained through legal matters. 179

8 Rest—A contrary dream meaning hard work and good luck in sporting matters. 125

2 Restaurant—To look at others eating in a restaurant signifies ill health; should you be eating also, small enjoyment among new friends. Eating with children at a restaurant: Wealth. Others eating at a restaurant: Will receive money soon. Eating at a restaurant with sweetheart: Bad financial conditions. Husband and wife eating in a restaurant alone: Long happy marriage. 326

6 Return—To dream you see someone who has been away for a long time is a sign of losses soon to be made good, and renewed prosperity. 726

6 Revelry—A contrary dream heralding misfortune unless you dream of looking on at the revelry of others. 240

9 Revolver—To dream of handling a revolver is a sign of danger by water. Try to avoid traveling by sea or river. Firing a revolver: You will be cheated. Killing with a revolver: Will have a long life. Officers with a revolver: Good harvest. 819

4 Revenge—Anxious times, humiliation, and a quarrel; but the latter will soon be made up. Seeking revenge against a man: Humiliation. Seeking revenge against a woman: You are considered to be very vulgar. Seeking revenge against the family: Small arguments solved. 283

6 Reward—Failure of your plans through overconfidence. Remember, there are things money cannot buy. 618

1 Rheumatism—To dream of suffering from this signifies a new lease on life and happiness. 613

7 Rhinoceros—Success in business affairs, but delays and disillusion to those in love. 304

6 Ribbon—A dream of light pleasure and careless spending of money. 276

8 Rice—Be careful of your plans, for they are ill advised. Eating rice with many people: Will make a good marriage. Giving rice to children: Trouble will cease. Eating rice pudding: Money will come easily to you. 350

8 Riches—Unfortunately, this is a dream of contrary meaning. The more flourishing your affairs in your visionary world, the worse they will be in real life. 134

6 Riding—It is a fortunate omen to dream that you are riding a horse unless the animal is out of control or throws you. Riding with others: Plans will turn out

unsatisfactorily. Riding fast in a car: Prosperity may develop. 609

4 Rings—To lose your ring is a warning of trouble coming through a friend or relation. It is a fortunate sign if someone makes you a present of a ring. Having a ring of precious stones: Wealth. An unmarried person dreaming of a ring with precious stones: Matrimony. Married person dreaming of a ring with precious stones: Birth of a child. Losing your ring: Large fortune. A single girl dreaming of losing her ring: She will be left by boyfriend. Giving a gift of rings: Loss of money. Receiving a wedding ring: Will have devoted lover. Having a ring on a chain: Good health. 598

8 Riot—This is a warning of financial failure, especially if you see many rioters fighting. Taking part in a riot: Misfortune in business. Friends taking part in a riot. Persecution by an enemy. Relatives taking part in a riot: Death of a friend. A riot ending: Will receive high honors. 458

8 Rival—This should be treated as an obstacle dream. If you defeat your rival or if he retires, you will prove successful in your business affairs. Being defeated by a rival: Shame and sorrow. A lover dreaming of having a rival: Will be lacking in love affairs. A young woman dreaming of having a rival: Will accept her present lover. 962

9 River—As with all dreams of water, whether of the sea, a lake, or a river, the meaning depends upon the clearness or muddiness of the water. If there are signs of a storm, then be very cautious in your plans, for troubles lies ahead. To fall or jump in shows domestic worries. 243

2 Road—A well-made broad road is a most fortunate omen, but lanes or narrow, winding paths should be treated as obstacles. Traveling on a straight road: Lasting happiness. Traveling on a crooked road: Discovery of a secret. Traveling on a bad road: New undertakings will bring sorrow and losses. 749

7 Roar—The roar of waters means a traveler will return. Of animals: An enemy is watching you. 610

6 Robber—It is considered fortunate to be molested by a

191

thief in your dream, provided you escape injury. Escaping injury by a robber: Good times ahead. Catching a robber: Triumph over enemies. Killing a robber: Will have a long life. A robber being arrested: Success in business. A robber getting away: Disappointment in love. 591

4 Robin—One of nature's most fortunate omens. 364

7 Rocket—Short-lived success is portended. You must build on firmer foundations next time. 394

1 Rocks—Another obstacle dream, the meaning of which depends upon the circumstances, but it certainly foretells difficulties and hard work. 613

1 Rope—These are obstacle dreams. If you find yourself securely bound by rope, then expect difficult times in your business affairs, for trouble is surely coming. Coming down on a rope: Will overcome all who may seek your downfall. 415

7 Room—This unusual dream signifies success after you have almost given up hope. Of a room: Will discover family secrets. A room that you live in: Financial worries. A hotel room: Death of a friend. A dark room: Loss of money. A bathroom: Sickness. 349

9 Roof—Prosperity and festive garments are soon to be yours. 594

6 Rosary—To dream of telling the beads on your own rosary means a reconciliation with a friend. To see someone else wearing a rosary signifies bereavement. 906

4 Roses—A most fortunate dream for everybody unless the blossoms are withered or fall to pieces in your hands. If the flowers are only slightly faded, it foretells success after some difficulties. 058

3 Rubber—To erase writing with an india rub is a presage of uncertainty of action. Take counsel of older heads than yours. 462

7 Rubbish—You are about to make a valuable discovery. Use it, but try not to hurt a friend by doing so. 232

9 Ruins—It is a fortunate dream in which you are wandering amid building ruins, but it is merely a modern house that has tumbled down, that is a bad sign. Be-

ware of speculation. Marriage being ruined: You are well known for being stingy. A ruined city: Will receive unexpected fortune. A financially ruined family: Will receive money unexpectedly. 216

9 Running—This is generally an obstacle dream. If you succeed in reaching your goal, then all will go well; but if you tire or stop running, then expect business difficulties. A woman running: Will lose her virginity. Running because of being scared: Security. Running because of being afraid: Will go into exile. Running naked: Will be robbed by relatives. Running to catch someone: Good fortune. A woman running naked: Will go crazy. Wanting to run but can't: Will have a serious illness. 835

S

3 Sable—The color betokens tidings of loss; the fur is a warning against extravagance. Others having sable furs: A false friend is nearby. 831

9 Saddle—To dream that you are riding a horse without a saddle foretells ill health through your own carelessness. Revise your plans at once and guard against mistakes. Riding a horse with a new saddle: Joy without profit. Riding a horse without a saddle: Bad health. Others riding horses without saddles: A catastrophe is ahead. Children riding horses without saddles: Reverse your plans. 540

5 Sadness—A good omen for your future; lasting joys. 401

8 Sailing—This is another form of the water dream, and its meaning depends upon whether or not the water is smooth and your voyage pleasant. If not, then you can expect trouble and worry according to the severity of the storm. The smaller the boat, the greater your success in overcoming your misfortune. 314

8 Salmon—Family troubles. Catching salmon: Accord

193

with friends. Eating salmon: You have a loyal friend. Canned salmon: Approaching money. 809

7 Salt—This is a fortunate dream in every way, but if you spill the salt you can expect some difficulty and hard work before you succeed. Using salt on food: Will have religious arguments. Cooking food with salt: Good days are ahead. Putting too much salt in food: Will squander money. 340

2 Sand—Many small vexations. Working with sand: Years of hard work are ahead. Mixing sand with cement: Success. A sand dune: Will be justified by friends. 947

9 Satin—A fortunate dream for the business man, but the lover should beware of false and flattering words. White satin: Abundant means. Blue satin: Will have damages in own affairs. Red satin: Will be wounded by a bullet. A business man dreaming of satin: Business is secured. A lover dreaming of satin: Beware of false and flattering talk. A beautiful single girl dreaming of satin: Will have an ardent love. A married woman dreaming of satin: Will deceive her husband. 648

1 Sausage—Domestic troubles, often through ill health. Buying sausages: Contentment in life. Eating pork sausages: Will win in gambling. Eating liver sausages: Poverty. 568

1 Savage—Small worries through the dishonesty of another. To dream of many savages signifies rescue by a friend from a trouble of your own making. Being hurt by a savage person: Leading a wild life. Many savages: Rescue by a friend. Fighting with a savage person: Small worries through dishonesty of others. 190

1 Savings—To dream you are accumulating savings foreshadows poverty. 847

7 Saw—It is not a fortunate omen to dream that you are sawing wood. It indicates difficulties to be overcome. 151

3 Scald—A dream of contrary meaning. Good fortune will follow after the first difficulties have been overcome. Children being scalded: Family quarrels. 498

9 School—To dream you begin again and go to school, and cannot say your lessons right, shows you are

about to undertake something which you do not understand. Going to school: Business will be in good standing. Taking children to school: Will set a good example for children. Going to swimming school: Anxiety. Going to dancing school: Your morals make you unfit to fill a position. 270

4 Scissors—A warning of false friends. Beware of giving your confidence too fully. Buying scissors: You are a very precise and proper person. Using manicure scissors: Will live a long life. Lovers handling scissors: Will have a big argument about love matters. 319

1 Scorpion—Will receive damages caused by enemies. Several scorpions: Enemies are talking behind your back. A nest of scorpions: Will overcome your enemies. Scorpions eating lizards: You are an idealist. A scorpion in a cage: You are surrounded by boisterous people. Being bitten by a scorpion: Business will succeed. Killing a scorpion: Will suffer loss through pretended friends. 865

9 Scratched—To dream of being scratched foretells hurt. Scratching own back: Approaching money. Drawing blood from a scratch: Will receive bad news. Being scratched by a woman's nails: Your love is secured. Being scratched by a cat: Sickness. Being scratched by a dog: Will be cheated by friends. 108

5 Scream—It is considered a fortunate sign to find yourself screaming in a dream. Others screaming: An enemy is seeking your ruin. 455

7 Sculptor—Change in present position. Being friendly with a sculptor: Will bring about love but less money. Posing for a sculptor: Social activities of a happy nature. A married woman posing for a sculptor: Will be left by her husband. A virgin posing for a sculptor: Will marry a rich man. A widow posing for a sculptor: Suitable time to pursue her desires. 639

7 Sea—Of the open sea with small waves: Great joy. A blue sea: Business affairs are running smoothly. A dead, calm sea: Will make money from a business transaction. Falling into the sea: Beware of jealous friends. Being thrown by force into the sea: Sickness. Traveling across the smooth sea: Devoted love within the family. Man

and wife traveling on a rough sea: Great and lasting love. A girl dreaming of a stormy sea: Deep anguish because of a double cross. 142

2 Seals—You are pushed on by ambitions but will never attain your goals. A seal coming onto the beach: Will soon become pregnant. A sealskin coat: Approaching money. A small seal in an aquarium: Security in love. 821

7 Secret—To dream of a secret being whispered into your ear means a public indignity is to be bestowed on you. Having a secret: Will have a large fortune. Being told a secret: Must control passions. Telling a secret: Misfortune in love affairs. Couples keeping secrets from each other: Diligence and hard work. Friends telling you a secret: Approaching money. 259

2 Seduce—Will have plenty of money during life. Seducing a very young girl: Business will run as you desire. Seducing a woman by force: Good events will happen to you. Own daughter being seduced: Financial gains. A married person dreaming of being seduced: Will live comfortable life. A widow dreaming of being seduced: Will be robbed. A man being arrested for seducing a woman: Will have many perplexities. A teenager seducing girl of same age: Death in family very soon. 434

1 Separation—To dream that you are separated from those you love foretells the failure of some cherished plan. Husband and wife separated: Gossip by friends. Separation of sweethearts: Idle talk by people around you. Friends being separated: Sickness of children. Sweetheart wanting a separation: Be cautious in business transactions. Separating from a business partner: Success in business. Separating from those you love: Failure of some cherished plan. 154

7 Serpent—Ungrateful people surround you. A serpent with several heads: Will seduce a beautiful girl. Catching a serpent with several heads: Will go fishing. Killing a serpent with several heads: Victory over enemies. Being bitten by a serpent: Enemies are accusing you. 124

9 Servant—For a woman to dream that she is a servant is an obstacle dream. Persevere and stick close to your job. To dream that you employ several servants is an

unfortunate omen. A female servant: Gossip by other people. A male servant: You are disliked by people. Employing several servants: Persevere and stick close to your affairs. Servants at work: Infidelity. Firing a servant: Will sustain heavy losses. Paying a servant: Great joy. 513

3 Sex—A boy of the male sex: Luck and prosperity. A woman of the female sex: Will live a long life. A man having sexual desire: Public disgrace. A woman having sexual desire: Immediate success of hopes. 156

2 Sexual Organs—Sexual organs being in good condition: Will have abundance of money. A man having a disease of the sexual organs: Warning of trouble. A man having a deformed sexual organ: Will be punished for a crime done. A woman having deformed sexual organs: Will have a virtuous son. A man having unusual sexual organs: Will have a death of a son. A woman having unusual sexual organs: Children will have a good reputation. A woman having ovaries removed: Death of a member of the family. Exposing sexual organs: Danger. 614

2 Sew—An obstacle dream. If your sewing is successful and you complete the garment or other article, all will be well. But if you leave off before finishing the work, then look out for troubles. Sewing for the house: Good results in business. Sewing clothes for yourself: Dishonor. A tailor sewing: Will receive news from abroad. 191

3 Shark—This presages a narrow escape from serious trouble or illness. Catching a shark: Affairs are running smoothly. Being killed by a shark: Will overcome obstacles. Being bitten by a shark but not killed: Bad results in business. Others being bitten by sharks: Will escape from serious trouble. 129

1 Shave—To dream that you are shaving or that someone else is shaving you is a warning of difficulty ahead. Be careful in whom you trust and do not lend money, buy shares and stocks. 415

9 Shawl—Deep affection from one you love. Buying a shawl: Will receive a visit from a doctor. Relatives wearing a shawl: Will go to a funeral parlor. Young girls wearing shawls: You are surrounded by fast-talking peo-

ple. A large white shawl: Purity and virtue. A black shawl: Grief. A red shawl: You are too loose with your affections. Giving a shawl as a gift: You will have deep affection from one you love. 315

8 Sheep—A fortunate dream, for it tells of coming success through well-conceived plans. A shepherd leading sheep: Will make much money. Buying sheep: Good earnings in stock speculation. Selling sheep: Death of an enemy. 683

2 Shell—To dream of a shell with the fish alive in it predicts prosperity, but an empty seashell is a bad omen. A clean shell: Will go into bankruptcy. A smooth shell: Will have changes in your life. Gathering shells: Fleeting pleasures. A live shellfish: Prosperity. A dead shellfish: Will receive news of the death of a friend. 767

2 Shepherd—This is considered a bad omen if you see no sheep at the time. If the flock is there also, then the presence of the shepherd increases your difficulties but will not stop your ultimate success. 209

8 Ship—To dream that you are traveling in a ship shows good fortune if you reach your destination safely. A man dreaming of a ship's docking: Unexpected good news. A woman dreaming of a ship's docking: Unexpected bad news. Lovers dreaming of a ship docking: Marriage will not be realized. A ship sinking: Abundance of money. Being on the bridge of a ship: Will take a short trip. A small ship with sails: Will receive unexpected good news. 638

6 Shipwreck—A certain omen of disaster. Losing your life in shipwreck: Arrival of an unexpected friend. Being saved from a shipwreck: Will have emotional sorrow. Being shipwrecked with the one you love: Big catastrophe is ahead. 591

2 Shirt—It is always a fortunate omen when you dream of your shirt or your chemise. Good fortune follows your efforts. An everyday shirt: Prosperous future. A nightshirt: Victory over enemies. Putting on a shirt: Will be neglected. Taking off a shirt: Will be disillusioned in love. Washing a shirt: You will be loved. A dirty shirt: Will contract a contagious disease. 596

9 Shiver—New garments will soon be yours, and they will be very much to your liking. 450

3 Shoes—This might almost be called a dream of contrary meaning, for if you see yourself without shoes, then you may expect success in business. To dream that your shoes are worn or patched is a certain sign of difficulties, but with care and hard work you will succeed. New shoes show some fortunate enterprise with unexpected results. Having black shoes: Bad times are ahead. Having white shoes: Future is completely secure. Having suede shoes: Will have easy and happy days. Having high boots: Happiness. Buying new shoes: Will have a large profit. Being without shoes: Expect success in business. 183

8 Shooting—It is a very bad omen if you kill or shoot some living creature in your dream. To shoot and miss shows some success over your difficulties. Shooting with a shotgun: You are being deceived. Shooting at a target: Will take a long trip. Shooting enemies: Domestic troubles. Shooting and killing someone: Disappointments and grief. 125

4 Shop—To dream that you are keeping shop indicates hard work before you prosper, depending on to what extent your dream shop does business. A dress shop: Everything will be wonderful. A food shop: Ruin of other people. A shop burning: Loss of possessions. 607

8 Showers—A setback in your plans through a deceitful enemy. 206

4 Shroud—News of a wedding is at hand. 436

7 Signature—Loyal companions will uphold you at all times. Putting signature on wedding license: Good health. Putting signature on diploma: Joy. Putting signature on a birth certificate: Riches. Putting signature on death certificate: Be careful of eyesight. 142

4 Silver—To dream of silver is a sign of some loss. Do not be hasty in your plans. If the coins are of large value, you may escape if you are careful. Counting silver: Big gains. Finding silver money: Prosperity. Changing silver money: Will be visited by a friend. Buying silver things: Beware of enemies. Selling silver things: Will receive money losses. 526

7 Singing—This is a dream of contrary meaning, for it foretells troubles to come; but they will soon pass, so do not despair. To dream that you hear other people singing shows that the difficulties will come through your dealings with other people. Hearing a soprano singing: Good news. Singing operatic songs: Will be afflicted by tears. Watching a singer perform: Small sickness in family. Hearing melancholy songs sung: Illness. Hearing birds singing: Love and joy. Hearing a love song: A happy event to come. 493

1 Sisters—To dream you see your brothers and sisters signifies long life. Arguing with sisters: Family disgrace. A sister arguing with a sister-in-law: Expect small fortune. Two sisters-in-law arguing with a sister: Family shame and sorrow. A sister arguing with a brother-in-law: Good fortune ahead. 271

9 Skating—Generally considered a warning of some coming danger. 315

1 Skeleton—To dream that you see a skeleton is a sign of domestic trouble. 505

8 Skin—Dreaming of your own skin, if it is healthy, means good fortune; if it appears disfigured, kindness from those of whom you least expect it. 521

3 Skull—An engagement is in the near future for you. 354

1 Sky—This is a fortunate dream unless you see heavy clouds. A few clouds probably show difficulties that you will overcome, but watch carefully to see whether the clouds are gathering or disbursing. A red sky: Increase of wealth. Ascending into the sky: Can expect honors to be bestowed. Descending from the sky: Beware of falling. A rainbow in the sky: A peril is near at hand. Stars falling from the sky: Will be unable to have children. 712

3 Sleep—To dream that you sleep foretells evil. A man sleeping with a woman: Enjoyment in life. Sleeping with a little child: Return of love and domestic joy. Sleeping with a person of oppostite sex: Affairs will go well. Sleeping with a handsome young man: Pleasures followed by disgust. Sleeping with a beautiful young girl: Annoyance and worry. Sweethearts sleeping together:

Delightful events to come. Sleeping alone: Beware of temptation. A man sleeping naked with a beautiful woman: Happiness. A woman sleeping naked with a handsome man: Treachery. 498

8 Smuggling—This betokens a plan which will almost succeed but not quite. 035

9 Smoke—Some pleasant success, but you will not really benefit by it. The denser the smoke, the greater will be your disappointment. Smoke coming from a building: A friend is deceiving you. Very thick smoke: A very big disappointment will come. Being overcome by smoke: Beware of flattery. 109

6 Snakes—This dream is a warning of treachery where you least expect it, some unfortunate turn of events that you have not anticipated. Your plans will be wrecked. Killing a snake: Will have conquest over your enemies. Several snakes: Jealous people would like to call your ruin. 690

8 Snow—This is a very good dream, but you may have to work hard, especially if you find yourself walking in a snow storm. Snow falling during the winter: Abundance. Washing yourself with snow: Relief from pain. Eating snow: You have left your place of birth. Driving through snow: Grief. Snow in the mountains: Good profits in the future. Drifts of snow in a city: Will receive good news. 690

6 Soap—An unexpected encounter will result in a solution of matters that have puzzled you. Washing your own body with soap: Will be asked for help by friends. Washing clothes with soap: Will receive money from a rich relative. 834

2 Soldier—Loss of employment, and probably many changes before you settle down once more. Soldiers drilling: Realization of hopes and desires. Wounded soldiers: Loss of sleep. Many soldiers marching: Complete change of life. A young girl dreaming of soldiers: Will have many changes before settling down. Soldiers fighting: The dreamer will be victorious. 209

9 Spade—A new vista of contentment opens before you. Having a spade: Will receive some money. Using a spade: Stay on beaten track when out alone. 198

6 Spear—A good sign of wordly success and renown to come soon. Using a spear to catch fish: Abundance. A spear stabbing a fish: Rapid success of hopes. 762

7 Spending—Be careful to economize for a time; money matters will improve after a long while. Spending money in traveling: Frivolity. Spending money on family: Loss of good friends. Spending money for food: Will have happy days. Spending money foolishly: Be careful and economize for a short time. Spending money for a charity: Affairs will improve after a long while. 250

8 Spider—Good fortune is on the way, especially in your business ventures. Seeing a spider in the morning: Will have a lawsuit. A spider spinning a web: Domestic happiness. Being bitten by a spider: Marital unfaithfulness. 278

2 Spring—To dream of a spring in winter is an omen of a wedding soon to take place. Drinking a glass of spring water: Small disputes. A dry spring: Poverty and sickness. A spring of gushing water: Wealth and honor. 173

6 Spy—Adventure will come your way; but someone will have a protective influence over you, and you will meet with no harm. 915

3 Squirrels—Be content. Hard work is your lot, so stay cheerful, and persevere. A woman dreaming of a squirrel: Will be surprised while doing wrong. A young girl dreaming of a squirrel will be untrue to her boyfriend. Killing a squirrel: Will acquire a few new friends. Being bitten by a squirrel: Will marry for money. 813

4 Stable—A good companion will be yours for life. Racetrack's stables: Will make much money. 875

9 Stain—To dream of stained garments presages scandal to their wearer. Several stains on garments of ladies: Laziness. Stains on children's clothes: Children will grow up healthy. Stains on a tablecloth: Disappointments of own hopes. A stain on a woman's breast: Illness to come. 648

5 Stairs—To decend a staircase means your wish will be granted; to tumble down them means the reverse. Very high stairs: Will be jilted by your lover. 824

7 Stamps—Association with someone in a high official position will cause you some worry but much gain.

Buying stamps: Misery. Collecting stamps: Great joy. Giving stamps away: Reconciliation with an enemy. 214

4 Star—Shooting stars: Great and good fortune. Seeing stars at night: Important and very beneficial event to come. An unusually bright star: Losses in business. A star shining into a room: Danger of death for head of family. Stars falling from the sky: Disaster. 157

6 Statues—To dream of seeing statues moving signifies riches. 645

3 Stealing—A gift of jewelry will be offered you. 192

1 Steeple—An unfortunate dream unless you are climbing one, which means achievement of your greatest wish. 208

9 Stockings—To see light-colored socks on: Sorrow. Dark-colored socks: Pleasure. A hole in one: You will lose something. Woolen socks: Affluence. Silk socks: Hardships. Torn stockings: Financial losses. Taking off stockings: Good days ahead. Putting on stockings: Honor and profit. Knitting stockings: Will meet with opposition. 297

6 Stones—Angry discussions and new surroundings. Walking on stones: Will have to suffer for a while. Of precious stones: Good business. Buying precious stones: Good earnings. Admiring precious stones: Sickness. Wearing precious stones: Abundance. Losing precious stones: Misfortune. Selling precious stones: Loss of money. 150

2 Stork—A promise of ill tidings. Two storks together: Will marry and have good children. Seeing a stork in the winter: Big disaster ahead. A stork flying in the air: Robbers are close by. 695

4 Storm—Another obstacle dream. Watching a storm: Unhappiness in love. Being in a storm: Separation of loved ones. A storm hitting own house: Discovery of a secret. A storm demolishing your house: People with evil intention are nearby. 328

4 Strangers—A dream of contrary meaning. If you dream of strangers, the more of them you see, the better. It means the assistance of kind friends who will help you on in life. 202

4 Strangle—To dream of being strangled: Trouble caused

203

by the one you dream of. To think you are strangling someone: Your wish will come true. 913

9 Straw—A warning of difficulties. You must work hard in order to overcome your troubles. Several bundles of straw: Joy and honor. Straw in a stable: Happiness in domestic matters. Burning straw: Will attend big festivities. 513

6 String—Strong powers of attraction are yours, which you must use carefully. A voyage is in your near future. 123

1 Struggle—To dream of struggling to escape from something or someone means great improvement in your health and strength. Struggling with a wild animal: Good fortune. Struggling with a woman: Will suffer through own foolish actions. 829

3 Sugar—This means sweet words and a happy future. Cooking with sugar: Will be cheated by friends. Putting sugar on fruit: Will have a happy future. 912

7 Suicide—A sign of an overstraining mind and a warning to change your surroundings for a time. Planning to commit suicide: Troubles were brought on by yourself. Having committed suicide: Unhappiness. Thinking of committing suicide: Must conform yourself to real life. A woman committing suicide: Opposition in love and despair. A husband or wife committing suicide: Permanent change in surroundings. 799

8 Summons—Adverse criticism and scandal will vex you. 323

9 Sun—Success in money matters and love. A beautiful sunset: Will be told false news. A woman dreaming of a beautiful sunset: A child will be born. The sun shining on your bed: Apprehension. The sun peeping through the clouds: Troubles will soon vanish. 702

3 Sunrise—This is a token of ambitions soon to be realized, while to dream of watching the sunset signifies the reverse. 912

1 Surf—You will need all your tact to avoid the attentions of an unwelcome admirer. 631

9 Surgeon—The slight illness of a friend will cause a deeper relationship between you. Being a surgeon: Joy and profit. 270

204

3 Swan—A good omen, but it only affects your business affairs. A white swan: Riches and good standing in life. A black swan: Domestic troubles and sorrow. Killing a swan: Business affairs need care. 246

6 Swearing—Bad language in a dream is always unfortunate, whether you are yourself to blame or someone else. 249

7 Sweetheart—To dream that your lover is beautiful and pleasing to you is a good omen; but be cautious if you dream he or she is fickle and changeable. 925

8 Swimming—Hard work confronts you; but if you swim to shore or reach your objectives, then you will succeed in the end. Swimming on your back: Will have a bad quarrel. Swimming in a pool: Success. Swimming and reaching your objective: Will be successful in everything. 143

5 Swoon—To dream you see a person swoon is unfortunate to the maid. To the married it is a sign they will become rich and prosperous. 158

8 Swords—All sharp-edged weapons or tools indicate bad news. Being wounded by a sword: Great danger is ahead. A broken sword: Deep discouragement. Wounding another with a sword: Good results in your business. Wounded by an acquaintance's sword: Will receive a service. Blood coming from a sword wound: Will receive a great favor. 953

T

4 Table—It is not fortunate to be seated at a table in your dream; but it is fortunate to see others thus seated. A banquet table: Enjoyment in life. A table with a marble top: Will have a comfortable life. A broken table: Misery and poverty. Breaking a table: Loss of fortune. An empty table: Will fall into poverty. Sitting at a table with sweetheart: Triumph over enemies. 346

3 Tailor—To a girl this dream signifies that she will marry an inferior. A male dreaming about a tailor: Exercise caution in business ventures. Being a tailor: Change of surroundings. Ordering clothes from a tailor: Joy without profit. 309

8 Talk—Talking too much: Will be exposed to some malicious plans. Talking with friends: Will come out of present peril. Talking to parents: Will be granted what you ask for. Talking to a sweetheart: Beware of jealous friends. Talking to your superior: Will become a victim and suffer humiliation. 214

7 Tapestry—Great enjoyment will come to you from small causes. Admiring tapestry: Abuse of confidence. Buying tapestry: Enjoyment will come to you. 142

8 Taxi—Hasty news will be sent to you; be on guard against false information. Riding in a taxi: Will have success in your business. Calling a taxi: New interests and surroundings. Escaping from the path of an oncoming taxi: Avoid rivals. 269

7 Tea—To dream that you are making or drinking tea is a warning of many small difficulties ahead. Persevere and all will go well. Drinking tea: Domestic unhappiness. Tea grounds: Will have many social duties. Tea bags: Will be disappointed in a love affair. 124

6 Teacher—If the dreamer is teaching, an invitation to a solemn occasion is portended; if being taught, anger about a trifling slight will vex him. 501

8 Tears—A sign of contrary meaning. Happiness awaits you. Crying: Will receive a gift. Children shedding tears: Recovery of money due you. Sweethearts shedding tears: Will have consolation. 404

5 Tease—Your secret hopes will be discovered and much discussed, yet you will gain them in the end. Teasing a dog: Will have good earnings. Being teased by friends: Will be offended by enemies. Being teased by sweetheart: You are deeply in love. 491

4 Teeth—It is always unfortunate to dream about your teeth; watch your health. A gold tooth: Corruption and sorrow. Infected teeth: Must give much explanation to other people. Having dirty teeth: Prosperity. Not brushing teeth: Faithful friends. Having teeth pulled: Finan-

cial losses. Teeth falling out: Death. Losing teeth in a fight: Loss of a relative. Having teeth knocked out: Sudden misfortune. Brushing teeth: Misery. 408

9 Telegram—It is more fortunate to receive a telegram than to send one, but neither event is a happy omen. Sending a business telegram: Decline in business. Receiving a business telegram: Will collect money past due you. 135

1 Telephone—Your curiosity will be satisfied. Making a telephone call: Advantages in business. Receiving a telephone call: Postponement of a date. Talking long distance on the telephone: Happiness. Being without a phone: Desires will be realized. 325

1 Telescope—You are apt to exaggerate your troubles. Cares will lessen if they are faced cheerfully. 307

3 Temple—A foreign temple is a portent of curious experiences to be yours before long. Discretion will bring you a big reward. 390

7 Temptation—Obstacles are barring your way to what is rightfully yours; guard your tongue and your good sense will surmount all difficulties. 124

5 Tent—You will find great pleasure in helping the love affairs of some youthful friend of yours. Living in a tent with family: Will undergo great changes in life. Living in a tent with sweetheart: Arguments over love. A military camp of tents: Will take a tiresome trip. 257

5 Theater—To dream that you witness a performance at the theater is a warning of treachery from someone you trust. Be cautious in discussing your plans, otherwise you will lose money. 617

6 Thimble—It is considered very fortunate for a woman to dream that she has lost her thimble. 159

4 Thirst—An obstacle dream: If you satisfy your thirst you will overcome your troubles. 463

2 Thread—To wind thread denotes wealth gained by thrift; to break it, hard times. To unravel knotted thread means a mystery will be solved. 346

9 Thunder—A thunderstorm is a sign of great difficulties in store for you. Like all obstacle dreams, it depends upon what happens in your dream. Lightning following thunder: Death of a friend. Being hit by lightning fol-

lowed by thunder: A woman who is overly sexual. 324

5 Ticket—Good tidings long expected will come at last. 212

6 Tickle—A misunderstanding will be cleared up. If the tickle is in the nose or throat so that you sneeze, you will surely be asked to lend money. 897

5 Tiger—Another obstacle dream. If you are caught by a wild beast, look out for heavy losses. A tiger performing at a circus: Will have helpful friends. A tiger in a cage at the zoo: Death of a prominent person. Hearing a tiger roar: Will suffer grief. 275

7 Tin—A dream signifying that counterfeit friendship will be taken for true. Test your friends before you trust them. 205

3 Toad—Loss and difficulties are shown; but if the creature hops away, hard work may save the situation. Catching toads: A self-inflicted injury will come. Killing toads: A false friend is nearby. Stepping on a toad: Friends will desert you when needed most. 912

5 Tobacco—Your fancied troubles will soon vanish, like smoke. A tobacco shop: A lot of gossip behind your back. Smoking a cigarette: You are squandering money. Women dreaming of smoking cigarettes: Troubles will soon vanish. 716

4 Toboggan—You will soon be involved in someone else's affairs so deeply that it will be difficult for you to extricate yourself. Be careful of every step. 913

9 Tomatoes—A portent of comfortable circumstances, which you will attain by your own efforts. 567

6 Tombs—To dream that you are walking among tombs foretells marriages; to dream that you are ordering your own tomb denotes that you will shortly be married; but to see a tomb fall to ruins denotes sickness and trouble to your family. To dream that you, with another person, are admiring tombs, denotes your future partner to be very suitable for you. To dream you are inspecting the tombs of the illustrious dead denotes your speedy advancement to honor and wealth. 437

5 Toothache—You will have much to be grateful for in a letter from a distant friend. Child having a toothache: Happiness over letter from an old friend. Having a

persisting toothache: Fortune in the future. Receiving relief from a toothache: Love quarrels. 130

1 Torch—This signifies that if you will hold the light of reason to your troubles you will quickly see your way out of them. Woman holding torches: Will fall in love. Holding a flaming torch: A secret will be revealed to you. 136

6 Tornado—A dream warning you against strife in your home or in business. It will surely bring disaster in either. A furious tornado: Loss of friends. A mild tornado: Will have disaster in own affairs. Damages caused by a tornado: Honesty will bring victory for you. 123

3 Torpedo—A presage of love at first sight which will completely alter your life. A torpedo exploding: You are surrounded by envious people. A torpedo hitting a target: Will have joy with children. 831

9 Torture—To dream of being tortured signifies domestic bliss. Torturing animals: Big money losses. Lovers torturing each other: You are unreasonable. 639

3 Towel—You will undergo a brief illness but will recover very quickly. 219

9 Tower—The higher you ascend, the greater your loss will be. It is an obstacle dream. 243

7 Toys—This dream indicates that your family will be very clever and successful. 897

9 Traffic—Many friends and some public dignity are promised. An accident in traffic: Loss of money. Others being hurt in a traffic accident: Will undergo persecution. Being stopped by a traffic officer: You enjoy an active life. 999

8 Trains—Traveling on a train alone: A lawsuit will be ruled in your favor. Traveling on a train with your family: Advantages in life. A cargo train: Will meet a pleasant person. 215

5 Tramp—An absent friend is thinking of you. A letter from that friend is on its way. 302

6 Travel—Difficulties in your business ventures. Success depends upon hard work. Traveling alone: Will avoid unpleasant events. Traveling with loved ones: Delays in personal matters. Traveling in a carriage: Will enjoy a

large fortune. Traveling in a car: Happiness and family love. Traveling on a horse: Will have dealings with obstinate people. Traveling to foreign countries: Consider the results before acting. 915

8 Treasure—It is a most unfortunate omen to dream that you have discovered a treasure. Beware of treachery among those you trust. Finding a hidden treasure: Danger. Finding a treasure chest: Inheritance. Digging for a treasure: Disgrace. Stealing a treasure: Beware of double cross from those you now trust. 854

4 Trees—If you dream of trees in full leaf, it is a very fortunate omen, for nature is kind to you. If you see a tree cut down, then expect loss in business. To dream of climbing trees is a certain omen of hard work and little luck, whatever else happens in your dream. Falling out of a tree: Loss of employment. A barren tree: Someone is cheating you. Heavily ladened fruit trees: Riches and fortune in business. Blossoming trees: Joys and sweet satisfaction. A Christmas tree: Joy and happiness. Escaping from a forest fire: Will have an unusual accident. 832

6 Trial—You have an admirer whose merits you have not hitherto valued. You would be wise to study and develop this friendship. Being on trial: Will enjoy lifelong security. Being unjustly accused on trial: You are enjoying much passion. Being on trial for wrongdoings against a woman: Will receive bad news. Being on trial for wrongdoings against a man: Hard days ahead. 636

3 Trunk—A traveler will return from abroad. A wish will be granted in connection with the home. 264

3 Trouble—If you find yourself in trouble in your dream, it is a sign of change in residence. A married person being in trouble: Disaster is ahead for you. A single person being in trouble: Shame and sorrow. A girl being in trouble: Will have many sweethearts. A widow being in trouble: She will be pregnant. Facing trouble: Will have success. Avoiding trouble: Troubles will come to you. 435

8 Trousers—This dream signifies flirtations to the married and quarrels to the single dreamer. Having a hole in trousers: Flirtations with a married woman. A single girl

210

dreaming of a man's trousers: Will have quarrels. 242

3 Tug—Merry company and a wedding between middle-aged lovers. 102

5 Tunnel—Another obstacle dream. If you escape from the tunnel, all will go well. Driving a car through the tunnel: Unsatisfactory business undertaking. Going through a tunnel on a train: You have many false friends. 284

1 Turkey—Trouble with your friends, with your husband or wife, and your business customers or associates. Visiting the country of Turkey: Loss of all possessions. Killing a turkey: Infidelity. Eating turkey: Great joy. Carving a turkey: Quarrels with business partners. 730

6 Turtle—These creatures are omens of unfulfilled wishes or ambitions. With hard work you may succeed. Catching a sea turtle: A mystery will be solved. Eating a sea turtle: You have secret enemies. Drinking bouillon made from a sea turtle: Long life and success. 204

4 Twins—Babies are not considered fortunate omens in a dream, though young children are favorable. Twin babies make the omen more dangerous. 931

U

7 Ugliness—It is a fortunate omen to dream of an ugly person. 403

9 Undertaker—This is one of the contrary dreams and denotes a wedding. An undertaker removing a body. from the house: Happiness. Going to an undertaker's parlor: Will live a long life. 639

1 Undress—If you dream of being in public not fully dressed, be cautious of word and act; gossip will distress you. Undressing in privacy: A guarded secret will be discovered. Undressing before others: People are talking badly behind your back. Undressing in a hotel room:

Satisfactory love life. Husband and wife undressing in same room: Business affairs will go badly. Undressing in public: Disaster and worry will come to you. 856

1 Unfaithful—A dream of contrary meaning. All will go well with your future. If you dream that your husband, wife, or lover is unfaithful, there is a lot of good fortune in store for you. 982

4 Unhappy—A dream of contrary meaning. The more miserable you are in your dream, the better for you in real life. A woman being unhappy with her husband: Receive invitation by prominent person. Sweethearts being unhappy with each other: Doubt and distrust without reason. 409

7 Uniform—This dream signifies a change for the better, a promotion which will bring you good fortune in love as well as a better position. A member of own family in uniform: Glory and dignity. Wearing a uniform: Valor and prominence. Woman wearing uniforms for her business: You are too arrogant. 304

9 University—A sign that you are fortunate in your talents and in your friends. 153

4 Unmarried—For married people to dream of being single again is a sign of danger from jealousy and gossip. Be sure and trust each other, and all will be well. A single person desiring to get married: Will receive good news. An old bachelor wanting to get married: Will marry a healthy woman. An old maid wanting to get married: She will marry a young man. 805

1 Uproar—To dream of scenes and confusion and uproar signifies a decision which will be arrived at soon after long delay; it will be as you wish. 109

3 Vaccination—You are in danger of giving more affection than its recipient is worth; keep a guard on your

212

heart and obey your head. Children being vaccinated: Beware of squandering money. Being vaccinated by a nurse: Will have opposition in life. Others being vaccinated: Enemies will occupy your time. 102

3 Valentine—This predicts news of an old sweetheart who still thinks much of you. Sending valentines: Will lose an opportunity to make money. Receiving a valentine: Will take advantage of available opportunities. A sweetheart receiving a valentine: Victory over enemies. A sweetheart sending a valentine: Contradiction. 534

5 Valley—To dream that you are in a valley is a warning of ill health. Do not overtax yourself or your powers. A beautiful valley: Be cautious in all your affairs. Crossing a green valley: Contentment and ease. A barren valley: Dissatisfaction and want. 248

3 Vampire—A bad omen. You will marry for money and find it a bad bargain. Fighting with a vampire: Will receive good news. 525

2 Vase—You are apt to give too much thought to appearances; try to value useful qualities in one who loves you. 362

4 Vault—To dream that you are in a vault is a sign of difficulties in your path. If eventually you escape, all will be well once more; but be careful of undertaking new ventures. 832

8 Vegetables—Hard work for little result will surely follow a dream of these green offerings of nature. Persevere, and do not lose heart. 152

3 Veil—To dream that you are wearing a veil is a bad omen, even if it is a bridal veil, unless you remove it before the dream is concluded. Opening a veil or folding it: Favorable circumstances. 453

5 Velvet—A fortunate dream, but it will depend largely upon the color. Sewing with velvet: Will receive assistance from a friend. 329

9 Vermin—Nearly all unpleasant dreams of this sort go by contraries and mean good luck. 612

5 Village—This dream promises an offer of a change which will prove most important to your future. A village burning: Will make a pilgrimage. The village where you live: Improved conditions in the future. 392

7 Villain—To dream of a ruffian or villain denotes a letter or present from one you love. 313

4 Vinegar—Useless toil. Fresh vinegar: Sickness. Cooking with vinegar: Disaster in your industry. Making vinegar sauce for a salad: Will participate in an orgy. Eating foods made with vinegar: Poverty. Buying vinegar: Abundance. 193

5 Vine—One of the most fortunate dreams, especially if the vine is in full leaf. You may have to work hard, but success is certain to come. 140

3 Violets—Very fortunate for the lover. Picking violets: Will have a happy marriage. Buying violets: Will have a lawsuit. 399

4 Violence—If you are violently attacked, it portends better times for you; to see violence to others means festivities and cheerful friends. 580

9 Violin—To hear sweet music is a sign of social and domestic happiness, but beware if one of the strings should break, for it foretells a quarrel. Playing a violin: Bliss between husband and wife. Playing a violin in solitude: Will attend a funeral. 594

3 Virgin—To dream of an effigy of the virgin is a warning of threatened trouble; be reserved and on guard with all but trusted friends. Being introduced to a virgin: Pleasures without secrecy. Realizing a person is not a virgin: Much personal grief. Knowing a virgin with many boyfriends: Be on guard and don't trust friends. A sick person dreaming of a virgin saint: Will recover completely. 102

8 Visit—To pay a visit means obstacles to your plans; to receive a visit from a friend signifies travel for pleasure. A doctor visiting you: Will have advantages over others. Visiting your friends: Your situation is not good. Receiving business visits: Will have sorrow that will cause tears. 376

5 Visitors—It is not a good omen to dream of visitors; the more people there are around you, the greater will your business difficulties be. 104

9 Voice—To hear people speaking is a dream of contrary meaning. If they appear to be happy and merry, then expect reverses in business and many worries. 234

1 Volcano—To dream of a volcano foretells great disagreements, family jars, and lover's quarrels. To a man of commerce it portends dishonest servants and a robbery of some sad convulsion. To lovers it is a sign that all deceit, intrigue, and base designs on one side or the other will be exploded; and the designer will be branded with the contempt and execration so justly deserved. 901

7 Vomit—To dream of vomiting, whether of blood, meat, or phlegm, signifies to the poor, profit, and to the rich, hurt. Vomiting wine: Will lose in real estate dealings. Vomiting after drinking liquor: Will easily spend money won in gambling. 358

8 Voting—You must be more confident if you wish to fulfill your hopes; you are favored but too difficult. 492

3 Voyage—A message from a distance is soon to be received. Taking a voyage to a foreign country with relatives: Fortune. Taking a voyage alone: Good times ahead. 901

2 Vulture—Dangerous enemies. To kill a vulture indicates conquest of misfortune; To see one devouring its prey—your troubles will cease and fortune smile upon you. 839

W

6 Wade—It is considered a good sign for lovers if they dream of wading in clear water, if the water is muddy or rough, disillusion will soon come. 564

9 Wager—This portends losses. Act cautiously. Accepting a wager: You are very confused in your thinking. Losing a wager: Will acquire wealth dishonorably. 819

1 Wages—To receive them, danger of loss; to pay them, money from legacy. Being refused payment of wages:

Will have lawsuit. Receiving your own wages: Loss. 280

3 Wailing—To dream you hear wailing and weeping from unseen voices is a bad sign of loss of someone dear to you. 903

4 Waiter—To dream of being at a table where you are waited upon is a sign of an invalid whom you will have to nurse shortly. 328

1 Wallet—This portends important news from an unexpected source. An empty wallet: Fortune. A full wallet: Discovery of a secret. Finding a woman's wallet: Will receive a small amount of money. 217

5 Walking—Small worries that will vanish if you tackle them bravely. Walking forward: Will have a change in fortune that will bring profit. Walking backward: Loss of money. Walking at night: Annoyance. Walking along muddy streets: Will be molested. Walking on crutches: Losses in gambling. Walking in water: Triumph and success. 203

4 Walls—These are obstacles and, if you climb over them, all will be well for you. But you will have to face hard work. A wall falling down: Personal and business losses. Climbing a wall with a ladder: Joy. 562

1 Waltz—An admirer is concealing his affection from you. Be kind. Dancing a waltz: Good humor and happiness. Waltzing with husband or wife: Sickness. Waltzing with lover or sweetheart: An admirer is concealing his affections. 208

6 War—To dream of war and affairs of war signifies trouble and danger. Watching a war: Misfortune. Being in a war: Danger of illness. 735

9 Warts—To see warts on your hands in a dream indicates that as many sums of money as you can see warts will come to you; on the hands of others, warts signify rich friends. 612

5 Wasps—Enemies among those whom you trust. 923

1 Watch—A journey by land. Watching someone you don't care for: The moon will bring rain. Watching from a high window: People are spying on you. Wearing a wristwatch: Loss in business. A young girl receiving a

gift of a wristwatch: Will receive marriage proposal. Buying a wristwatch: Joy and tranquility. 154

4 Water—Drawing water from a well: Will be tormented by wife. Bathing in clear water: Good health. Bathing in dirty water: Sickness. Drinking water from a glass of water: Prompt matrimony. Drinking ice water: Prosperity and triumph over enemies. Breaking a glass of ice water: Death of mother and health for children. Falling in to water and waking immediately: Entire life ruined by woman you marry. Water flooding house and ruining furniture: Will quarrel with enemies. A river flooding: Will receive good news concerning pending lawsuits. Falling into rough water from a boat: Loss of fortune. Pouring water on fire: Will lose lawsuit. Water on your head: Profit. Swimming pool water: Fortune. 526

8 Waterfall—An invitation to a place of amusement. You are observed and gossiped about. 583

3 Web—Travel and gratified wishes. A sign of wealth. 534

3 Wedding—A dream of contrary: Expect trouble in your family circle. Attending a sister's wedding: Big danger. Attending a brother's wedding: Will make money. Attending the wedding of a son: Approaching money. Attending the wedding of a daughter: Wealth. Attending the wedding of a widow: Will make abundant money. 183

6 Wedding ring—A parting. To take it off in a dream means the parting you see will be final. 492

7 Weeping—To dream one weeps is joy and mirth. Weeping along with grief: Will enjoy pleasures. 340

7 Well—To draw water means success and profit; to fall in; danger that can scarcely be avoided. A well full of clear water: Luck and prosperity. An overflowing well: Death of children and losses in business. A dry well: Will have some damages in own affairs. Throwing someone in a well of water: Death for the dreamer. 529

1 Whale—Misunderstandings that will be cleared up in time. A delayed wedding is indicated. 121

9 Wheels—Property will be left to you. A broken wheel: New interest and surroundings. The wheel of a mill: You are faced with great danger. The wheel of a car:

217

Unhappiness, in married life. A gambling wheel: Will suffer much embarrassment. 324

2 Whip—An affectionate message. Good tidings will come shortly. 101

2 Whirland—Beware of dangerous reports. 506

6 Whirlpool—Advice will be given to you well worth following. An inheritance in the future. 924

8 Whispering—A rumor will be confirmed. Financial gains are at hand. 395

6 Whistle—To hear scandal is being spread about you; to dream that you are whistling merrily indicates sad news coming. 591

1 Whiskey—This is a foreboding of ill; it signifies debts and difficulties. Offering whiskey to relatives: Be on the lookout for a double cross. Offering whiskey to mate: Realization of high ambitions. Offering whiskey to a lover: Temptation will come to you. Being offered a drink of whiskey: A mystery will be solved. 406

7 Wife—Of your own wife: Must control your passions. Taking a wife: Accomplishment of desires. Arguing with your wife: Will have a quarrel lasting several days. Wife being beautifully dressed: Warning of trouble. Own wife undressing: You must mend your ways of life. Own wife being naked: She is unfaithful to you. Wife being in a bathtub: Misfortune in love affairs. A wife dreaming of being married to another man: Sudden separation, or death, of husband. 574

3 Wig—Two proposals to come. The darker man loves you best. A woman wearing a blond wig: Will have many admirers. A man wearing a light colored wig: Will be refused by several women. A man wearing a dark colored wig: Will be loved best by one woman. A woman wearing a white wig: Will marry a rich man. A woman wearing a dark wig: Should mend her ways in life. A woman wearing a brunette wig: Will marry a poor man. 183

2 Widow—To dream that you are conversing with a widow foreshadows that you will lose your wife by death. For a woman to dream that she is a widow portends the infidelity of her husband. For a young woman

to dream of being a married widow: Prognosticates that her lover will abandon her. 353

7 Widower—To dream that you are one denotes the sickness of your wife. For a young woman to dream she is married to a widower denotes much trouble with false lovers, but she will be happily married at last to a man of good sense and good conduct. 349

5 Wind—Good news is coming; the stronger the gale of wind, the sooner you may expect good fortune. Battling with the wind: Attending success and untrying energy. The wind blowing own hat away: Future conditions will improve. The wind turning umbrella inside out: Joy. A ship battling against the wind: Will discover a secret. A wind blowing away a boat sail: Approaching troubles. The wind sinking or destroying a vessel. Money will come easily. 923

5 Windmill—Some gain but only of small character. Windmill stopped: Will receive inheritance from a rich relative. 428

7 Window—An open one: Success will attend you. A closed one: You will suffer desertion by your friends. A broken window: Be suspicious of robbery by friends. Jumping from a window: Will have a lawsuit. Climbing from a window on ladder: Will become bankrupt. A very big window: Very good success in business. Seeing people kissing in front of a window: Death of a pet bird. Viewing something from a window: Victory over enemies. Throwing things from a window: Advancement within own position. 943

6 Wine—A sign of comfortable home life, it does not refer to business and love matters. Drinking wine: Will receive many good things. Spilling wine: Someone will be injured and lose much blood. Buying wine: New employment. Receiving wine as a gift: Doomed for disappointment. Making wine: Good results in all affairs. Getting drunk on wine: Big success. 195

8 Winter—To dream of a wintry scene with snow on the ground is an omen of prosperity but to dream of summer in winter is the reverse. Being sick during the winter: Relatives are envious of you. Living through a severe winter: Will receive a gift. 215

1 Witness—To dream of being a witness in court is a warning to be on your guard against false accusations that will be made against you. Witnesses testifying on your behalf: Good results in business affairs. Being a witness for someone else: A big catastrophe is ahead. 910

9 Witch—An ill omen in every way. Being scared by a witch: Abuse of confidence. Becoming nervous because of a witch: Damages to your health. 360

2 Wolf—Enmity. To kill one, success. To pursue one, dangers overcome. Pursued by one, danger. A wolf running: Will have dealing with smart and treacherous enemies. 794

3 Woman—To see many women is a dream of wealth and renown; a beautiful woman, a happy marriage; an ugly woman, worry and vexation, a woman's voice changes in position. A woman lying on a bed: Security. A beautiful naked woman: Big unhappiness. A woman making advances to a man: Jealousy. A man dreaming of a woman of ill repute: Serious disaster ahead. Being a woman of ill repute: Will suffer humiliation. A woman dreaming of being a man: Birth of a son who brings honor to family. A woman with white hair: Dignity and distinction. A woman with long beautiful blond hair: Will enjoy a happy life. A married woman dreaming of being pregnant: Will receive happy news. 912

7 Worms—Danger of infectious diseases. Destroying worms: Will have money. Worms being on plants: Will receive unexpected money. Worms being on own body: Big riches. 169

6 Wounds—To dream that you are wounded is a favorable dream. 303

6 Wreck—Threatened trouble to health and business. Broken pieces of a ship after a wreck: Peril of death. People in a raft after a wreck: Must endure trouble before realizing desires. People being saved from a wreck: Danger in business affairs. An automobile wreck: Dishonor. Being killed in an automobile wreck: Unhappiness in family. Being injured in an automobile wreck: Joy and profit. Family being killed in automobile

wreck: Will require welfare aid. Friends being in an automobile wreck: Will suffer humiliation. 627

9 Wrestling—An unfortunate dream for it means loss of money through ill-health. 243

3 Wrinkles—Compliments and social pleasures. Having wrinkles in own face: Long life after a sickness. An elderly person without wrinkles: Compliments and social pleasures. Being wrinkled at middle age. You are very gullible. 715

1 Writing—Written or printed matter is always an unfavorable omen. If you dream that you are writing, you are creating difficulties by your own actions. 316

8 Yacht—To see one means good luck if the sea is smooth; to be in one, ambition is realized unless the sea be rough which means disappointment. 152

2 Yard—News of an engagement among your friends. The wedding will bring you a new admirer. Working in a yard: An admirer will soon be married. Having a well-kept yard: Family arguments. A ship yard: Fortune. A lumber yard: Riches. Planting things in a yard: Joy. Picking flowers from a yard: Death. 281

4 Yarn—You will receive a fine present from an unexpected quarter. A man dreaming of yarn: Will attain business success. A woman dreaming of yarn: Will have plenty of money. 724

3 Yawning—An obstacle dream but not of serious importance. 309

9 Yearning—To dream of a strong feeling of longing means that you will be confidently indifferent where you would like to be kind. 394

9 Yell—To dream of hideous yells and noises is a sign of peace after strife. An introduction will alter your plans.

Yelling yourself: Family quarrels. Hearing others yelling: Will have strife followed by peace. 819

1 Yield—To dream of yielding to persuasive words is a warning against pride; do not believe flatterers. Yielding to persuasive words: False friend is near by. Lovers yielding to persuasive stories: Danger in love affairs. 415

7 Young—To dream that you have become young again is a favorable omen. But the change for the better will not last long. 340

Z

7 Zebra—Disagreement with friends. A zebra being attacked by wild animals: Your honor is in danger. A zebra being fed at a zoo: Ingratitude. 412

4 Zeppelin—A dream signifying an ambition far beyond your reach. Being in a zeppelin: Will be molested. Coming down in a zeppelin: Will receive good news. Watching a zeppelin moving slowly: People are meddling in your affairs. 346

2 Zoo—Although wild animals in captivity are not generally good omens in themselves, it is considered fortunate to visit a zoological gardens. Going to the zoo alone: Will be molested. Going to zoo with family and children: Good hopes for the future. Going to the zoo with sweetheart: Danger of misfortune. 524

LUCKY DAYS

In every human mind is a spark of the gambling instinct—a desire to take chances that afford the thrill of gaining or losing in such a venture. Life itself is a speculation: a child is born—perhaps it will live, perhaps it will not; a merchant opens a business—perhaps he will succeed, perhaps he won't; an aviator takes a long flight—perhaps he will make a safe landing, perhaps he will not. The desire to take chances is innate in all humanity, primitive or civilized.

Emerson said, "Astrology is Astronomy brought to earth and applied to the affairs of men." Astrology, the oldest science in the world, has outlined the proper courses for people to follow for many thousands of years. "There is a time and a place for all things," and no more practical science in the world can be applied to mankind's daily affairs than the sciences of astrology and numerology.

Ptolemy, a great astrologer and philosopher of ancient times, has said, "Judgment must be regulated by thyself, as well as by the science—it is advantageous to make choice of days and hours at a time constituted by the nativity."

Although the author of this book does not recommend or encourage promiscuous gambling in any form, he is mindful that so long as human beings remain constituted as they are, they are going to indulge in some form of speculation, whether for pleasure and amusement; starting businesses; taking trips; buying and selling stocks, real estate, commodities; and so on. Hence, if people MUST speculate, this book will be of value to anyone by showing how to combine the laws that rule and regulate the universe with one's own judgment. You will remember that accurate judgment is also necessary for the success of any enterprise, yet by combining this with the fundamental laws of cause and effect outlined by the science of the universe herein treated, a greater measure of success may be attained than by attempting things at a time that might prove to be very inopportune.

We present this information for what it may be worth. It may appeal to you as a pastime flavored with the thrill of sport, or a test of skill tempered by your judgment. We would have all readers pleased and interested, but none enslaved by it.

For those who have read the contents of this book with interest and wish to test it out for results, we suggest that you keep tabs on the schedule outlined; it will save you considerable money and will bring excellent results.

YOUR FORTUNATE NUMBERS

These methods, based on the science of numerology, are different for every person. The author has spent many years studying the occult meaning of numbers, and although results cannot be guaranteed, many use them with great success.

What You Must Know

FIRST; Learn how to tell magic time, as follows:

Magic Time

A.M. 1-2-3-4-5-6-7-8-9-10-11-12

P.M. 13-14-15-16-17-18-19-20-21-22-23-24

SECOND: Note the day of the week. Monday is 1; Tuesday is 2; Wednesday is 3; Thursday is 4; Friday is 5; Saturday is 6; Sunday is 7.

THIRD: Count the number of letters in your name. *Example:* Jack Brown has four letters in his first name and five in his second name. 4 plus 5 equals 9. This number is always lucky for Jack Brown.

FOURTH: A lucky number is found by combining the values of the day and month in which you were born. *Example:* If you were born on June 25 (June is the sixth

226

month), combine 6 and 25 to get 625 or 67. Add these figures: 6 plus 2 plus 5 equals 13. Add again, 1 plus 3 equals 4. This gives four magic numbers, all with the same strength: 625, 67, 13, 4. Use the one that suits you best. January equals 1; February 2; March 3; April 4; May 5; June 6; July 7; August 8; September 9; October 10; November 11 (or 2); December 12 (or 3).

Four Methods for Using Your Fortunate Numbers

1. THE MAGIC HOUR: Use the number of the day of the week and the number of the hour at which you play or bet. *Example:* Suppose it is 4 P.M. on Friday. See the clock: 4 P.M. is 16 o'clock. Friday is 5. Combine these to make 165 or 75. Then add 1 plus 6 plus 5 equals 12. Add again, 1 plus 2 equals 3. This gives four magic numbers: 165, 75, 12, 3 with the same strength. Use the one that suits you best.

2. STRIKE THE KEYNOTE: Use the number of letters in your name and the hour of play. *Example:* Suppose Jack Brown (9) wants a lucky number at 8 P.M. Combine 9 and 20 to make 920. Add these: 9 plus 2 plus 0 equals 11. Add again, 1 plus 1 equals 2. This gives four magic numbers: 920, 29, 11, 2. Use the one that suits you best.

3. YOUR PINNACLE OF SUCCESS: Use the number of the day on which you were born and the number of the month. *Example:* Suppose you were born on August 24. Combine 24 and 8. This gives 248 or 68. Add 2 plus 4 plus 8 equals 14. Add again, 1 plus 4 equals 5. This gives you four lucky numbers of the same magic power: 248, 68, 14, 5.

4. LADY LUCK METHOD: Count the number of letters in your sweetheart's name and combine with the number of letters in your own name. *Example:* Maybelle Jones (13 letters) and Jack Brown (9 letters) makes 139 or 49. Add these: 1 plus 3 plus 9 equals 13. Add again, 1 plus 3 equals 4. This gives you four lady luck num-

227

bers: 139, 49, 13, 4. Use the one that suits the occasion best.

NOTE: If you want more than one lucky number in a day, combine your lady luck number with the hour. *Example:*At 20 o'clock (8 P.M.), combine Maybelle Jones (13) with Jack Brown (9): 20, 139. Add these to suit your convenience. ALWAYS NOTE THE HOUR. The time figure changes only when the hour changes. Adding, transposing, or combining a magic number does not alter its strength. *Example:* 165, 75, 12 or 3. Also, a zero in a number can be used or not—200, 20, 2.

Astrology indicates the exact periods when you should speculate and when you should not do so. The earth going through the twelve signs of the zodiac forms certain configurations which indicate your prospects in any game of chance. Thus, there are regular periods every year when you may win or lose. It is up to you to make use of this information. For the most accurate reading, your sign has been divided into three sections. This division, by decanate, gives you about ten days, which are influenced by the sun's transits.

LUCKY DAYS — ARIES

For All Those Born Between March 21
and April 20, Any Year

If you were born on March 21, 22, 23, 24, 25, 26, 27, 28, 29, and 30. You may speculate during the following periods, and may expect to win:

January	21	to	31
May	21	to	31
July	23	to	August 3
November	23	to	December 3

From March 21 to 31, you will be tempted to speculate, but you must determine for yourself whether or not this period is fortunate. Do not speculate from June 22 to July 2, September 23 to October 4, and December 22 to January 3 of any year.

If you were born on April 1, 2, 3, 4, 5, 6, 7, 8, 9, and 10. You may speculate during the following periods of any year, and may expect to win:

February	1	to	11
June	1	to	12
August	3	to	14
December	2	to	13

From April 1 to 12, you will also be tempted to speculate, but you must find out for yourself whether or not you can win. Do not speculate from January 2 to 13, July 2 to 14, and October 3 to 15.

If you were born on April 11, 12, 13, 14, 15, 16, 17, 18, 19, and 20. You may speculate during the following periods of any year, and may expect to win:

February	9	to	20
June	10	to	21
August	12	to	23
December	11	to	13

From April 10 to 20, you will also be tempted to speculate, but you must find out for yourself whether or not you can win. Do not speculate from January 12 to 19, from July 13 to 23, and October 14 to 23.

All Aries-born are inclined to take chances between July 22 and August 23. When you speculate in cooperation with others, it would be advisable to have a partner born under one of the following signs:

Aquarius—January 21 to February 19
Gemini—May 22 to June 21
Leo—July 24 to August 23
Sagittarius—November 23 to December 22
Libra—September 24 to October 23

Miscellaneous Things to Observe

Those born between March 21 and March 28 will have better chances in speculation during the new moon.

Those born between March 29 and April 5 will have better chances in speculation during the second quarter of the moon.

Those born between April 6 and April 13 will have better chances in speculation during the full moon.

Those born between April 14 and April 20 will have better chances in speculation during the fourth quarter of the moon.

Nearly all calendars give the four quarters of the moon.

Numerology

According to the science of numerology, the celestial number of Aries is 7. Mars, the ruling planet of this sign, has the number 6 for its numerical value. Combining these two numbers we have 7 plus 6, which equals 13. This number must now be reduced to a single digit. Therefore, 1 plus 3 equals 4. The number 4 is then the key number for all persons born in Aries. Bear this in mind on all occasions. When you buy a ticket of any sort, make sure that the serial number has 4 as the predominating number. Room number 4 in a hotel, a street number containing a 4 or several 4's, horse number 4 in a race, player number 4 in a sport game, a card that totals 4 in a card game, a 4 rolled with dice, 4 on a spin wheel, and so on, are considered fortunate for you.

Illustration: Suppose you have two cards in your hand: a 10-spot and a 3-spot. 10 plus 3 equals 13, and 1 plus 3 equals 4. Therefore, such a hand of cards or any other combination that could be reduced to 4, would be fortunate for you. If you have a combination that totals 31, that would also reduce to 4, because 3 plus 1 equals 4, and so on. Use the same method of reduction to a single digit with other combinations.

To Find Your Best Days for Speculation

Any day of any month that totals 4 is considered fortunate for you. Thus, the 13th, the 22nd, and the 31st of a month are fortunate for you because any of these dates reduced to a single digit make 4. The days of the month that are best for speculation are the 4th, 13th, 22nd, and 31st. However, you should engage in speculation only in your proper months or periods, as explained below.

Proper Hours for Speculation

The proper hour for speculation is when your ruling planet is governing. Refer to your daily paper, almanac, or calendar to find the time of sunrise. Then, count the hours after sunrise. These hours are the same every week, month, and year. Only the time of sunrise changes.

Hours for Speculation: Sunday: 7th, 14th, 21st hour after sunrise. Monday: 4th, 11th, 18th hour after sunrise. Tuesday: 1st, 8th, 15th, 22nd hour after sunrise. Wednesday: 5th, 12th, 19th hour after sunrise. Thursday: 2nd, 9th, 16th, 23rd hour after sunrise. Friday: 6th, 13th, 20th hour after sunrise. Saturday: 3rd, 10th, 17th, 24th hour after sunrise.

*For All Those Born Between April 21 and
May 21, Any Year*

**If you were born on April 21, 22, 23, 24, 25, 26, 27, 28,
29, and 30, and May 1.** You may speculate during the
following periods, and may expect to win:

February	20	to	March 1
June	22	to	July 3
August	24	to	September 4
December	23	to	January 3

From April 21 to May 2, you will also be tempted to
speculate, but you must determine for yourself whether
or not you can win. Do not speculate from January 21
to February 2, from July 24 to August 4, and from October 24 to November 3.

**If you were born on May 2, 3, 4, 5, 6, 7, 8, 9, 10, and
11.** You may speculate during the following periods, and
may expect to win:

January	2	to	12
March	1	to	11
July	2	to	13
September	2	to	14

From May 1 to 12, you will also be tempted to speculate, but you must determine for yourself whether or not
you can win. Do not speculate from February 1 to 11,
from August 2 to 14, and from November 2 to 13.

**If you were born on May 12, 13, 14, 15, 16, 17, 18, 19,
20, and 21.** You may speculate during the following periods, and may expect to win:

January	10	to	20
March	11	to	20
July	12	to	23
September	12	to	23

From May 10 to 21, you will also be tempted to speculate, but you must determine for yourself whether or not you can win. Do not speculate from February 9 to 19, from August 10 to 23, and from November 11 to 23.

All Taurus-born are inclined to take chances between August 24 and September 23. When you speculate in cooperation with others, it would be advisable to have a partner born under one of the following signs:

Pisces—February 20 to March 20
Taurus—April 21 to May 21
Cancer—June 22 to July 23
Virgo—August 24 to September 23
Scorpio—October 24 to November 22
Capricorn—December 23 to January 20

Miscellaneous Things to Observe

Those born between April 21 and April 28 will have better chances in speculation during the new moon.

Those born between April 29 and May 5 will have better chances in speculation during the second quarter of the new moon.

Those born between May 6 and May 14 will have better chances in speculation during the full moon.

Those born between May 15 and May 21 will have better chances in speculation during the fourth quarter of the moon.

Nearly all calendars give the four quarters of the moon.

Numerology

According to the science of numerology, the celestial number of Taurus is 9. Venus, the ruling planet of this sign also has the number 9. Combining these two numbers we have: 9 plus 9 which equals 18. This number must now be reduced to a single digit. Therefore, 1 plus 8 equals 9. The number 9 is the key number for all persons born in Taurus. Bear this in mind on all occasions. When you buy a ticket of any sort, make sure that the serial number has 9 as the predominating number: room number 9 in a hotel, a street number containing a 9 or several 9's, horse number 9 in a race. Player number 9 in a sport game, cards that total 9 in a card game, a 9 rolled with dice, 9 on a spin wheel, and so on, are considered fortunate for you.

Illustration: Suppose you have two cards in your hand: a 4-spot and a 5-spot. Since 4 plus 5 equals 9, such a hand of cards or any other combination that could be reduced to 9 would be fortunate for you. If you should have a combination that totals 36, that would also reduce to 9, and so on. Use the same method of reduction to a single digit with other combinations.

To Find Your Best Days for Speculation

Any day of the month that totals 9 is considered fortunate for you. Thus, the 18th and the 27th are fortunate because these dates reduce to a single digit making 9. The days of the month that are best for speculation are the 9th, 18th, and 27th. However, you should engage in speculation only in your proper months or periods as explained below.

Proper Hours for Speculation

The proper hour for speculation is when your ruling planet is governing. Refer to your daily paper, almanac, or calendar to find the time of sunrise. Then count the hours after sunrise. These hours are the same every week, month, and year, only the time of sunrise changes.

Hours for speculation: Sunday: 2nd, 10th, 16th hour after sunrise. Monday: 6th, 13th, 20th hour after sunrise. Tuesday: 3rd, 8th, 15th, 24th hour after sunrise. Wednesday: 7th, 14th, 21st hour after sunrise. Thursday: 4th, 11th, 18th hour after sunrise. Friday: 1st, 8th, 15th, 22nd hour after sunrise. Saturday: 5th, 12th, 19th hour after sunrise.

LUCKY DAYS — GEMINI

For All Those Born Between May 22 and June 21

If you were born on May 22, 23, 24, 25, 26, 27, 28, 29, 30, and 31, and June 1. You may speculate during the following periods, and may expect to win:

January	21	to	30
March	21	to	31
July	24	to	August 3
September	23	to	October 3

From May 22 to June 1, you will also be tempted to speculate, yet must determine for yourself whether or not you can win. Do not speculate from February 20 to 29, August 24 to September 3, and November 23 to December 2.

If you were born on June 2, 3, 4, 5, 6, 7, 8, 9, 10, and 11. You may speculate during the following periods, and may expect to win:

January	31	to	February 9
April	1	to	10
August	4	to	13
October	4	to	13

From June 2 to 11, you will also be tempted to speculate, yet must determine for yourself whether or not you can win. Do not speculate from March 1 to 10, September 4 to 13, and December 3 to 12.

If you were born on June 12, 13, 14, 15, 16, 17, 18, 19, 20, and 21. You may speculate during the following periods, and may expect to win:

February	10	to	19
April	11	to	20
August	13	to	23
October	14	to	23

From June 12 to 21, you will also be tempted to speculate, yet you must determine for yourself whether or not you can win. Do not speculate from March 11 to 20, September 13 to 23, and December 13 to 22.

All Gemini-born are inclined to take chances between September 24 and October 23. When you speculate in

235

cooperation with others, it would be advisable to have a partner born under one of the following signs:

Aquarius—January 21 to February 19
Aries—March 21 to April 20
Gemini—May 22 to June 21
Leo—July 24 to August 23
Libra—September 24 to October 23
Sagittarius—November 23 to December 22

Miscellaneous Things to Observe

Those born between May 22 and May 29 will have a better chance in speculation during the new moon.

Those born between May 30 and June 6 will have a better chance in speculation during the second quarter of the moon.

Those born between June 7 and June 14 will have a better chance in speculation during the full moon.

Those born between June 15 and June 21 will have a better chance in speculation during the fourth quarter of the moon.

Nearly all calendars give the four quarters of the moon.

Numerology

According to the science of numerology, the celestial number of Gemini is 3. Mercury, the ruling planet of this sign, has the numerical value 4. Combining these two numbers we have 3 plus 4 which equals 7. The number 7 is the key number for all persons born in Gemini. Bear this in mind on all occasions. When you buy a ticket of any sort, make sure that the serial number has 7 as the predominating number. Room number 7 in a hotel, a street number containing a 7 or several 7's, horse number 7 in a race, player number 7 in a sport game, cards that total 7 in a card game, a 7 rolled with dice, 7 on a spin wheel, and so on, are considered fortunate for you.

Illustration: Suppose you have two cards in your hand: a 3-spot and a 4-spot. Since 3 plus 4 equals 7, such a hand of cards or any other combination that could be reduced to 7, would be fortunate for you. If you should have a combination that totals 52, that will also reduce to 7. Use the same method of reduction to a single digit with other combinations.

To Find Your Best Days for Speculation

Any day of any month that totals 7 is considered fortunate for you. Thus, the 16th, and the 25th are fortunate because these dates reduced to a single digit total 7. The days of the month that are best for speculation are the 7th, 16th, and 25th, however, you should engage in speculation only in your proper months or periods as explained below.

Proper Hours for Speculation

The proper hour for speculation is when your ruling planet is governing. Refer to your daily paper, almanac, or calendar to find the time of sunrise, then count the hours after sunrise. These hours are the same every week, month, and year. Only the time of sunrise changes.

Hours for speculation: Sunday: 3rd, 10th, 17th, 24th hour after sunrise. Monday: 7th, 14th, 21st hour after sunrise. Tuesday: 4th, 11th, 18th hour after sunrise. Wednesday: 1st, 8th, 15th, 22nd hour after sunrise. Thursday: 5th, 12th, 19th hour after sunrise. Friday: 2nd, 9th, 16th, 23rd hour after sunrise. Saturday: 6th, 13th, 20th hour after sunrise.

LUCKY DAYS — CANCER

*For All Those Born Between June 22 and
July 23*

If you were born on June 22, 23, 24, 25, 26, 27, 28, 29, 30, and July 1, and 2. You may speculate during the following periods and may expect to win:

February	20	to	29
April	21	to	May 1

237

August	24	to	September 3
October	24	to	November 2

From June 22 to July 2, you will also be tempted to speculate, but you must determine for yourself whether or not you can win. Do not speculate from March 21 to 31, September 24 to October 3, and December 22 to 31.

If you were born on July 3, 4, 5, 6, 7, 8, 9, 10, 11, 12, and 13. You may speculate during the following periods and may expect to win:

March	1	to	10
May	2	to	12
September	4	to	13
November	3	to	12

From July 3 to 13, you will also be tempted to speculate, but you must determine for yourself whether or not you can win. Do not speculate from April 1 to 10, October 4 to 13, and January 1 to 12.

If you were born on July 14, 15, 16, 17, 18, 19, 20, 21, 22, and 23. You may speculate during the following periods, and may expect to win:

March	11	to	20
May	12	to	21
September	14	to	23
November	13	to	22

From July 14 to 23, you will also be tempted to speculate, but you must determine for yourself whether or not you can win. Do not speculate from April 11 to 20, October 13 to 23, and January 10 to 20.

All Cancer-born are inclined to take chances between October 24 and November 22. When you speculate in cooperation with others, it would be advisable to have a partner born under one of the following signs:

Pisces—February 20 to March 20
Taurus—April 21 to May 21
Cancer—June 22 to July 23

Virgo—August 24 to September 23
Scorpio—October 24 to November 22
Capricorn—December 23 to January 20

Miscellaneous Things to Observe

Those born between June 22 and June 29 will have better chances in speculation during the new moon.

Those born between June 30 and July 7 will have better chances in speculation during the second quarter of the moon.

Those born between July 8 and July 17 will have better chances in speculation during the full moon.

Those born between July 18 and July 23 will have better chances in speculation during the fourth quarter of the moon.

Nearly, all calendars give the four quarters of the moon.

Numerology

According to the science of numerology, the celestial number of Cancer is 8. The moon, the ruling planet of this sign, has the numerical value of 3. Combining these two numbers we have 8 plus 3, which equals 11. This must be reduced to a single digit, therefore, 1 plus 1 equals 2. The number 2 is the key number for all persons born in Cancer. Bear this in mind on all occasions. When you buy a ticket of any sort, make sure that the serial number has the predominating number 2 in it. Room number 2 in a hotel, a street number containing a 2 or several 2's, horse number 2 in a race, player number 2 in a sport game, cards that total 2 in a card game, a 2 rolled in dice, 2 on a spin wheel, and so on, are considered fortunate for you.

Illustration: Suppose you have two cards in your hand; a 9-spot and a 2-spot. 9 plus 2 equals 11, and 11 added (1 plus 1) equals 2. Therefore, such a hand, or any other combination of cards that could be added and reduced to 2, would be fortunate for you. If you have a combination that totals 45, it would reduce to 2. Use the same method with other combinations and totals.

To Find Your Best Days for Speculation

Any day of the month that totals 2 is considered fortunate for you. Thus, the 11th, 20th, 29th are fortunate because these dates reduce to a single digit 2. Therefore, the days of the month that are best for speculation are the 2nd, 11th, 20th, and 29th. However, you should engage in speculation only in your proper months or periods as explained below.

Proper Hours for Speculation

The proper hour for speculation is when your ruling planet is governing. Refer to your daily paper, almanac, or calendar to find the time of sunrise; then count the hours after sunrise. These hours are the same every week, month, and year. Only the time of sunrise changes.

Hours for speculation: Sunday: 4th, 11th, 18th hour after sunrise. Monday: 1st, 8th, 15th, 22nd hour after sunrise. Tuesday: 5th, 12th, 19th hour after sunrise. Wednesday: 2nd, 9th, 16th, 23rd hour after sunrise. Thursday: 6th, 13th, 20th hour after sunrise. Friday: 3rd, 10th, 17th hour after sunrise, also the 24th. Saturday: 7th, 14th, 21st hour after sunrise.

LUCKY DAYS — LEO

For All Those Born Between July 24 and August 23

If you were born on July 24, 25, 26, 27, 28, 29, 30, and 31, and August 1, 2, and 3. You may speculate during the following periods, and may expect to win:

March	21	to	31
May	22	to	June 1
September	24	to	October 3
November	23	to	December 2

From July 24 to August 5, you will also be tempted to

240

speculate, but you must determine for yourself whether or not you can win. Do not speculate from January 21 to 30, April 21 to May 2, and October 23 to November 3.

If you were born on August 4, 5, 6, 7, 8, 9, 10, 11, 12, and 13. You may speculate during the following periods and may expect to win:

April	1	to	11
June	2	to	12
October	3	to	13
December	3	to	12

From August 2 to 14, you will also be tempted to speculate, but you must determine for yourself whether or not you can win. Do not speculate from January 31 to February 10, May 2 to 12, and November 2 to 13.

If you were born on August 14, 15, 16, 17, 18, 19, 20, 21, 22, and 23. You may speculate during the following periods and may expect to win:

April	10	to	20
June	12	to	21
October	13	to	23
December	12	to	22

From August 12 to 23, you will also be tempted to speculate, yet must determine for yourself whether or not you can win. Do not speculate from February 12 to 19, May 11 to 21, and November 12 to 22.

All Leo-born are inclined to take chances between November 23 and December 22. When you speculate in cooperation with others, it would be advisable to have a partner born under one of the following signs:

Aquarius—January 21 to February 19
Aries—March 21 to April 20
Gemini—May 22 to June 21
Leo—July 24 to August 23
Libra—September 24 to October 23
Sagittarius—November 23 to December 22

Miscellaneous Things to Observe

Those born between July 24 and July 31 will have better chances in speculation during the new moon.

Those born between August 1 and August 7 will have better chances in speculation during the second quarter of the moon.

Those born between August 8 and August 16 will have better chances in speculation during the full moon.

Those born between August 17 and August 23 will have better chances in speculation during the fourth quarter of the moon.

Nearly all calendars give the four quarters of the moon.

Numerology

According to the science of numerology, the celestial number of Leo is 5. The sun, the ruling planet of this sign, has 9 as its numerical value. Combining these two numbers we have 5 plus 9, which equals 14. This must be reduced to a single digit. Therefore, 1 plus 4 equals 5. The number 5 is the key number for all persons born in Leo. Bear this in mind on all occasions. When you buy a ticket of any sort, make sure that 5 is the predominating number. Room number 5 in a hotel, a street number containing a 5 or several 5's, horse number 5 in a race, player number 5 in a sport game, cards that total 5 in a card game, a 5 rolled with dice, 5 on a spin wheel, and so on, are considered fortunate for you.

Illustration: Suppose you have two cards in your hand: a 2-spot and a 3-spot. Since 2 plus 3 equals 5, such a hand, or any other combination of cards that could be added and reduced to 5, would be fortunate for you. If you have a combination that totals 41, it would also reduce to 5; 4 plus 1 equals 5. Use the same method with other combinations and totals.

To Find Your Best Days for Speculation

Any day of the month that totals 5 is considered fortunte for you. Thus, the 14th or 23rd are fortunate be-

242

cause these dates reduce to a single digit 5. Therefore, the days of the month that are best for speculation for you are the 5th, 14th, and 23rd. However, you should engage in speculation only in your proper periods as explained below.

Proper Hours for Speculation

The proper hour for speculation is when your ruling planet is governing. Refer to your daily paper, almanac, or calendar to find the time of sunrise; then count the hours after sunrise. These hours are the same every week, month, and year. Only the time of sunrise changes.

Hours for speculation: Sunday: 1st, 8th, 15th, 22nd hour after sunrise. Monday: 5th, 12th, 19th hour after sunrise. Tuesday: 2nd, 9th, 16th, 23rd hour after sunrise. Wednesday: 6th, 13th, 20th hour after sunrise. Thursday: 3rd, 10th, 17th, 24th hour after sunrise. Friday: 7th, 14th, 21st hour after sunrise. Saturday: 4th, 11th, 18th hour after sunrise.

LUCKY DAYS — VIRGO

For All Those Born Between August 24 and September 23

If you were born on August 24, 25, 26, 27, 28, 29, 30, and 31, and September 1, 2, and 3. You may speculate during the following periods, and may expect to win:

April	21	to	May 1
June	22	to	July 2
October	24	to	November 3
December	22	to	December 31

From August 23 to September 3, you will also be tempted to speculate, yet must determine for yourself whether or not you can win. Do not speculate from February 20 to 29, May 22 to June 1, and November 23 to December 3.

If you were born on September 4, 5, 6, 7, 8, 9, 10, 11, 12, and 13. You may speculate during the following periods, and may expect to win:

January	1	to	11
May	2	to	12
July	3	to	13
November	2	to	12

From September 3 to 14 you will be tempted to speculate, yet must determine for yourself whether or not you can win. Do not speculate from March 1 to 11, June 2 to 12, and December 2 to 13.

If you were born on September 14, 15, 16, 17, 18, 19, 20, 21, and 22. You may speculate during the following periods and may expect to win:

January	11	to	21
May	11	to	21
July	12	to	23
November	12	to	22

From September 12 to 23, you will be tempted to speculate, but you must determine for yourself whether or not you can win. Do not speculate from March 9 to 20, June 11 to 21, and December 12 to 22.

All Virgo-born are inclined to take chances from December 23 to January 20. When you speculate in cooperation with others, it would be advisable to have a partner born under one of the following signs:

Pisces—February 20 to March 20
Taurus—April 21 to May 21
Cancer—June 22 to July 23
Virgo—August 24 to September 23
Scorpio—October 24 to November 22
Capricorn—December 23 to January 20

Miscellaneous Things to Observe

Those born between August 24 and August 31 will have better chances in speculation during the new moon.

244

Those born between September 1 and September 7 will have better chances of speculation during the second quarter of the moon.

Those born between September 8 and September 17 will have better chances of speculation during the full moon.

Those born between September 18 and September 23 will have better chances in speculation during the fourth quarter of the moon.

Nearly all calendars give the four quarters of the moon.

Numerology

According to the science of numerology, the celestial number of Virgo is 8. Mercury, the ruling planet of this sign, has the numerical value of 4. Combining these 2 numbers, we have 8 plus 4, which equals 12. This number must be reduced to a single digit. Therefore, 1 plus 2 equals 3. Number 3 is the key number for all people born in Virgo. Bear this in mind on all occasions. When you buy a ticket of any sort, make sure that 3 is the predominating number, if it contains a serial number. Room number 3 in a hotel, a street number containing a 3 or several 3's, horse number 3 in a race, player number 3 in a sports game, cards that total 3 in a card game, a 3 rolled with dice, 3 on a spin wheel, and so on, are considered fortunate for you.

Illustration: Suppose you have two cards in your hand: a 10-spot and a 2-spot. Now, 10 plus 2 equals 12 and reducing to a single digit, 1 plus 2 equals 3. Therefore, such a hand would be fortunate for you. Any other combination of cards that could be added and reduced to 3 can also be used. If you have a combination that equals 21, it would reduce to 3, and so on. Use the same method with other combinations or totals.

To Find Your Best Days for Speculation

Any day of any month that totals 3 is considered fortunate for you. Thus, the 12th, 21st, 30th, would be fortunate because these dates reduce to the single digit 3.

Therefore, the days of the month that are best for speculation for you are the 3rd, 12th, 21st, 30th. However, you should engage in speculation only in your proper periods as explained below.

Proper Hours for Speculation

The proper hour for speculation is when your ruling planet is governing. Refer to your daily paper, almanac, or calendar to find the time of sunrise, then count the hours after sunrise. These hours are the same every week, month, and year. Only the time of sunrise changes.

Hours for speculation: Sunday: 3rd, 10th, 17th, 24th hour after sunrise. Monday: 7th, 14th, 21st hour after sunrise. Tuesday: 4th, 11th, 18th hour after sunrise. Wednesday: 1st, 8th, 15th, 22nd hour after sunrise. Thursday: 5th, 12th, 19th hour after sunrise. Friday: 2nd, 9th, 16th, 23rd hour after sunrise. Saturday: 6th, 13th, 20th hour after sunrise.

LUCKY DAYS — LIBRA

*For All Those Born Between
September 24 and October 23*

If you were born on September 24, 25, 26, 27, 28, 29, and 30, and October 1, 2, and 3. You may speculate during the following periods and may expect to win:

January	21	to	30
May	22	to	June 1
July	24	to	August 3
November	23	to	December 3

From September 23 to October 5, you will also be tempted to speculate, yet must determine for yourself whether or not you can win. Do not speculate from March 21 to 31, June 22 to July 3, and December 22 to 31.

If you were born on October 4, 5, 6, 7, 8, 9, 10, 11, 12, and 13. You may speculate during the following periods and may expect to win:

January	31	to	February 9
June	1	to	12
August	3	to	14
December	2	to	12

From October 2 to 14 you will also be tempted to speculate, but you must determine for yourself whether or not you can win. Do not speculate from January 1 to 12, April 1 to 11, and July 2 to 15.

If you were born on October 14, 15, 16, 17, 18, 19, 20, 21, 22, and 23. You may speculate during the following periods and may expect to win:

February	9	to	19
June	11	to	21
August	12	to	23
December	11	to	22

From October 10 to 23, you will also be tempted to speculate, but you must determine for yourself whether or not you can win. Do not speculate from January 9 to 20, April 10 to 20, and July 12 to 23.

All Libra-born are inclined to take chances between January 21 and February 19. When you speculate in co-operation with others, it would be advisable to have a partner born under one of the following signs:

Aquarius—January 21 to February 19
Aries—March 21 to April 20
Gemini—May 22 to June 21
Leo—July 24 to August 23
Libra—September 24 to October 23
Sagittarius—November 23 to December 22

Miscellaneous Things to Observe

Those born between September 24 and September 30

will have better chances in speculation during the new moon.

Those born between October 1 and October 7 will have better chances in speculation during the second quarter of the moon.

Those born between October 8 and October 17 will have better chances in speculation during the full moon.

Those born between October 18 and October 23 will have better chances in speculation during the fourth quarter of the moon.

Nearly all calendars give the four quarters of the moon.

Numerology

According to the science of numerology, the celestial number of Libra is 6. Venus, the ruling planet of this sign, has a numerical value of 9. Combining these two numbers we have: 6 plus 9, which equals 15. This number must be reduced to a single digit. Therefore, 1 plus 5 equals 6. The number 6 is the key number of all persons born under Libra. Bear this in mind at all times. When you buy a ticket of any sort, make sure that the serial number has 6 as the predominating number. Room number 6 in a hotel, a street number containing a 6 or several 6's, horse number 6 in a race, player number 6 in a sport game, cards that total 6 in a card game, a 6 rolled with dice, 6 on a spin wheel, and so on, are considered fortunate for you.

Illustration: Suppose you have two cards in your hand: a 4-spot and a 2-spot. Since 4 plus 2 equals 6, such a hand, or any other combination that totals and reduces to 6, would be fortunate for you. If you have a combination that totals 51, it would reduce to 6, and so on. Use the same method with other combinations and totals.

To Find Your Best Days for Speculation

Any day of the month that totals 6 is considered fortunate for you. Thus, the 15th and 24th are fortunate because these dates reduce to the single digit 6. There-

248

fore, the days of the month that are best for speculation for you are the 6th, 15th, and 24th. However, you should engage in speculation only in your proper periods as explained below.

Proper Hours for Speculation

The proper hour for speculation is when your ruling planet is governing. Refer to your daily paper, almanac, or calendar to find the time of sunrise, then count the hours after sunrise. These hours are the same every ·week, month, and year. Only the time of sunrise changes.

Hours for speculation: Sunday: 2nd, 9th, 16th, 23rd hour after sunrise. Monday: 6th, 13th, 20th hour after sunrise. Tuesday: 3rd, 8th, 15th, 24th hour after sunrise. Wednesday: 7th, 14th, 21st hour after sunrise. Thursday: 4th, 11th, 18th hour after sunrise. Friday: 1st, 8th, 15th, 22nd hour after sunrise. Saturday: 5th, 12th, 19th hour after sunrise.

LUCKY DAYS — SCORPIO

For All Those Born Between October 23 and November 22

If you were born on October 24, 25, 26, 27, 28, 29, 30, and 31 and November 1 and 2. You may speculate during the following periods and may expect to win:

February	20	to	29
June	22	to	July 2
August	24	to	September 3
December	21	to	31

From October 23 to November 3, you will also be tempted to speculate, but you must determine for yourself whether you can win. Do not speculate from January 20 to 31, April 21 to May 2, and July 23 to August 4.

If you were born on November 3, 4, 5, 6, 7, 8, 9, 10, 11,

and 12. You may speculate during the following periods and may expect to win:

January	1	to	11
March	1	to	10
July	2,	to	13
September	3	to	14

From November 1 to 13, you will also be tempted to speculate, but you must determine for yourself whether you can win. Do not speculate from February 1 to 12, May 1 to 12, and August 2 to 15.

If you were born on November 13, 14, 15, 16, 17, 18, 19, 20, 21, and 22. You may speculate during the following periods and may expect to win:

January	11	to	20
March	10	to	20
July	12	to	23
September	13	to	23

From November 10 to 23, you will also be tempted to speculate, but you must determine for yourself whether you can win. Do not speculate from February 8 to 20, May 11 to 21, and August 13 to 23.

All Scorpio-born are inclined to take chances from February 20 to March 20. When you speculate in co-operation with others, it would be advisable that your partner is born under one of the following signs:

Capricorn—December 23 to January 20
Pisces—February 20 to March 20
Taurus—April 21 to May 21
Cancer—June 22 to July 23
Virgo—August 24 to September 23
Scorpio—October 24 to November 22

Miscellaneous Things to Observe

Those born between October 24 and October 30 will have better chances in speculation during the new moon. Those born between October 31 and November 8 will have better chances in speculation during the second quarter of the moon.

Those born between November 9 and November 16 will have better chances in speculation during the full moon.

Those born between November 17 and November 22 will have better chances in speculation during the fourth quarter of the moon.

Nearly all calendars give the four quarters of the moon.

Numerology

According to the science of numerology, the celestial number of Scorpio is 5. Pluto, the ruling planet of this sign, has the numerical value of 3. Combining these two numbers we have: 5 plus 3 equals 8. Number 8 is the key number for all persons born in Scorpio. Bear this in mind on all occasions. When you buy a ticket of any sort, make sure that the serial number has 8 as the predominating number. Room number 8 in a hotel, a street number containing an 8 or several 8's, horse number 8 in a race, player number 8 in a sport game, cards that total 8 in a card game, an 8 rolled with dice, 8 on a spin wheel, and so on, are considered fortunate for you.

Illustration: Suppose you have two cards in your hand: a 4-spot and another 4-spot. Since 4 plus 4 equals 8, such a hand or any other combination of cards that would total 8 would be fortunate for you. If you have a combination that totals 26 or 53, that would also reduce to 8. Use the same methods with other combinations and totals.

To Find Your Best Days for Speculation

Any day of any month that totals 8 is considered fortunate for you. Thus, the 17th and 26th are fortunate because these days reduce to the single digit 8. Therefore, the best days for speculation for you are: the 8th, 17th, and 26th. However, you should engage in speculation only in your proper periods as explained below.

251

Proper Hours for Speculation

The proper hour for speculation is when your ruling planet is governing. Refer to your daily paper, almanac, or calendar to find the time of sunrise; then count the hours after sunrise. These hours are the same every week, month, and year. Only the time of sunrise changes.

Hours for speculation: Sunday: 7th, 14th, 21st hour after sunrise. Monday: 4th, 11th, 18th hour after sunrise. Tuesday: 1st, 8th, 11th, 22nd hour after sunrise. Wednesday: 5th, 12th, 19th hour after sunrise. Thursday: 2nd, 9th, 16th, 23rd hour after sunrise. Friday: 6th, 13th, 20th hour after sunrise. Saturday: 3rd, 10th, 17th, 24th hour after sunrise.

LUCKY DAYS — SAGITTARIUS

For All Those Born Between November 23 and December 22

If you were born on November 23, 24, 25, 26, 27, 28, 29, and 30 and December 1 and 2. You may speculate during the following periods and may expect to win:

January	21	to	30
March	21	to	31
July	23	to	August 3
September	23	to	October 4

From November 22 to December 3, you will also be tempted to speculate, but you must determine for yourself whether or not you can win. Do not speculate from February 19 to 29, May 21 to June 3, and August 22 to December 4.

If you were born on December 3, 4, 5, 6, 7, 8, 9, 10, 11, and 12. You may speculate during the following periods and may expect to win:

January	31	to	February 9
April	1	to	11

August	12	to	23
October	3	to	14

From December 1 to 14, you will also be tempted to speculate, but you must determine for yourself whether or not you can win. Do not speculate from March 1 to 13, June 1 to 12, and September 2 to 14.

If you were born on December 13, 14, 15, 16, 17, 18, 19, 20, 21, and 22. You may speculate during the following periods and may expect to win:

February	9	to	20
April	10	to	20
August	13	to	23
October	12	to	23

From December 10 to 22, you will also be tempted to speculate, but you must determine for yourself whether or not you can win. Do not speculate from March 10 to 21, June 11 to 21, and September 12 to 23.

All Sagittarius-born are inclined to take chances between March 21 and April 20. When you speculate in cooperation with others, it would be advisable to have a partner born under one of the following signs:

Aquarius—January 21 to February 19
Aries—March 21 to April 20
Gemini—May 22 to June 21
Leo—July 24 to August 23
Libra—September 24 to October 23
Sagittarius—November 23 to December 22

Miscellaneous Things to Observe

Those born between November 23 and November 29 will have better chances in speculation during the new moon.

Those born between November 30 and December 7 will have better chances in speculation during the second quarter of the moon.

Those born between December 8 and December 16 will have better chances in speculation during the full moon.

253

Those born between December 17 and December 22 will have better chances in speculation during the fourth quarter of the moon.

Nearly all calendars give the four quarters of the moon.

Numerology

According to the science of numerology, the celestial number of Sagittarius is 8. Jupiter, the ruling planet of this sign, has the numerical value of 9. Combining these two numbers we have 8 plus 9 equals 17. Now this must be reduced to a single digit. Thus, 1 plus 7 equals 8. The key number for all persons born in Sagittarius is 8, the same as for Scorpio. Since there are only 9 digits, and there are 12 signs, some Zodiacal signs have duplicate numbers. Bear in mind at all times that 8 is your celestial number. When you buy a ticket of any sort, make sure that the serial number has a predominance of 8 in it. Room number 8 in a hotel, player number 8 in a sport game, horse number 8 in a race, a street number with an 8 or several 8's, cards that total 8 in a card game, an 8 rolled with dice, 8 on a spin wheel, and so on, are considered fortunate for you.

Illustration: Suppose you have two cards in your hand: a 6-spot and a 2-spot. Since 6 plus 2 equals 8, such a hand or any combination of cards that would total 8, would be fortunate for you. If you have a combination that totals 35 or 53, that would also reduce to 8. Use this same method for other combinations.

To Find Your Best Days for Speculation

Any day of any month that totals 8 is considered fortunate for you. Thus the 17th and the 26th are fortunate because these dates reduce to a single digit 8. Therefore, the best days for speculation for you are the 8th, 17th, and 26th. However, you should speculate only in your proper periods as explained below.

Proper Hours for Speculation

The proper hour for speculation is when your ruling

planet is governing. Refer to your daily paper, almanac, or calendar to find the time of sunrise, then count the hours after sunrise. These hours are the same every week, month, and year. Only the time of sunrise changes.

Hours for speculation: Sunday: 6th, 13th, 20th hour after sunrise. Monday: 3rd, 10th, 17th, 24th hour after sunrise. Tuesday: 7th, 14th, 21st hour after sunrise. Wednesday: 4th, 11th, 18th hour after sunrise. Thursday: 1st, 8th, 15th, 22nd hour after sunrise. Friday: 5th, 12th, 19th hour after sunrise. Saturday: 2nd, 9th, 16th, 23rd hour after sunrise.

LUCKY DAYS — CAPRICORN

For All Those Born Between December 23 and January 20

If you were born on December 22, 23, 24, 25, 26, 27, 28, 29, 30, and 31. You may speculate during the following periods and may expect to win:

February	20	to	29
April	21	to	May 2
August	23	to	September 3
October	22	to	November 2

From December 20 to 31, you will also be tempted to speculate, but you must determine for yourself whether you can win. Do not speculate from March 21 to 31, June 22 to July 3, and September 24 to October 4.

If you were born on January 1st, 2nd, 3rd, 4th, 5th, 6th, 7th, 8th, 9th, and 10th. You may speculate during the following periods and may expect to win:

March	1	to	10
May	2	to	12
September	4	to	14
November	2	to	12

From January 1 to 12 you will also be tempted to speculate, but you must determine for yourself whether

255

or not you can win. Do not speculate from April 1 to 11, July 2 to 13, and October 3 to 14.

If you were born on January 11, 12, 13, 14, 15, 16, 17, 18, 19, and 20. You may speculate during the following periods and may expect to win:

March	10	to	20
May	11	to	21
September	13	to	24
November	13	to	22

From January 9 to 21, you will also be tempted to speculate, but you must determine for yourself whether or not you can win. Do not speculate from April 10 to 20, July 13 to 23, and October 12 to 23.

All Capricorn-born are inclined to take chances between April 21 to May 21. When you speculate in cooperation with others, it would be advisable to have a partner born under one of the following signs:

Capricorn—December 23 to January 20
Pisces—February 20 to March 20
Taurus—April 21 to May 21
Cancer—June 22 to July 23
Virgo—August 24 to September 23
Scorpio—October 24 to November 22

Miscellaneous Things to Observe

Those born between December 23 and December 30 will have better chances in speculation during the new moon.

Those born between December 31 and January 6 will have better chances in speculation during the second quarter of the moon.

Those born between January 7 and January 14 will have better chances in speculation during the full moon.

Those born between January 15 and January 20 will have better chances in speculation during the fourth quarter of the moon.

Nearly all calendars give the four quarters of the moon.

256

Numerology

According to the science of numerology, the celestial number of Capricorn is 8. Saturn, the ruling planet of this sign, has the numerical value of 3. Combining those numbers we have 8 plus 3, which equals 11. This must be reduced to a single digit. Thus, 1 plus 1 equals 2. The key number for all persons born in Capricorn is 2, the same as for those born in Cancer. There are only nine digits, but there are twelve signs, therefore some signs have duplicate numbers. Bear in mind at all times that 2 is your celestial number. When you buy a ticket of any sort, see that the serial number has 2 predominating, room number 2 in a hotel, player number 2 in a sport game, horse number 2 in a race, a street number with 2 or several 2's in it, cards that total 2 in a card game, a 2 rolled with dice, 2 on a spin wheel, and so on, are considered fortunate for you.

Illustration: Suppose you have two cards in your hand: a 10-spot and an ace. Now 10 plus 1 equals 11 and that reduced to a single digit equals 2, therefore, such a hand would be fortunate for you, or any other combination of cards that total 2. If you have a combination that totals 20, that would also reduce to 2. Use this same method for other combinations.

To Find Your Best Days for Speculation

Any day of any month that totals 2 is considered fortunate for you. Thus, the 11th, 29th, and so on, because these reduce to the single digit 2. Therefore, the best days for speculation for you are the 2nd, 11th, and 29th. However, you should speculate only in your proper periods as explained below.

Proper Hours for Speculation

The proper hour for speculation is when your ruling planet is governing. Refer to your daily paper, almanac, or calendar to find the time of sunrise, then count the hours after sunrise. These hours are the same every week, month, and year. Only the time of sunrise changes.

Hours for speculation: Sunday: 5th, 12th, 19th hour after sunrise. Monday: 2nd, 9th, 23rd hour after sunrise. Tuesday: 6th, 13th, 20th hour after sunrise. Wednesday: 3rd, 8th, 15th, 24th hour after sunrise. Thursday: 7th, 14th, 21st hour after sunrise. Friday: 4th, 11th, 18th hour after sunrise. Saturday: 1st, 10th, 17th, 22nd hour after sunrise.

LUCKY DAYS — AQUARIUS

*For All Those Born Between January 21
and February 19*

If you were born on January 21, 22, 23, 24, 25, 26, 27, 28, 29, and 30. You may speculate during the following periods and may expect to win:

March 21 to 31
May 22 to June 2

From January 20 to 31, you will also be tempted to speculate, yet must determine for yourself whether or not you can win. Do not speculate from April 21 to May 2, July 23 to August 3, and October 24 to November 3.

If you were born on January 31 and February 1, 2, 3, 4, 5, 6, 7, 8, and 9. You may speculate during the following periods and may expect to win:

April	1	to	12
June	1	to	11
October	3	to	13
December	3	to	13

From January 30 to February 10 you will also be tempted to speculate, yet you must determine for yourself whether or not you can win. Do not speculate from May 2 to 12, August 2 to 14, and November 1 to 12.

If you were born on February 10, 11, 12, 13, 14, 15, 16,

17, 18, and 19. You may speculate during the following periods and may expect to win:

April	11	to	20
June	11	to	21
October	13	to	23
December	11	to	22

From February 9 to 20 you will also be tempted to speculate, yet must determine for yourself whether or not you can win. Do not speculate from May 10 to 22, August 13 to 23, and November 11 to 22.

All Aquarius-born are inclined to take chances between May 22 and June 21. When you speculate in co-operation with others, it would be advisable that your partner is born under one of the following signs:

Aries—March 21 to April 20
Gemini—May 22 to June 21
Aquarius—January 21 to February 19
Leo—July 24 to August 23
Libra—September 24 to October 23
Sagittarius—November 23 to December 22

Miscellaneous Things to Observe

Those born between January 21 and January 28 will have better chances in speculation during the new moon.

Those born between January 29 and February 6 will have better chances in speculation during the second quarter of the moon.

Those born between February 7 and February 14 will have better chances in speculation during the full moon.

Those born between February 15 and February 19 will have better chances in speculation during the fourth quarter of the moon.

Nearly all calendars give the four quarters of the moon.

Numerology

According to the science of numerology, the celestial number of Aquarius is 8. Uranus, the ruling planet of this sign, has the numerical value of 4. Combining these two numbers we have, 8 plus 4, which equals 12. This must be reduced to a single digit. Thus, 1 plus 2 equals 3. The key number for all persons born in Aquarius is 3, the same as Virgo. There are only 9 digits, but there are 12 signs, therefore some signs must have duplicate numbers. Bear in mind at all times that 3 is your celestial number. When you buy a ticket of any sort make sure that the serial number has 3 or several 3's. Room number 3 in a hotel, a street number containing 3 or several 3's, horse number 3 in a race, player number 3 in a sport game, cards that total 3 in a card game, a 3 rolled with dice, 3 on a spin wheel, and so on, are considered fortunate for you.

Illustration: Suppose you have two cards in your hand: a 9-spot and a 3-spot. Since 9 plus 3 equals 12 and that reduced to a single digit equals 3, such a hand or any other combination of cards that would total 3, would be fortunate for you. If you have a combination that totals 48 or 66, that would total 12 and this reduced gives 3. Use the same method with other combinations and totals.

To Find Your Best Days for Speculation

Any day of any month that totals 3 is considered fortunate for you. Thus, the 12th, 21st, and 30th are fortunate because these reduce to the single digit 3. Therefore, the best days for speculation for you are the 3rd, 12th, 21st, and 30th. However, you should speculate only in your proper periods, as explained below.

Proper Hours for Speculation

The proper hour for speculation is when your ruling planet is governing. Refer to your daily paper, almanac, or calendar to find the time of sunrise, then count the hours after sunrise. These hours are the same every week, month, and year. Only the time of sunrise changes.

Hours for speculation: Sunday: 3rd, 10th, 17th, 24th

hour after sunrise. Monday: 7th, 14th, 21st hour after sunrise. Tuesday: 4th, 11th, 18th hour after sunrise. Wednesday: 5th, 12th, 19th hour after sunrise. Thursday: 2nd, 9th, 16th, 23rd hour after sunrise. Friday: 6th, 13th, 20th hour after sunrise. Saturday: 1st, 8th, 15th, 22nd hour after sunrise.

LUCKY DAYS — PISCES

For All Those Born Between February 20 and March 20

If you were born on February 20, 21, 22, 23, 24, 25, 26, 27, 28, and 29. You may speculate during the following periods and may expect to win:

April	21	to	May 2
June	22	to	July 3
October	23	to	November 2
December	22	to	31

From February 19 to 29 you will also be tempted to speculate, yet must determine for yourself whether or not you can win. Do not speculate from May 21 to June 2, August 23 to September 4, and November 21 to December 4.

If you were born on March 1, 2, 3, 4, 5, 6, 7, 8, 9, and 10. You may speculate during the following periods and may expect to win:

January	1	to	10
May	1	to	12
July	2	to	13
November	1	to	12

From March 1 to 12 you will also be tempted to speculate, yet must determine for yourself whether or not you can win. Do not speculate from June 1 to 13, September 2 to 13, and December 1 to 12.

If you were born on March 11, 12, 13, 14, 15, 16, 17,

18, 19, and 20. You may speculate during the following periods and may expect to win:

January	10	to	20
May	11	to	21
July	13	to	23
November	11	to	22

From March 9 to 21 you will also be tempted to speculate, yet must determine for yourself whether or not you can win. Do not speculate from June 10 to 22, September 12 to 23, and December 10 to 22.

All Pisces-born are inclined to take chances between June 22 and July 23. When you speculate in cooperation with others, it would be advisable to have a partner born under one of the following signs:

Capricorn—December 23 to January 20
Pisces—February 20 to March 20
Taurus—April 21 to May 21
Cancer—June 22 to July 23
Virgo—August 24 to September 23
Scorpio—October 24 to November 22

Miscellaneous Things to Observe

Those born between February 20 and February 26 will have better chances in speculation during the new moon.

Those born between February 27 and March 5 will have better chances in speculation during the second quarter of the moon.

Those born between March 6 and March 13 will have better chances in speculation during the full moon.

Those born between March 14 and March 20 will have better chances for speculation during the fourth quarter of the moon.

Nearly all calendars give the four quarters of the moon.

Numerology

According to the science of numerology, the celestial number of Pisces is 8. Neptune, the ruling planet of this sign, has the numerical value of 5. Combining these two

262

numbers we have 8 plus 5 equals 13. This must be reduced to a single digit. Thus, 1 plus 3 equals 4. Number 4 is the key number for all persons born in Pisces, the same as for those born in Aries. There are only 9 digits. Since there are 12 signs, some signs will have duplicate numbers. Bear in mind that your key number is 4. When you buy a ticket of any sort, make sure that the serial number 4 is the predominating number. Room number 4 in a hotel, a street number containing 4 or several 4's, horse number 4 in a race, player number 4 in a sport game, cards that total 4 in a card game, a 4 rolled with dice, 4 on a spin wheel, and so on, are considered fortunate for you.

Illustration: Suppose you have two cards in your hand: a 9-spot and a 4-spot. Since 9 plus 4 equals 13, and this reduced equals 4, so this or any other combination that could be reduced to 4, would be a fortunate hand for you. Use the same method with other combinations, such as 31 or 67, which reduce to 4.

To Find Your Best Days for Speculation

Any day of the month that totals 4 is considered fortunate for you. Thus, the 13th, 22nd, and 31st of a month would be fortunate for you, because these days reduce to a single digit, making 4. The days of the month that are best for speculation are the 4th, 13th, 22nd, and 31st. However, you should engage in speculation only in your proper periods as explained below.

Proper Hours for Speculation

The proper hour for speculation is when your ruling planet is governing. Refer to your daily paper, almanac, or calendar to find the time of sunrise, then count the hours after sunrise. These hours are the same every week, month, and year. Only the time of sunrise changes.

Hours for speculation: Sunday: 2nd, 9th, 16th, 23rd hour after sunrise. Monday: 5th, 12th, 19th hour after

263

sunrise. Tuesday: 6th, 13th, 20th hour after sunrise. Wednesday: 3rd, 10th, 17th, 24th hour after sunrise. Thursday: 7th, 14th, 21st hour after sunrise. Friday: 1st, 8th, 15th, 22nd hour after sunrise. Saturday: 4th, 11th, 18th hour after sunrise.

FORTUNATE AND ADVERSE CYCLES

Jupiter, the largest planet in our solar system, plays an important part in human life. In size alone, Jupiter is three times as big as all the rest of the planets put together. It takes twelve years for this planet to go through the twelve signs of the Zodiac and during this period it influences all human beings. Just as its power is great enough to change the course of comets, so it changes the destiny of empires and men. Its cycle means that every twelve years, this planet is at the same place in the Heavens as at your birth, marking the beginning of a new cycle for you. This law holds true for every man and woman. Thus, it is possible to calculate, for each one of us, the fortunate years as well as those years when we are wasteful, extravagant, and careless, and face losses. The following interpretation of the Jupiter cycle is the same for all of us, but this does not mean that it is general; this planet takes one year to go through one sign and therefore it is easy to calculate its exact position for every year of your life.

King Solomon said: "To everything there is a season, and a time for every purpose under the Heaven." This means that human life should be planned in accordance with the planetary influences operating at one's birth and those influencing each of us now. But everyone is given the freedom to work in harmony with those great natural Laws or to act contrary to them. It is up to us to plan our lives in such a way that we expand under favorable influences and to hold back when the planets are at critical angles. Those that do not understand those laws go blindly ahead and blame destiny for their ill-luck. All of us, regardless of when born, have periods when we are fortunate and success smiles upon us, but from time to time, we are under a cycle when our affairs go wrong and opportunities are few. Luckily, those cycles come at regular intervals and it is possible to indicate exactly the cycle you are under at a certain age of your life.

Regardless of other planetary influences operating in your life, the following cycles are fortunate for you and it is up to you to make use of them.

Fortunate cycles: At the ages of 16, 20, 22, 26, 28, 32, 34, 38, 40, 44, 46, 50, 56, 58, 62, 64, 68, 70, 74, 76, and 80. Of course, you may have some difficulties those years but some good fortune will come your way, somebody will help you, an opportunity will present itself, and chances for making money are good. To those out of work, it means that they will be able to find employment, even if it is not what they would like to have. Changes made will prove profitable and business will increase. It marks a fortunate time for expanding in business, to take long journeys, for legal affairs or to establish yourself securely. It is a time when things come our way, when we receive many gifts, when we win at games of chance or when the opposite sex favors us. Your fortunate cycles last about nine months and start about four months before your birth month to four months afterwards. For many of us, those are the years of prosperity.

Next to consider are the adverse cycles, also called cycles of restrictions. They mark periods in your life when you will not feel well, when your blood will be impure, and when you will be careless and extravagant. It is an adverse time to speculate or gamble and those in business should not expand and should beware of wild schemes that will end in lawsuits. Others will refuse to cooperate, and some of us may even lose our jobs. Do not take foolish chances. Thus, you will protect yourself against illusion and disappointments.

Cycles of restriction also operate for nine months. You will feel them about four months before your birth month and the fourth month afterwards.

Adverse cycles: At the ages of 15, 18, 21, 27, 30, 33,

39, 42, 45, 51, 54, 57, 63, 66, 69, 75, 78, 81. A new cycle starts about every twelve years of your life and marks a complete change in your affairs. No doubt you know that the world conditions are influenced by the sun spots, whose cycle is about eleven and a half years, similar to your own cycle. Without consulting the planets on the day and year you were born, it is not possible to tell you whether you will have success or misfortune when such a cycle begins. Perhaps if you go back in your life and go over the events that took place at the age of 12 and 24, you can tell if the beginning of a new cycle is good or bad for you. New cycles start for everybody at the ages of 12, 24, 36, 48, 60, 72, 84, 96.

History records many amazing predictions about the destiny of nations, rulers, and individuals, all based on cycles—this was the secret of the Egyptians and all past civilizations. It is up to every one of us to make use of those cycles in our affairs. Before anyone makes a plan for the future, he should see if he is under a fortunate cycle or an adverse cycle. If it is a fortunate cycle, then he can go ahead with his plans, expand, take chances, and make radical changes in his affairs. If the cycle is adverse, it means that he must wait for at least one more year before launching new ventures or making any radical changes.

There are, of course, other cycles yet we cannot go into them any further until you have learned to apply what you just have read. It would be very interesting for you to look back into your past and see how many fortunate happenings you can trace to the fortunate cycles and how many losses or sorrows you can show for the adverse cycles. Thus, you will learn one of the fundamental laws of life.

It is hoped that with this information, you will be more successful and find greater happiness, also protected and warned against pitfalls and losses. Nothing can be more valuable than to know whether you are lucky now or whether you must be on your guard. Realize how many times fate has been kind to you and you did not take the opportunity. When your affairs are going smoothly and success is yours and you know that it is part of a fortunate cycle, you can time its end and thus not expect your luck to last longer than it really will. You may be successful now but in a few months you may come under a critical cycle. Prepare yourself for it and do not live or act as if your good fortune will keep on going on for many more months. Establish yourself and enjoy the good things that come your way. But if fate is unkind to you, when every hope is gone, you will want to know just when luck, success, and happiness will be yours again. Consult these pages and see when your next favorable cycles will come and prepare yourself for your ship to come in. Perhaps it would be well for you to ponder the words of Dryden:

The lucky have whole days, and those they choose.
The unlucky have but hours, and those they lose.